1988 Supplement

LAND-USE CONTROLS

D1434684

1988 Supplement

LAND-USE CONTROLS
Cases and Materials

Robert C. Ellickson
Professor of Law
Yale University

A. Dan Tarlock
Professor of Law
Illinois Institute of Technology
Chicago-Kent College of Law

Little, Brown and Company   *Boston and Toronto*

Library of Congress Catalog Card No. 80-84029
ISBN 0-316-23301-3

FG

Published simultaneously in Canada
by Little, Brown and Company (Canada) Limited

PRINTED IN THE UNITED STATES OF AMERICA

Contents

Table of Cases

Italics indicate principal cases.
All references are to Supplement page numbers.

Table of Cases

Table of Cases

Preface

After a period of quiescence in the early 1980s, land-use law erupted in 1987 when the Supreme Court of the United States decided three important cases construing the Taking Clause of the Fifth Amendment. In two of these cases—*First English* and *Nollan*—the Court ruled in favor of the plaintiff landowner. In the third case—*Keystone Bituminous*—the Court undermined Justice Holmes' venerable *Pennsylvania Coal* opinion that has served as the foundation of regulatory taking claims. These decisions went in conflicting directions and provoked vigorous dissenting opinions signed by at least three justices. As a result, land-use law is likely to be in ferment in the coming years.

We have begun working on a new edition of the Casebook, but these 1987 decisions called for the immediate updating of the prior Supplement. This volume also includes materials on other major legal developments. For example, it describes how federal antitrust law has become increasingly lenient in regard to local anticompetitive activities, and presents innovations in the law of exclusionary zoning, especially the New Jersey Supreme Court's *Mount Laurel II* decision and that decision's legislative aftermath.

We have adhered to the practice, followed in the Casebook, of often deleting citations in judicial opinions without ellipses. Footnotes retain the numbers they had in the original.

We thank Jean Castle and the editors at Little, Brown for their assistance.

Robert C. Ellickson
A. Dan Tarlock

May 1988

1988 Supplement

LAND-USE CONTROLS

Chapter Two
Zoning and the Rights of Landowners

Page 51. After Note 4, add:

4a. *Attack on* Euclid. In 1981 President Reagan appointed Bernard Siegan, Professor of Law at the University of San Diego, to the President's Commission on Housing, a policy taskforce. Professor Siegan helped convince the Commission that the *Euclid* standard of review of local zoning measures is too lenient. The Report of the President's Commission on Housing (1982), included the following recommendations:

> To protect property rights and to increase the production of housing and lower its cost, all State and local legislatures should enact legislation providing that no zoning regulations denying or limiting the development of housing should be deemed valid unless their existence or adoption is necessary to achieve a vital and pressing governmental interest. In litigation, the governmental body seeking to maintain or impose the regulation should bear the burden for proving it complies with the foregoing standard. . . .
>
> The Commission believes that in recent years our legal system has weakened the property rights of owners of real property and largely ignored the implicit rights of newcomers deprived of affordable housing by excessive or exclusionary zoning. This imbalance should be redressed by State legislatures. But there is another potential source of protection — the courts.
>
> In the past 25 years, the courts and legislatures have expanded the traditional meanings of property in applying due process protections. Yet the ownership of real property continues to be governed by a 50-year-old precedent that constitutes a significant departure from the traditional judicial role of protecting such property rights against government interference. . . .
>
> . . . Accordingly, the Commission believes the *Euclid* doctrine should be reexamined. The Commission recommends that the Attorney General seek an appropriate case in which to request review of the *Euclid* doctrine in the context of modern land-use issues and the due process protections afforded other property rights in the 50 years since *Euclid* was decided. Most Commissioners believe that the "vital and pressing governmental interest" standard . . . represents an appropriate redress of the balance. Nonetheless, the Commission suggests the Attorney General consider the "vital and pressing" and other potential standards in his review.

1

Several Commissioners are concerned that adoption of this proposed new standard as a constitutional doctrine raises serious dangers of an expanded role for the judiciary and believe that judges are ill-equipped to balance the social and environmental concerns inherent in zoning. These commissioners are concerned that the police power, of which zoning is an example, not be so constrained; rather, it should be dynamic, and able to adjust as economic and social conditions vary. They would rely on the legislation recommended by the Commission to confine the exercise of discretionary local land-use decisions. [Id. at 200-202.]

Page 78. Before Note 5, insert:

WILLIAMSON COUNTY REGIONAL PLANNING COMMISSION v. HAMILTON BANK

473 U.S. 172, 105 S. Ct. 3108, 87 L. Ed. 2d 126 (1985)

Justice BLACKMUN delivered the opinion of the Court.

Respondent, the owner of a tract of land it was developing as a residential subdivision, sued petitioners, the Williamson County [Tennessee] Regional Planning Commission and its members and staff, in United States District Court, alleging that petitioners' application of various zoning laws and regulations to respondent's property amounted to a "taking" of that property. At trial, the jury agreed and awarded respondent $350,000 as just compensation for the "taking." Although the jury's verdict was rejected by the District Court, which granted a judgment notwithstanding the verdict to petitioners, the verdict was reinstated on appeal. . . .

. . . Because respondent has not yet obtained a final decision regarding the application of the zoning ordinance and subdivision regulations to its property, nor utilized the procedures Tennessee provides for obtaining just compensation, respondent's claim is not ripe.

A

As the Court has made clear in several recent decisions, a claim that the application of government regulations effects a taking of a property interest is not ripe until the government entity charged with implementing the regulations has reached a final decision regarding the application of the regulations to the property at issue. In Hodel v. Virginia Surface Mining & Reclamation Assn., Inc., 452 U.S. 264 (1981), for example, the Court rejected a claim that the Surface Mining Control and Reclamation Act of 1977, 91 Stat. 447, 30 U.S.C. §1201 et seq., effected a taking because:

2

"There is no indication in the record that appellees have availed themselves of the opportunities provided by the Act to obtain administrative relief by requesting either a variance from the approximate-original-contour requirement of §515(d) or a waiver from the surface mining restrictions in §522(e). If [the property owners] were to seek administrative relief under these procedures, a mutually acceptable solution might well be reached with regard to individual properties, thereby obviating any need to address the constitutional questions. The potential for such administrative solutions confirms the conclusion that the taking issue decided by the District Court simply is not ripe for judicial resolution." 452 U.S., at 297 (footnote omitted).

Similarly, in Agins v. Tiburon the Court held that a challenge to the application of a zoning ordinance was not ripe because the property owners had not yet submitted a plan for development of their property. 447 U.S., at 260. In Penn Central Transp. Co. v. New York City the Court declined to find that the application of New York City's Landmarks Preservation Law to Grand Central Terminal effected a taking because, although the Landmarks Preservation Commission had disapproved a plan for a 50-story office building above the terminal, the property owners had not sought approval for any other plan, and it therefore was not clear whether the Commission would deny approval for all uses that would enable the plaintiffs to derive economic benefit from the property. 438 U.S., at 136-137.

Respondent's claim is in a posture similar to the claims the Court held premature in *Hodel*. Respondent has submitted a plan for developing its property, and thus has passed beyond the *Agins* threshold. But, like the *Hodel* plaintiffs, respondent did not then seek variances that would have allowed it to develop the property according to its proposed plat, notwithstanding the Commission's finding that the plat did not comply with the zoning ordinance and subdivision regulations. It appears that variances could have been granted to resolve at least five of the Commission's eight objections to the plat. The Board of Zoning Appeals had the power to grant certain variances from the zoning ordinance, including the ordinance's density requirements and its restriction on placing units on land with slopes having a grade in excess of 25%. The Commission had the power to grant variances from the subdivision regulations, including the cul-de-sac, road grade, and frontage requirements. Nevertheless, respondent did not seek variances from either the Board or the Commission.

Respondent argues that it "did everything possible to resolve the conflict with the commission," Brief for Respondent 42, and that the Commission's denial of approval for respondent's plat was equivalent to a denial of variances. The record does not support respondent's claim, however. There is no evidence that respondent applied to the Board of Zoning Appeals for variances from the zoning ordinance. . . .

3

Respondent asserts that it should not be required to seek variances from the regulations because its suit is predicated upon 42 U.S.C. §1983, and there is no requirement that a plaintiff exhaust administrative remedies before bringing a §1983 action. Patsy v. Florida Board of Regents, 457 U.S. 496 (1982). The question whether administrative remedies must be exhausted is conceptually distinct, however, from the question whether an administrative action must be final before it is judicially reviewable. See FTC v. Standard Oil Co., 449 U.S. 232, 243 (1980). See generally, C. Wright, A. Miller & E. Cooper, Federal Practice and Procedure §3532.6 (1984). While the policies underlying the two concepts often overlap, the finality requirement is concerned with whether the initial decision-maker has arrived at a definitive position on the issue that inflicts an actual, concrete injury; the exhaustion requirement generally refers to administrative and judicial procedures by which an injured party may seek review of an adverse decision and obtain a remedy if the decision is found to be unlawful or otherwise inappropriate. Patsy concerned the latter, not the former.

The difference is best illustrated by comparing the procedure for seeking a variance with the procedures that, under Patsy, respondent would not be required to exhaust. While it appears that the State provides procedures by which an aggrieved property owner may seek a declaratory judgment regarding the validity of zoning and planning actions taken by county authorities, see Fallin v. Knox County Bd. of Commrs., 656 S.W.2d 338 (Tenn. 1983); Tenn. Code Ann. §§27-8-101, 27-9-101 to 27-9-113, and 29-14-101 to 29-14-113 (1980 and Supp. 1984), respondent would not be required to resort to those procedures before bringing its §1983 action, because those procedures clearly are remedial. Similarly, respondent would not be required to appeal the Commission's rejection of the preliminary plat to the Board of Zoning Appeals, because the Board was empowered, at most, to review that rejection, not to participate in the Commission's decision-making.

Resort to those procedures would result in a judgment whether the Commission's actions violated any of respondent's rights. In contrast, resort to the procedure for obtaining variances would result in a conclusive determination by the Commission whether it would allow respondent to develop the subdivision in the manner respondent proposed. The Commission's refusal to approve the preliminary plat does not determine that issue; it prevents respondent from developing its subdivision without obtaining the necessary variances, but leaves open the possibility that respondent may develop the subdivision according to its plat after obtaining the variances. In short, the Commission's denial of approval does not conclusively determine whether respondent will be denied all reasonable beneficial use of its property, and therefore is not a final, reviewable decision.

B

A second reason the taking claim is not yet ripe is that respondent did not seek compensation through the procedures the State has provided for doing so.[13] The Fifth Amendment does not proscribe the taking of property; it proscribes taking without just compensation. . . . If the government has provided an adequate process for obtaining compensation, and if resort to that process "yield[s] just compensation," then the property owner "has no claim against the Government for a taking." *Monsanto*, 104 S. Ct., at 2878, 2881 n.21. Thus, we have held that taking claims against the Federal Government are premature until the property owner has availed itself of the process provided by the Tucker Act, 28 U.S.C. §1491. *Monsanto*, 104 S. Ct., at 2880-2882. Similarly, if a State provides an adequate procedure for seeking just compensation, the property owner cannot claim a violation of the Just Compensation Clause until it has used the procedure and been denied just compensation. . . .

Under Tennessee law, a property owner may bring an inverse condemnation action to obtain just compensation for an alleged taking of property under certain circumstances. Tenn. Code Ann. §29-16-123 (1980). The statutory scheme for eminent domain proceedings outlines the procedures by which government entities must exercise the right of eminent domain. §§29-16-101 to 29-16-121. The State is prohibited from "enter[ing] upon [condemned] land" until these procedures have been utilized and compensation has been paid the owner, §29-16-122, but if a government entity does take possession of the land without following the required procedures,

> "the owner of such land may petition for a jury of inquest, in which case the same proceedings may be had, as near as may be, as hereinbefore provided; or he may sue for damages in the ordinary way. . . ." §29-16-123.

The Tennessee state courts have interpreted §29-16-123 to allow recovery through inverse condemnation where the "taking" is effected by restrictive zoning laws or development regulations. See Davis v. Metropolitan Govt. of Nashville, 620 S.W.2d 532, 533-534 (Tenn. App. 1981); Speight v. Lockhart, 524 S.W.2d 249 (Tenn. App. 1975). Re-

---

13. Again, it is necessary to contrast the procedures provided for review of the Commission's actions, such as those for obtaining a declaratory judgment, see Tenn. Code Ann. §§29-14-101 to 29-14-113 (1980), with procedures that allow a property owner to obtain compensation for a taking. Exhaustion of review procedures is not required. See Patsy v. Florida Board of Regents, 457 U.S. 496 (1982). As we have explained, however, because the Fifth Amendment proscribes takings *without just compensation*, no constitutional violation occurs until just compensation has been denied. The nature of the constitutional right therefore requires that a property owner utilize procedures for obtaining compensation before bringing a §1983 action.

spondent has not shown that the inverse condemnation procedure is unavailable or inadequate, and until it has utilized that procedure, its taking claim is premature.

[Reversed and remanded.]

Page 96.   Before "2. Constraints on Zoning Measures . . . ," add:

NOTE ON DEVELOPMENTS IN ANTITRUST LAW

1. *Update on* Mason City. After the District Court denied Mason City's motion to dismiss, the *Mason City* case went to trial. The District Court found that the city, although not immune from antitrust liability, had not committed an antitrust violation when it had denied the plaintiff developers the rezoning they had requested. The court also rendered a judgment of $250,000 in favor of the city in its counterclaim against the plaintiffs for tortious interference with business relationships. On appeal the Eighth Circuit affirmed that the city was not liable for an antitrust violation but reversed as too speculative the counterclaim award of $250,000. Mason City Center Assocs. v. City of Mason City, 671 F.2d 1146 (8th Cir. 1982).

Mason City was tried before a jury, which seems to have felt more sympathy for the city than for the developer who asserted a conspiracy to restrain trade. Might a self-interested juror be more alert to the certain impact of city antitrust liability on local tax rates than to the uncertain benefits to him of livelier competition in the retail sector?

2. *Other shopping center wars.* Frustrated shopping center developers have been plaintiffs in several other leading cases involving the applicability of federal antitrust statutes to local land-use decisions. For example, in Westborough Mall, Inc. v. City of Cape Girardeau, 693 F.2d 733 (8th Cir. 1982), *cert. denied,* 103 S. Ct. 2122 (1983), the would-be developers of the Westborough Mall asserted that city officials had conspired with the developers of the proposed West Park Mall to block the former project. The District Court held that Parker v. Brown immunized the city from antitrust liability. The Eighth Circuit reversed. It held that "a conspiracy to thwart normal zoning procedures and to directly injure the plaintiffs by illegally depriving them of their property is not in furtherance of any clearly articulated state policy." Id. at 746. The case was remanded for trial.

The owner of an existing shopping center who engages in shenanigans to prevent the entry of a competing center may have violated the antitrust laws. See, e.g., Landmarks Holding Corp. v. Bermant, 664 F.2d 891 (2d Cir. 1981), infra Supplement p. 72. Whom should an antitrust plaintiff prefer to sue—a city or a private firm?

3. *Academic commentary.* During the early 1980s, several commentators asserted that the narrowing of city antitrust immunities would result in unwarranted federal oversight of local decisionmaking. Professor Easterbrook, *in* Antitrust and the Economics of Federalism, 26 J.L. & Econ. 23 (1983), argued that state and local anticompetitive behavior should be exempt from the federal antitrust laws when consumers in *other* states do not as a consequence have to pay higher prices. Mason City would be exempt, for example, unless non-Iowans would suffer from the suppression of retail trade in Mason City. Professor Deutsch contended that a local government should be free from antitrust liability except in some cases where the government has itself acted as a developer, or where (as is alleged in the usual shopping-center case) the government has acted to enrich a small number of influential individuals to the detriment of the general welfare. See Deutsch, Antitrust Challenges to Local Land Use Controls, 6 Zoning & Plan. L. Rep. 169 (1983).

4. *The antitrust bubble bursts.* Three legal developments in the mid-1980s made antitrust actions against municipalities less enticing for landowners. In 1984 Congress enacted a statute that prospectively protected municipalities from liability for Clayton Act damages. The following year the Supreme Court eliminated the requirement that a municipality show active state supervision to qualify for antitrust immunity. Henceforth it need show only that its anticompetitive actions were taken pursuant to a clearly articulated state policy. Town of Hallie v. City of Eau Claire, 471 U.S. 34, 105 S. Ct. 1713, 85 L. Ed. 2d 24 (1985). These developments are described in the highly publicized decision that follows. The *Unity Ventures* decision itself was the third item of favorable legal news for local officials concerned about antitrust liability.

UNITY VENTURES v. COUNTY OF LAKE

631 F. Supp. 181 (N.D. III. 1986)

BUA, District Judge.
Before the Court is the defendants' motion for judgment notwithstanding the verdict or, in the alternative, for a new trial. For the reasons stated herein, the motion for a judgment n.o.v. is granted, and the motion for a new trial is denied.

I. Introduction

Unity Ventures, LaSalle National Bank, and William Alter brought this suit for damages and injunctive relief against Lake County, Illinois, the Village of Grayslake, Illinois, the members of the Lake County

Board, individually and as board members, Edwin M. Schroeder, as mayor of Grayslake, and the trustees of the Village of Grayslake. Plaintiffs alleged that defendants conspired to prevent the development of Alter's land by a series of wrongful acts, including denying access to sanitary sewer service, in violation of plaintiffs' rights under the due process and equal protection clauses of the Fourteenth Amendment and the Civil Rights Act of 1871, 42 U.S.C. §1983.

All claims, except for those based on procedural due process, were tried to a jury. On January 12, 1984, the jury returned a verdict in favor of the plaintiffs and against the defendants for $9,500,000 on the antitrust claim and on the civil rights claim. The verdict on the antitrust claim was trebled and the Court entered judgment in favor of the plaintiffs in the amount of $28,500,000. Thereafter, the defendants filed a timely motion for j.n.o.v. or, in the alternative, for a new trial.

II. Facts . . .

On April 20, 1976, Grayslake entered into an agreement with Lake County for sewage disposal whereby the County was to provide service to Grayslake through the Northeast Interceptor. Pursuant to this agreement, Grayslake was granted a "sphere of influence" that included areas of Lake County outside the boundaries of Grayslake, over which Grayslake had the right to approve all connections to Lake County's Northeast Interceptor. The pertinent part of the agreement provided:

> The County shall preserve the function of County interceptors located within the sphere of influence of the Village (as delineated in Exhibit "A" attached hereto and made a part hereof) by not permitting any direct connection hereto by any person, firm, corporation or municipality unless the Village consents in writing to such direct connection.

[The Village of Grayslake refused to consent to Unity Ventures' application to connect to the Northeast Interceptor.]

III. Discussion . . .

A. ANTITRUST IMMUNITY
1. The Local Government Antitrust Act of 1984

The Local Government Antitrust Act of 1984, P.L. No. 98-544, 130 *Cong. Rec.* H11850-51 (daily ed. Oct. 10, 1984) (the Act) prohibits damages from being entered against local governments for violations of the Clayton Act (15 U.S.C. §§15, 15a or 15c). The Act, which became effective September 10, 1984, is not retroactive unless specific conditions are met.

Defendants claim that this case meets the conditions necessary to trigger retroactive application of the Act, even though a jury verdict had been rendered prior to the passage of the Act. The plaintiffs contend that the Act does not apply retroactively to this case; an argument which, if successful, might enable the $28.5 million verdict to stand.

The language of the Act and the Conference Report is plain. Section 3(a) of the Act creates an immunity from damages:

> No damages, interest on damages, costs, or attorneys' fees may be recovered under Section 4, 4A, or 4C of the Clayton Act (15 U.S.C. §§15, 15a, or 15c) from any local government, or official or employee thereof acting in an official capacity.

But under Section 3(b), this immunity is not retroactive: "Subsection (a) shall not apply to cases commenced before the effective date of this Act" — unless stringent conditions are met:

> [U]nless the defendant establishes and the court determines, in light of all the circumstances, including the stage of litigation and the availability of alternative relief under the Clayton Act, that it would be inequitable not to apply this subsection to a pending case. In consideration of this section, existence of a jury verdict, district court judgment, or any stage of litigation subsequent thereto, shall be deemed to be prima facie evidence that [the immunity] shall not apply. . . .

The jury verdict for this case was rendered in January 1984, long before this Act was passed. The verdict will stand because the defendants have failed to meet their burden of proving that compelling equities necessitate the retroactive application of the Act. . . .

2. State Action Doctrine of Immunity

Defendants allege that the plaintiffs have failed to state a claim on the ground that the defendants' governmental activities were immune from antitrust challenge under the state action doctrine. Accordingly, defendants assert that they are entitled to judgment n.o.v. or, in the alternative, a new trial.

Exemption for anticompetitive actions by state governments was established by the Supreme Court in Parker v. Brown, 317 U.S. 341 (1943). The Supreme Court in City of Lafayette v. Louisiana Power & Light Co., 435 U.S. 389, 413 (1978) extended the *Parker* exemption to local government units acting "pursuant to state policy to displace competition with regulation or monopoly public service." Before it will be exempt from antitrust challenge, the activity must be supported by state policy which is "clearly articulated and affirmatively expressed." *City of Lafayette*, 435 U.S. at 410; Community Communications Company v. City of Boulder, 455 U.S. 40, 51 (1982).

Most recently, the Supreme Court has upheld the "clearly articulated state policy" test in Town of Hallie v. City of Eau Claire, 471 U.S. 34 (1985). This decision fully considers how clearly articulated a state policy must be in order for a municipality to establish that its anticompetitive conduct constitutes state action. Furthermore, *Town of Hallie* provides this Court with a standard for analyzing the Illinois statutes at issue in the present case.

In *Town of Hallie*, four towns surrounding the City of Eau Claire alleged that the City conditioned the provision of sewage treatment, over which it had a monopoly, upon a property owner's agreement to annex his property to the City. The towns alleged that this condition constituted a tying arrangement in violation of the Sherman Act. The Supreme Court affirmed the dismissal of the towns' claim, holding that the City of Eau Claire's actions reflected a "clearly articulated and affirmatively expressed" state policy to permit municipalities to condition the provision of sewage treatment upon an agreement to annex.

Town of Hallie established that, to pass the "clear articulation" test, a state statute must "clearly contemplate that a city may engage in anti-competitive conduct." The legislature, however, need not expressly have stated in either a statute or its legislative history that it intended for the action to have anticompetitive effects.

The Wisconsin statutes in *Hallie* provided that a city may: 1) define the area to be served by its sewer system [Wis. Stat. §62.18(1)(1982)]; 2) fix the limits of such service in unincorporated areas [Wis. Stat. Ann. §66.069(2c) (Supp. 1984); and 3) refuse to serve an area which refuses to annex to the city [Wis. Stat. Ann. §144.07(1m) (Supp. 1984)]. Thus, the Wisconsin statutes specifically authorized the City of Eau Claire to use its monopoly power over sewage treatment to force property owners to annex to the City as a condition of obtaining sewage service.

In analyzing the plain meaning of the statutes, the Supreme Court held that "the statutes clearly contemplate that a city may engage in anticompetitive conduct. Such conduct is a foreseeable result of empowering the City to refuse to serve unannexed areas."

Recently, the Seventh Circuit Court of Appeals addressed the issue of state action immunity in a case involving similar, if not identical, facts to the present case. LaSalle National Bank v. County of DuPage, 777 F.2d 377 (7th Cir. 1985). In *LaSalle National Bank*, plaintiffs' complaint alleged that the County and the Villages of Woodridge and Lisle violated antitrust laws by agreeing to a formula for allocating new sewage connections among themselves in response to IEPA (Illinois Environmental Protection Agency) charges that the consolidated County treatment plants were processing too much waste. The formula was apparently first contained in the two agreements which effected the consolidation of the ownership and management of all sewage treatment facilities in the County. As a part of the consideration for turning over ownership of their own treatment plants to the County, the Villages each reserved the right to a certain number of new connections in the event sewage treatment supply in the County became scarce. The Seventh Circuit also noted that "[a]mong the provisions in the sales agreements was one reserving for each Village the right to determine which users outside the Village would receive sewage treatment service from the sewage treatment plant the Village was selling to the County." Id., at 379. . . .

The Court concludes that, as in *LaSalle National Bank*, the relevant Illinois statutes authorize counties and municipalities to contract together and combine resources for the provision of sewage treatment. Id., at 381. The Court further concludes that the agreement between Lake County and Grayslake, including the "sphere of influence" provision for determining which users outside Grayslake's boundaries would receive sewage treatment, fell within the authorized cooperation between municipalities and counties found in the Illinois statutes in *LaSalle National Bank*.

Turning to the second part of the Seventh Circuit's analysis, the Court . . . excerpts the relevant portions of *LaSalle National Bank*:

> We think it clear that the Illinois statutory scheme which encourages local units of government to cooperate among themselves and with the IEPA in the provision of sewage treatment evinces legislative appreciation of the tension between intergovernmental competition for economic development and pollution control goals, and implicitly sanctions reduced intergovernmental competition.
>
> In sum, free competition and competitive pricing are not the policies underlying the Illinois scheme for sewage treatment. Rather the scheme is one in which local governmental units are encouraged to cooperate in providing sewage service to residences within their boundaries for the common good of the communities they serve. These local and regional decisions regarding sewage treatment are guided by political forces, minimal judicial review, see Krol v. County of Will, 38 Ill. 2d 587, 590 [233 N.E.2d 417] (1968), and state and national environmental protection laws. Under such a scheme anticompetitive effects are clearly foreseeable and contemplated.

Id., at 382. Finally, in *LaSalle National Bank*, the Seventh Circuit concluded that "the defendants' agreement allocating sewage treatment capacity was authorized and that the Illinois legislature intended that such cooperative agreements not be the subject of federal antitrust suits." Id.

In the present case, the Court finds the analysis and result in *LaSalle National Bank* controlling. . . . Accordingly, the Court holds that the doctrine of state action immunity under the antitrust laws applies here to the local government's alleged violative conduct. Since the state action doctrine under Parker v. Brown, 317 U.S. 341 (1943) applies, the jury's verdict and award for the federal antitrust action must be vacated and the action dismissed.

[The Court went on to hold that, even if its ruling on the immunity issue were incorrect, the plaintiffs could not prevail on the merits of either the antitrust or civil-rights claims.]

Page 111.   After the second line, insert:

KEYSTONE BITUMINOUS COAL ASSOCIATION v. DE BENEDICTUS

—U.S.—, 107 S. Ct. 1232, 94 L. Ed. 2d 472 (1987)

[This case involved the constitutionality of this second Pennsylvania statute (the Subsidence Act), which was much like the Kohler Act struck down in *Pennsylvania Coal.* The plaintiff, an association of coal mine operators, filed a complaint that sought to enjoin the Pennsylvania Department of Environmental Resources (DER) from enforcing the act. The lower federal courts rejected the plaintiff's taking claim. The Supreme Court affirmed by a 5-4 margin. In his majority opinion, Justice STEVENS distinguished the two statutes on grounds other than the different types of coal involved:]

Unlike the Kohler Act, which was passed upon in *Pennsylvania Coal,* the Subsidence Act does not merely involve a balancing of the private economic interests of coal companies against the private interests of the surface owners. The Pennsylvania Legislature specifically found that important public interests are served by enforcing a policy that is designed to minimize subsidence in certain areas. Section 2 of the Subsidence Act provides:

> This act shall be deemed to be an exercise of the police powers of the Commonwealth for the protection of the health, safety and general welfare of the people of the Commonwealth, by providing for the conservation of surface land areas which may be affected in the mining of bituminous coal by methods other than 'open pit' or 'strip' mining, to aid in the protection of the safety of the public, to enhance the value of such lands for taxation, to aid in the preservation of surface water drainage and public water supplies and generally to improve the use and enjoyment of such lands and to maintain primary jurisdiction over surface coal mining in Pennsylvania. Pa. Ann. Stat., Tit. 52, §1406.2 (Purdon Supp. 1986).

The District Court and the Court of Appeals were both convinced that the legislative purposes set forth in the statute were genuine, substantial, and legitimate, and we have no reason to conclude otherwise.

None of the indicia of a statute enacted solely for the benefit of private parties identified in Justice Holmes' opinion are present here. First, Justice Holmes explained that the Kohler Act was a "private benefit" statute since it "ordinarily does not apply to land when the surface is owned by the owner of the coal." 260 U.S., at 414. The Subsidence Act, by contrast, has no such exception. The current surface owner may only waive the protection of the Act if the DER consents. See 25 Pa. Code §89.145(b)(1983). Moreover, the Court was forced to reject the Commonwealth's safety justification for the Kohler Act because it found that the Commonwealth's interest in safety could as easily have been accomplished through a notice requirement to landowners. The Subsidence Act, by contrast, is designed to accomplish a number of widely varying interests, with reference to which petitioners have not suggested alternative methods through which the Commonwealth could proceed.

Petitioners argue that at least §6, which requires coal companies to repair subsidence damage or pay damages to those who suffer subsidence damage, is unnecessary because the Commonwealth administers an insurance program that adequately reimburses surface owners for the cost of repairing their property. But this argument rests on the mistaken premise that the statute was motivated by a desire to protect private parties. In fact, however, the public purpose that motivated the enactment of the legislation is served by preventing the damage from occurring in the first place—in the words of the statute—"by providing for the conservation of surface land areas." Pa. Stat. Ann., Tit. 52, §1406.2 (Purdon Supp. 1986). The requirement that the mine operator assume the financial responsibility for the repair of damaged structures deters the operator from causing the damage at all—the Commonwealth's main goal—whereas an insurance program would merely reimburse the surface owner after the damage occurs.

Thus, the Subsidence Act differs from the Kohler Act in critical and dispositive respects. With regard to the Kohler Act, the Court believed that the Commonwealth had acted only to ensure against damage to some private landowners' homes. Justice Holmes stated that if the private individuals needed support for their structures, they should not have "take[n] the risk of acquiring only surface rights." 260 U.S., at 416. Here, by contrast, the Commonwealth is acting to protect the public interest in health, the environment, and the fiscal integrity of the area. That private individuals erred in taking a risk cannot estop the State from exercising its police power to abate activity akin to a public nuisance. The Subsidence Act is a prime example that "circumstances may so change in time . . . as to clothe with such a [public] interest what at other times . . . would be a matter of purely private concern." Block v. Hirsh, 256 U.S. 135, 155 (1921). . . .

Chief Justice REHNQUIST, with whom Justice POWELL, Justice O'CONNOR, and Justice SCALIA join, dissenting. . . .

The Court opines that the decision in *Pennsylvania Coal* rested on the fact that the Kohler Act was "enacted solely for the benefit of private parties," and "served only private interests." Ante, at 12. A review of the Kohler Act shows that these statements are incorrect. The Pennsylvania legislature passed the statute "as remedial legislation, designed to cure existing evils and abuses." 274 Pa., at 495, 118 A., at 492 (quoting the Act). These were public "evils and abuses," identified in the preamble as "wrecked and dangerous streets and highways, collapsed public buildings, churches, schools, factories, streets, and private dwellings, broken gas, water and sewer systems, the loss of human life. . . ." Id., at 496, 118 A., at 493. The Pennsylvania Supreme Court recognized that these concerns were "such as to create an emergency, properly warranting the exercise of the police power. . . ." Id., at 497, 118 A., at 493. There can be no doubt that the Kohler Act was intended to serve public interests.

Though several aspects of the Kohler Act limited its protection of these interests, see *Pennsylvania Coal*, 260 U.S., at 414, this Court did not ignore the public interests served by the Act. When considering the protection of the "single private house" owned by the Mahons, the Court noted that "[n]o doubt there is a *public* interest even in this." Id., at 413 (emphasis added). . . .

. . . Thus, it is clear that the Court has severely understated the similarity of purpose between the Subsidence Act and the Kohler Act. The public purposes in this case are not sufficient to distinguish it from *Pennsylvania Coal*. . . .

Page 132.   Before Michelman excerpt, add:

ALLINGHAM v. CITY OF SEATTLE

109 Wash. 2d 947, 749 P.2d 160 (1988)

GOODLOE, Justice.

A group of landowners seeks to invalidate a Seattle zoning ordinance which requires that a large percentage of certain privately owned lots be retained in or restored to a natural state. The trial court held that §§23.70.40 and 23.70.50 of Seattle Ordinance 111568 (the Greenbelt Ordinance) constituted a taking of property without just compensation and that therefore the ordinance was invalid as a zoning regulation. The City of Seattle appealed directly to this court. We affirm.

The Greenbelt Ordinance was enacted on February 27, 1984, and regulates development in 14 designated greenbelt areas located throughout the City of Seattle. The ordinance affects approximately 900 acres of land, about half of which is privately owned. The designated greenbelts are primarily linear bands of undeveloped, treed hillsides. The fact that many of these hillsides are steep is one of the reasons these areas have not yet been developed.

The Greenbelt Ordinance creates an "overlay zone", superimposed upon the existing or underlying zoning regulations. The underlying zones affected include single-family residential zones, three levels of multi-family residential zones, and manufacturing and industrial zones. The underlying zones regulate the types of uses to which the land may be put, while the Greenbelt Ordinance reserves percentages of the land for "greenbelt preserve[s]" and "restored greenbelt preserve[s]". Sections 23.70.50 and 23.70.60.

The Greenbelt Ordinance requires that an owner of a residential lot 5,000 square feet or larger must reserve 50 percent of the lot in an undisturbed state called a greenbelt preserve, and replant an additional 20 percent of the lot to create a restored greenbelt preserve. Lots smaller than 5,000 square feet have a smaller greenbelt preserve percentage requirement, with the smallest percentage requirement being 30 percent reserved for a greenbelt preserve and 20 percent for a restored greenbelt preserve from residential lots of 3,000 square feet or less. Owners of lots within underlying zones specified as manufacturing, general industrial, or heavy industrial must reserve 40 percent of the lot area for a greenbelt preserve and 10 percent for a restored greenbelt preserve. Lots which are only partially within the designated greenbelt zone must reserve greenbelt preserves and restored greenbelt preserves calculated upon that portion of the lot which is within the greenbelt zone. The ordinance sets forth criteria for determining the specific locations of greenbelt preserves and restored greenbelt preserves, primarily to ensure the contiguity of the total greenbelt areas reserved out of lots under various ownership. . . .

The plaintiffs commenced this action shortly after the Greenbelt Ordinance was passed, seeking to have the ordinance declared invalid as a taking of private property in violation of the due process and equal protection requirements of the state and federal constitutions. The City moved for summary judgment on the ground that the plaintiffs failed to exhaust their administrative remedies; the motion was denied. The case was tried on December 5, 1985. The trial court found that the effect of §§23.70.40 and 23.70.50 of the ordinance was to take the property of the greenbelt owners without compensation and that therefore those sections of the ordinance were invalid use of the police power under the Washington State Constitution. . . .

15

I

The City argues that the land owners should be required to exhaust their administrative remedies by submitting development plans or seeking variances from the requirements of the Greenbelt Ordinance.

Generally, plaintiffs have no standing to seek declaratory and injunctive relief against a zoning ordinance until they have exhausted their administrative remedies. Ackerley Communications v. Seattle, 92 Wash. 2d 905, 602 P.2d 1177 (1979); Lange v. Woodway, 79 Wash. 2d 45, 483 P.2d 116 (1971). The rationale for this rule is that often a variance or other administrative remedy can alleviate the hardship the zoning ordinance would have created for the plaintiff, thereby making a challenge to the ordinance unnecessary. *Lange*, at 48, 483 P.2d 116. Exhaustion of administrative remedies is not required where such exhaustion would be a futile gesture. Orion Corp. v. State, 103 Wash. 2d 441, 693 P.2d 1369 (1985). As stated in *Ackerley*:

> We recognize that where no administrative remedy is available, or where such remedy is patently inadequate, a party may be allowed to raise constitutional issues in a declaratory judgment proceeding without being required to exhaust administrative channels needlessly or to the party's injury.

Ackerley, 92 Wash. 2d at 909, 602 P.2d 1177.

The present case is one in which the available administrative remedies are patently inadequate to relieve the hardship imposed by the ordinance. The Greenbelt Ordinance sets out specific circumstances under which variances may be granted and strictly limits the scope of the variances. For example, under §23.70.50 the location of the greenbelt preserve may be other than that generally required by the ordinance if such a location would further the intent of the Urban Greenbelt Plan. Under §23.70.70, if the location, contiguity and area requirements of the ordinance result in a building footprint of less than 25 percent of the lot, a variance may be granted to allow a 25 percent building footprint to be maintained. However, this provision may not be used to reduce the total greenbelt preserve by more than 10 percent of the lot size. Section 23.70.60 allows the size of the restored greenbelt preserve to be reduced by up to 10 percent of the total lot size, again only under certain unusual circumstances. In sum, even if a property owner were to seek and be granted all available variance remedies, the Greenbelt Ordinance would still deny the owner use of 40-50 percent of the property. The available administrative remedies, while available to reduce the most severe hardships created by the ordinance, are clearly inadequate to alleviate the basic hardship created by requiring a large percentage of these lots to be left in a natural state. Thus, we hold that exhaustion of these administrative remedies would be futile and as such is not required before resort to judicial review of the ordinance.

II

The central issue in this case is whether the Greenbelt Ordinance constitutes a taking of private property without just compensation in violation of Washington's Const. art. 1, §16 and the fifth amendment to the United States Constitution. We hold that it does. A zoning ordinance constitutes a taking of private property where it (1) does not substantially promote legitimate public interests, or (2) deprives the owner of any profitable use of the land. Agins v. Tiburon, 447 U.S. 255, 260-261 (1980); Carlson v. Bellevue, 73 Wash. 2d 41, 51, 435 P.2d 957 (1968).

We recognize that the Greenbelt Ordinance advances numerous legitimate public interests. As stated in the ordinance, it was intended to provide buffers between incompatible land uses, mitigate the effects of noise and air pollution, limit development of environmentally sensitive areas unsuitable for building, maintain habitat for wildlife, and relieve the monotony of continuous urban development. Section 23.70.10. All of these are legitimate public interests.

We find, however, that the ordinance deprives certain landowners of all profitable use of a substantial portion of their land. Under the ordinance, 50 to 70 percent of certain lots must be preserved in or returned to a natural state. The owner of a lot located within a greenbelt zone cannot make any profitable use of that portion of his land required to be reserved under the ordinance: he cannot build a home on it, drive his vehicles across it, or cut down the trees and plant a garden on it. Although he still holds title to the property reserved as greenbelt land, he is denied the control over his property typically accorded landowners. We deem this to be a taking.

The City argues that the Greenbelt Ordinance is a legitimate zoning regulation because even if 70 percent of a lot must be left in its natural state, the remaining 30 percent may be put to profitable use, and therefore the owner has not been deprived of *all* profitable use of his property. According to this argument, the City should be allowed to regulate away all rights of ownership to a portion of a person's property, so long as some part of the property remains usable. We find this argument unpersuasive. If the City were to take a portion of certain properties for the purpose of building a road, clearly we would hold that the City must pay for the land so taken. Likewise where, as here, the City takes a portion of certain properties for the purpose of preserving greenbelts, the City must pay for the land taken. To permit the City to accomplish the same purpose under the guise of a zoning regulation would be

inequitable and would constitute an unconstitutional taking of private property without just compensation. We therefore hold that the Greenbelt Ordinance is invalid. . . .
[Unanimous.]

Page 134.   Before Note 2, insert:

Loretto v. Teleprompter Manhattan CATV Corp., 458 U.S. 419, 102 S. Ct. 3164, 73 L. Ed. 2d 868 (1982), involved the stringing of a television cable across the roof of the plaintiff landlord's building without her consent. The New York Court of Appeals held that this incursion did not constitute a taking of property. The Supreme Court, with Justice Marshall writing for the majority, reversed. The Court proclaimed for the first time that a permanent physical occupation of real property is invariably a taking. Justice Blackmun, writing for the three dissenters, contended that the majority's per se rule is too rigid.

The Supreme Court remanded *Loretto* to the New York Court of Appeals for a determination of whether the plaintiff had received just compensation. The Court of Appeals in turn remanded the case, with instructions, to the trial level. 58 N.Y.2d 143, 446 N.E.2d 428, 459 N.Y.S.2d 743 (1983).

Professor Costonis criticized the *Loretto* rule *in* Presumptive and Per Se Takings: A Decisional Model for the Taking Issue, 58 N.Y.U.L. Rev. 465 (1983), a fresh examination of the takings conundrum.

Page 149.   Before Note on Adult Entertainment, add:

CITY OF RENTON v. PLAYTIME THEATRES, INC.
475 U.S. 41, 106 S. Ct. 925, 89 L. Ed. 2d 29 (1986)

Justice REHNQUIST delivered the opinion of the Court.
This case involves a constitutional challenge to a zoning ordinance, enacted by appellant, the city of Renton, Washington, that prohibits adult motion picture theaters from locating within 1,000 feet of any residential zone, single- or multiple-family dwelling, church, park, or school. Appellees, Playtime Theatres, Inc., and Sea-First Properties, Inc., filed an action in the United States District Court for the Western District of Washington seeking a declaratory judgment that the Renton ordinance violated the First and Fourteenth Amendments and a permanent injunction against its enforcement. The District Court ruled in favor of Renton and denied the permanent injunction, but the Court of Appeals for the Ninth Circuit reversed and remanded for reconsideration. We

noted probable jurisdiction, and now reverse the judgment of the Ninth Circuit. . . .

At first glance, the Renton ordinance, like the ordinance in *American Mini Theatres*, does not appear to fit neatly into either the "content-based" or the "content-neutral" category. To be sure, the ordinance treats theaters that specialize in adult films differently from other kinds of theaters. Nevertheless, as the District Court concluded, the Renton ordinance is aimed not at the *content* of the films shown at "adult motion picture theatres," but rather at the *secondary effects* of such theaters on the surrounding community. The District Court found that the City Council's *"predominate* concerns" were with the secondary effects of adult theaters, and not with the content of adult films themselves. But the Court of Appeals, relying on its decision in Tovar v. Billmeyer, 721 F.2d 1260, 1266 (CA9 1983), held that this was not enough to sustain the ordinance. According to the Court of Appeals, if *"a motivating factor"* in enacting the ordinance was to restrict respondents' exercise of First Amendment rights the ordinance would be invalid, apparently no matter how small a part this motivating factor may have played in the City Council's decision. 748 F.2d, at 537 (emphasis in original). This view of the law was rejected in United States v. O'Brien, 391 U.S. 367, 382-386 (1968), the very case that the Court of Appeals said it was applying:

> It is a familiar principle of constitutional law that this Court will not strike down an otherwise constitutional statute on the basis of an alleged illicit legislative motive. . . .
> What motivates one legislator to make a speech about a statute is not necessarily what motivates scores of others to enact it, and the stakes are sufficiently high for us to eschew guesswork. Id., at 383-384.

The District Court's finding as to "predominate" intent, left undisturbed by the Court of Appeals, is more than adequate to establish that the city's pursuit of its zoning interests here was unrelated to the suppression of free expression. The ordinance by its terms is designed to prevent crime, protect the city's retail trade, maintain property values, and generally "protec[t] and preserv[e] the quality of [the city's] neighborhoods, commercial districts, and the quality of urban life," not to suppress the expression of unpopular views. . . .

We hold that Renton was entitled to rely on the experiences of Seattle and other cities, and in particular on the "detailed findings" summarized in the Washington Supreme Court's *Northend Cinema* opinion, in enacting its adult theater zoning ordinance. The First Amendment does not require a city, before enacting such an ordinance, to conduct new studies or produce evidence independent of that already generated by other cities, so long as whatever evidence the city relies upon is reasonably believed to be relevant to the problem that the city addresses. That was the case here. Nor is our holding affected by the fact that Seattle ultimately chose a different method of adult theater zoning than that chosen by Renton, since Seattle's choice of a different remedy to combat the secondary effects of adult theaters does not call into question either Seattle's identification of those secondary effects or the relevance of Seattle's experience to Renton.

We also find no constitutional defect in the method chosen by Renton to further its substantial interests. Cities may regulate adult theaters by dispersing them, as in Detroit, or by effectively concentrating them, as in Renton. "It is not our function to appraise the wisdom of [the city's] decision to require adult theaters to be separated rather than concentrated in the same areas. . . . [T]he city must be allowed a reasonable opportunity to experiment with solutions to admittedly serious problems." American Mini Theatres, 427 U.S., at 71 (plurality opinion). Moreover, the Renton ordinance is "narrowly tailored" to affect only that category of theaters shown to produce the unwanted secondary effects, thus avoiding the flaw that proved fatal to the regulations in Schad v. Mount Ephraim, 452 U.S. 61 (1981), and Erznoznik v. City of Jacksonville, 422 U.S. 205 (1975). . . .

Finally, turning to the question whether the Renton ordinance allows for reasonable alternative avenues of communication, we note that the ordinance leaves some 520 acres, or more than five percent of the entire land area of Renton, open to use as adult theater sites. The District Court found, and the Court of Appeals did not dispute the finding, that the 520 acres of land consists of "[a]mple, accessible real estate," including "acreage in all stages of development from raw land to developed, industrial, warehouse, office, and shopping space that is criss-crossed by freeways, highways, and roads."

Respondents argue, however, that some of the land in question is already occupied by existing businesses, that "practically none" of the undeveloped land is currently for sale or lease, and that in general there are no "commercially viable" adult theater sites within the 520 acres left open by the Renton ordinance. The Court of Appeals accepted these arguments, concluded that the 520 acres was not truly "available" land, and therefore held that the Renton ordinance "would result in a substantial restriction" on speech. 748 F.2d, at 534.

We disagree with both the reasoning and the conclusion of the Court of Appeals. That respondents must fend for themselves in the real estate market, on an equal footing with other prospective purchasers and lessees, does not give rise to a First Amendment violation. . . .

Reversed.

Justice BRENNAN joined by Justice MARSHALL, dissenting.

Renton's zoning ordinance selectively imposes limitations on the location of a movie theater based exclusively on the content of the films shown there. The constitutionality of the ordinance is therefore not correctly analyzed under standards applied to content-neutral time, place, and manner restrictions. But even assuming that the ordinance may fairly be characterized as content-neutral, it is plainly unconstitutional under the standards established by the decisions of this Court. . . .

Page 151. Before "4. Landowner Remedies," add:

NOTE ON ABORTION CLINICS IN MASSACHUSETTS

Delays stemming from the *Framingham Clinic* litigation caused the plaintiff clinic to lose its lease on the building in the Southborough industrial park. It then leased another building in the town of Framingham. The opening of that clinic was delayed when the Building Commissioner interpreted Framingham's zoning ordinance to require the clinic to apply for a special permit. When the town's zoning board of appeals sustained the Commissioner's decision, the clinic again sought relief in the Massachusetts courts and eventually won both trial court and Supreme Judicial Court rulings that the Commissioner had been wrong in his interpretation. See Framingham Clinic, Inc. v. Zoning Board of Appeals, 382 Mass. 283, 415 N.E.2d 840 (1981). How can courts prevent or otherwise deter Massachusetts towns from engaging in stalling tactics of this sort? See infra Casebook pp. 169-172, Notes 3 & 4.

SCHAD v. BOROUGH OF MOUNT EPHRAIM

452 U.S. 61, 101 S. Ct. 2176, 68 L. Ed. 2d 671 (1981)

Justice WHITE delivered the opinion of the Court.

In 1973, appellants began operating an adult bookstore in the commercial zone in the Borough of Mount Ephraim in Camden County, N.J. The store sold adult books, magazines, and films. Amusement licenses shortly issued permitting the store to install coin-operated devices by virtue of which a customer could sit in a booth, insert a coin, and watch an adult film. In 1976, the store introduced an additional coin-operated mechanism permitting the customer to watch a live dancer, usually nude, performing behind a glass panel. Complaints were soon filed against appellants charging that the bookstore's exhibition of live dancing violated §99-15B of Mount Ephraim's zoning ordinance, which described the permitted uses in a commercial zone,[1] in which the store was located, as follows:

> B. Principal permitted uses on the land and in buildings.
>
>   (1) Offices and banks; taverns; restaurants and luncheonettes for sit-down dinners only and with no drive-in facilities; automobile sales; retail stores, such as but not limited to food, wearing apparel, millinery, fabrics, hardware, lumber, jewelry, paint, wallpaper, appliances, flowers, gifts, books, stationery, pharmacy, liquors, cleaners, novelties, hobbies and toys; repair shops for shoes, jewels, clothes and appliances; barbershops and beauty salons; cleaners and laundries; pet stores; and nurseries. Offices may, in addition, be permitted to a group of four (4) stores or more without additional parking, provided the offices to not exceed the equivalent of twenty percent (20%) of the gross floor area of the stores.
>
>   (2) Motels. [Mount Ephraim Code §99-15B(1), (2) (1979).]

Section 99-4 of the Borough's code provided that "[a]ll uses not expressly permitted in this chapter are prohibited."

Appellants were found guilty in the Municipal Court and fines were imposed. Appeal was taken to the Camden County Court, where a trial de novo was held on the record made in the Municipal Court and appellants were again found guilty. The County Court first rejected appellants' claim that the ordinance was being selectively and improperly enforced against them because other establishments offering live entertainment were permitted in the commercial zones.[3] Those establishments, the court held, were permitted, nonconforming uses that had existed prior to the passage of the ordinance. In response to appellants' defense based on the First and Fourteenth Amendments, the court recognized that "live nude dancing is protected by the First Amendment" but was of the view that "First Amendment guarantees are not involved" since the case "involves solely a zoning ordinance" under which "[l]ive entertainment is simply not a permitted use in any establishment" whether the entertainment is a nude dance or some other form of live presentation. App. to Juris. Statement 8a, 12a. Reliance was placed on the statement in Young v. American Mini Theatres, Inc., 427 U.S. 50, 62 (1976), that "[t]he mere fact that the commercial exploitation of material

---

1. The zoning ordinance establishes three types of zones. The "R-1" residential district is zoned for single-family dwellings. The "R-2" residential district is zoned for single-family dwellings, townhouses, and garden apartments. The "C" district is zoned for commercial use, as specified in §99-15 of the Mount Ephraim Code.

3. The building inspector, who is responsible for enforcing the zoning ordinance, testified that three establishments located in commercial zones of the Borough offered live music. However, he stated that they were permitted to do so only because this use of the premises preceded the enactment of the zoning ordinance and thus qualified as a "nonconforming" use under the ordinance. Munic. Ct. Tr., 21-25, 35-36, 55-59. . . .

protected by the First Amendment is subject to zoning and other licensing requirements is not a sufficient reason for invalidating these ordinances." The Appellate Division of the Superior Court of New Jersey affirmed. . . . The Supreme Court of New Jersey denied further review.

Appellants appealed to this Court. Their principal claim is that the imposition of criminal penalties under an ordinance prohibiting all live entertainment, including nonobscene, nude dancing, violated their rights of free expression guaranteed by the First and Fourth Amendments of the United States Constitution. We . . . now set aside appellants' convictions.

I

As the Mount Ephraim Code has been construed by the New Jersey courts—a construction that is binding upon us—"live entertainment," including nude dancing, is "not a permitted use in any establishment" in the Borough of Mount Ephraim. App. to Juris. Statement 12a. By excluding live entertainment throughout the Borough, the Mount Ephraim ordinance prohibits a wide range of expression that has long been held to be within the protections of the First and Fourteenth Amendments. Entertainment, as well as political and ideological speech, is protected; motion pictures, programs broadcast by radio and television, and live entertainment, such as musical and dramatic works fall within the First Amendment guarantee. [Citations omitted.] Nor may an entertainment program be prohibited solely because it displays the nude human figure. "[N]udity alone" does not place otherwise protected material outside the mantle of the First Amendment. Jenkins v. Georgia, 418 U.S. 153, 161 (1974). Furthermore, as the state courts recognized, nude dancing is not without its First Amendment protections from official regulation. [Citations omitted.]

Whatever First Amendment protection should be extended to nude dancing, live or on film, however, the Mount Ephraim ordinance prohibits all live entertainment in the Borough: no property in the Borough may be principally used for the commercial production of plays, concerts, musicals, dance, or any other form of live entertainment.[5] Because appellants' claims are rooted in the First Amendment, they are entitled to rely on the impact of the ordinance on the expressive activities of others as well as their own. "Because overbroad laws, like vague ones, deter

5. The Borough's counsel asserted at oral argument that the ordinance would not prohibit noncommercial live entertainment, such as singing Christmas carols at an office party. Tr. of Oral Arg. 33. Apparently a high school could perform a play if it did not charge admission. However, the ordinance prohibits the production of plays in commercial theaters. Id., at 34.

privileged activit[ies], our cases firmly establish appellant's standing to raise an overbreadth challenge." Grayned v. City of Rockford, 408 U.S. 104, 114 (1972).

II

The First Amendment requires that there be sufficient justification for the exclusion of a broad category of protected expression as one of the permitted commercial uses in the Borough. . . .

. . . In Schneider v. State, 308 U.S. 147 (1939), for example, the Court recognized its obligation to assess the substantiality of the justification offered for a regulation that significantly impinged on freedom of speech: "Mere legislative preferences or beliefs respecting matters of public convenience may well support regulation directed at other personal activities, but be insufficient to justify such as diminishes the exercise of rights so vital to the maintenance of democratic institutions. And so, as cases arise, the delicate and difficult task falls upon the courts to weigh the circumstances and to appraise the substantiality of the reasons advanced in support of the regulation of the free enjoyment of [First Amendment] rights." Id., at 161.[8]. . . Because the ordinance challenged in this case significantly limits communicative activity within the Borough, we must scrutinize both the interests advanced by the Borough to justify this limitation on protected expression and the means chosen to further those interests.

As an initial matter, this case is not controlled by Young v. American Mini Theatres, Inc., the decision relied upon by the Camden County Court. Although the Court there stated that a zoning ordinance is not invalid merely because it regulates activity protected under the First Amendment, it emphasized that the challenged restriction on the location of adult movie theaters imposed a minimal burden on protected speech. 427 U.S., at 62. The restriction did not affect the number of adult movie theaters that could operate in the city; it merely dispersed them. The Court did not imply that a municipality could ban all adult theaters—much less all live entertainment or all nude dancing—from its commercial districts citywide. Moreover, it was emphasized in that

---

8. Several municipalities argued in *Schneider* that their antileafletting ordinances were designed to prevent littering of the streets. The Court did not deny that the ordinances would further that purpose, but it concluded that the cities' interest in preventing littering was not sufficiently strong to justify the limitation on First Amendment rights. The Court pointed out that the cities were free to pursue other methods of preventing littering, such as punishing those who actually threw papers on the streets. 308 U.S., at 162.

case that the evidence presented to the Detroit Common Council indicated that the concentration of adult movie theaters in limited areas led to deterioration of surrounding neighborhoods, and it was concluded that the city had justified the incidental burden on First Amendment interests resulting from merely dispersing, but not excluding, adult theaters.

In this case, however, Mount Ephraim has not adequately justified its substantial restriction of protected activity. None of the justifications asserted in this Court was articulated by the state courts and none of them withstands scrutiny. First, the Borough contends that permitting live entertainment would conflict with its plan to create a commercial area that caters only to the "immediate needs" of its residents and that would enable them to purchase at local stores the few items they occasionally forgot to buy outside the Borough. No evidence was introduced below to support this assertion, and it is difficult to reconcile this characterization of the Borough's commercial zones with the provisions of the ordinance. Section 99-15A expressly states that the purpose of creating commercial zones was to provide areas for "local and *regional* commercial operations." (Emphasis added.) The range of permitted uses goes far beyond providing for the "immediate needs" of the residents. Motels, hardware stores, lumber stores, banks, offices, and car showrooms are permitted in commercial zones. The list of permitted "retail stores" is nonexclusive, and it includes such services as beauty salons, barbershops, cleaners, and restaurants. Virtually the only item or service that may not be sold in a commercial zone is entertainment, or at least live entertainment.[14] The Borough's first justification is patently insufficient.

Second, Mount Ephraim contends that it may selectively exclude commercial live entertainment from the broad range of commercial uses permitted in the Borough for reasons normally associated with zoning in commercial districts, that is, to avoid the problems that may be associated with live entertainment, such as parking, trash, police protection, and medical facilities. The Borough has presented no evidence, and it is not immediately apparent as a matter of experience, that live

---

14. At present, this effect is somewhat lessened by the presence of at least three establishments that are permitted to offer live entertainment as a nonconforming use. See n.3, supra. These uses apparently may continue indefinitely, since the Mount Ephraim Code does not require nonconforming uses to be terminated within a specified period of time. See Mount Ephraim Code §99-24 (1979). The Borough's decision to permit live entertainment as a nonconforming use only undermines the Borough's contention that live entertainment poses inherent problems that justify its exclusion.

entertainment poses problems of this nature more significant than those associated with various permitted uses. . . .

The Borough also suggests that §99-15B is a reasonable "time, place, and manner" restriction; yet it does not identify the municipal interests making it reasonable to exclude all commercial live entertainment but to allow a variety of other commercial uses in the Borough. . . . Mount Ephraim asserts that it could have chosen to eliminate all commercial uses within its boundaries. Yet we must assess the exclusion of live entertainment in light of the commercial uses Mount Ephraim allows, not in light of what the Borough might have done.[18]

To be reasonable, time, place, and manner restrictions not only must serve significant state interests but also must leave open adequate alternative channels of communication. [Citations omitted.] Here, the Borough totally excludes all live entertainment, including nonobscene nude dancing that is otherwise protected by the First Amendment. As we have observed, Young v. American Mini Theatres, Inc., supra, did not purport to approve the total exclusion from the city of theaters showing adult, but not obscene, materials. It was carefully noted in that case that the number of regulated establishments was not limited and that "[t]he situation would be quite different if the ordinance had the effect of suppressing, or greatly restricting access to, lawful speech." 427 U.S., at 71, n.35.

The Borough nevertheless contends that live entertainment in general and nude dancing in particular are amply available in close-by areas outside the limits of the Borough. Its position suggests the argument that if there were countywide zoning, it would be quite legal to allow live entertainment in only selected areas of the county and to exclude it from primarily residential communities, such as the Borough of Mount Ephraim. This may very well be true, but the Borough cannot avail itself of that argument in this case. There is no countywide zoning in Camden County, and Mount Ephraim is free under state law to impose its own zoning restrictions, within constitutional limits. Furthermore, there is no evidence in this record to support the proposition that the kind of entertainment appellants wish to provide is available in reasonably nearby areas. The courts below made no such findings; and at least in their absence, the ordinance excluding live entertainment from the commercial zone cannot constitutionally be applied to appellants so as to criminalize the activities for which they have been fined. "[O]ne is not to have the exercise of his liberty of expression in appropriate places abridged

18. Thus, our decision today does not establish that every unit of local government entrusted with zoning responsibilities must provide a commercial zone in which live entertainment is permitted.

on the plea that it may be exercised in some other place." Schneider v. State, 308 U.S., at 163.

Accordingly, the convictions of these appellants are infirm, and the judgment of the Appellate Division of the Superior Court of New Jersey is reversed and the case is remanded for further proceedings not inconsistent with this opinion.

So ordered.

Justice BLACKMUN, concurring. . . .

. . . It would be a substantial step beyond *Mini Theatres* to conclude that a town or county may legislatively prevent its citizens from engaging in or having access to forms of protected expression that are incompatible with its majority's conception of the "decent life" solely because these activities are sufficiently available in other locals. I do not read the Court's opinion to reach, nor would I endorse, that conclusion.

Were I a resident of Mount Ephraim, I would not expect my right to attend the theater or to purchase a novel to be contingent upon the availability of such opportunities in "nearby" Philadelphia, a community in whose decisions I would have no political voice. . . .

Justice POWELL, with whom Justice STEWART joins, concurring.

I join the Court's opinion as I agree that Mount Ephraim has failed altogether to justify its broad restriction of protected expression. This is not to say, however, that some communities are not free — by a more carefully drawn ordinance — to regulate or ban all commercial public entertainment. In my opinion, such an ordinance could be appropriate and valid in a residential community where all commercial activity is excluded. Similarly, a residential community should be able to limit commercial establishments to essential "neighborhood" services permitted in a narrowly zoned area.

But the Borough of Mount Ephraim failed to follow these paths. The ordinance before us was not carefully drawn and, as the Court points out, it is sufficiently overinclusive and underinclusive that any argument about the need to maintain the residential nature of this community fails as a justification.

Justice STEVENS, concurring in the judgment.

The record in this case leaves so many relevant questions unanswered that the outcome, in my judgment, depends on the allocation of the burden of persuasion. . . .

. . . [T]he record indicates that what actually happens in [the Borough's] commercial zone may bear little resemblance to what is described in the text of the zoning ordinance.

The commercial zone in which appellants' adult bookstore is located is situated along the Black Horse Pike, a north-south artery on the eastern fringe of the Borough. The parties seem to agree that this commercial zone is relatively small; presumably, therefore, it contains only a handful of commercial establishments. Among these establishments are Al-Jo's, also known as the Club Al-Jo, My Dad's, and Capriotti's all of which offer live entertainment.[4] In addition, the zone contains the Mount Ephraim Democratic Club, the Spread Eagle Inn, and Guiseppi's. The record also contains isolated references to establishments known as the Villa Picasso and Millie's. Although not mentioned in the record, Mount Ephraim apparently also supports a commercial motion picture theater.

The record reveals very little about the character of most of these establishments, and it reveals nothing at all about the motion picture theater....

Without more information about this commercial enclave on Black Horse Pike, one cannot know whether the change in appellants' business in 1976 introduced cacophony into a tranquil setting or merely a new refrain in a local replica of Place Pigalle. If I were convinced that the former is the correct appraisal of this commercial zone, I would have no hesitation in agreeing with The Chief Justice that even if the live nude dancing is a form of expressive activity protected by the First Amendment, the Borough may prohibit it. But when the record is opaque, as this record is, I believe the Borough must shoulder the burden of demonstrating that appellants' introduction of live entertainment had an identifiable adverse impact on the neighborhood or on the Borough as a whole....

... Because neither the text of the zoning ordinance nor the evidence in the record indicates that Mount Ephraim applied narrowly drawn content-neutral standards to the appellants' business, for me this case involves a criminal prosecution of appellants simply because one of their employees has engaged in expressive activity that has been assumed, arguendo, to be protected by the First Amendment.[11] Accordingly, and

4. See Munic. Ct. Tr. 21-22, 35-37, 55, 58-59, 67. My Dad's, which is located directly across the street from appellants' bookstore, features a musical combo that plays music from a stage; a vocalist also performs there on occasion. Id., at 25, 35-36. Capriotti's, a dinner club/discotheque, and Al-Jo's also feature live performances by musical groups. Id., at 22, 36, 55, 58-59. The Borough permits live entertainment in these establishments as a prior nonconforming use.

11. Like Justice POWELL, ante (concurring opinion), I have no doubt that some residential communities may, pursuant to a carefully drawn ordinance, regulate or ban commercial public entertainment within their boundaries. Surely, a municipality zoned entirely for residential use need not create a special commercial zone solely to accommodate purveyors of entertainment. Cf. Valley View Village v. Proffett, 221 F.2d 412, 417-418 (C.A.6 1955) (Stewart, J.) (zoning ordinance that provides only for residential use is not per se invalid). Mount Ephraim, however, is not such a municipality.

without endorsing the overbreadth analysis employed by the Court, I concur in its judgment.

Chief Justice BURGER, with whom Justice REHNQUIST joins, dissenting. . . .

The Black Horse Turnpike cuts through the center of Mount Ephraim. For 250 feet on either side of the turnpike, the Borough has established a commercial zone. The rest of the community is zoned for residential use, with either single- or multi-family units permitted. Most of the inhabitants of Mount Ephraim commute to either Camden or Philadelphia for work.

The residents of this small enclave chose to maintain their town as a placid, "bedroom" community of a few thousand people. To that end, they passed an admittedly broad regulation prohibiting certain forms of entertainment. Because I believe that a community of people are—within limits—masters of their own environment, I would hold that, as applied, the ordinance is valid.

At issue here is the right of a small community to ban an activity incompatible with a quiet, residential atmosphere. The Borough of Mount Ephraim did nothing more than employ traditional police power to provide a setting of tranquility. This Court has often upheld the power of a community "to determine that the community should be beautiful as well as healthy, spacious as well as clean, well-balanced as well as carefully patrolled." Berman v. Parker, 348 U.S. 26, 33 (1954). Justice Douglas, speaking for the Court, sustained the power to zone as "ample to lay out zones where family values, youth values, and the blessings of quiet seclusion and clean air make the area a sanctuary for people." Village of Belle Terre v. Boraas, 416, U.S. 1, 9 (1979). Here we have nothing more than a variation on that theme. . . .

The fact that a form of expression enjoys some constitutional protection does not mean that there are not times and places inappropriate for its exercise. The towns and villages of this Nation are not, and should not be, forced into a mold cast by this Court. Citizens should be free to choose to shape their community so that it embodies their conception of the "decent life." This will sometimes mean deciding that certain forms of activity—factories, gas stations, sports stadia, bookstores, and surely live nude shows—will not be allowed. That a community is willing to tolerate such a commercial use as a convenience store, a gas station, a pharmacy, or a delicatessen does not compel it also to tolerate every other "commercial use," including pornography peddlers and live nude shows. . . .

I am constrained to note that some of the concurring views exhibit an understandable discomfort with the idea of denying this small residential enclave the power to keep this kind of show business from its very doorsteps. The Borough of Mount Ephraim has not attempted to suppress the point of view of anyone or to stifle any category of ideas. To say that there is a First Amendment right to impose every form of expression on every community, including the kind of "expression" involved here, is sheer nonsense. To enshrine such a notion in the Constitution ignores fundamental values that the Constitution ought to protect. To invoke the First Amendment to protect the activity involved in this case trivializes and demeans that great Amendment.

NOTE ON SCHAD

1. *The* Schad *state of affairs.* How many of the Justices would allow a small residential suburb to ban *all* commercial uses, including, for example, bookstores and newsstands? How many would allow a small residential suburb to permit in its commercial zones ordinary bookstores but not adult bookstores? If a seller of adult books were to attack the municipality's policy in the latter case, what evidence might help the suburb's attorney justify the content-based difference in treatment? See also Metromedia, Inc. v. City of San Diego, 453 U.S. 490 (1981), infra Supplement p. 86.

2. *Space Invaders.* The video-parlor boom of the early 1980s spawned a spate of cases on the power of a local government to regulate this threat to the morals of teenagers. Parlor operators argued that video games are a form of speech and thus that courts should actively review restrictions on their location. Most judges did not agree. For example, in America's Best Family Showplace Corp. v. City of New York, 536 F. Supp. 170 (E.D.N.Y. 1982), the District Court held that video games are not a form of speech because they are designed only to entertain, not to inform. It also held that New York City had proved that its restrictions on video games were rationally related to a legitimate state interest. See also Marshfield Family Skateland, Inc. v. Town of Marshfield, 389 Mass. 436, 450 N.E.2d 605 (1983), *appeal dismissed,* 464 U.S. 987 (1983), where the Massachusetts court saw no legal barrier to the enforcement of an ordinance that would purge the town of all coin-operated video games, including machines already in place.

What complications would arise if a video game were to have informative value, say because it improved language skills? Is Mr. Schad constitutionally entitled to place beside his coin-operated windows on nude dancers coin-operated "adult" video-game machines?

See generally Ziegler, Trouble in Outer Galactica: The Police Power, Zoning, and Coin-Operated Video-Games, 34 Syracuse L. Rev. 453 (1983).

Page 173.   Delete Gordon v. City of Warren and Notes 1 & 2 in the Note that follows *Gordon* and substitute:

SAN DIEGO GAS & ELECTRIC CO. v. CITY OF SAN DIEGO

450 U.S. 621, 101 S. Ct. 1287, 67 L. Ed. 2d 551 (1981)

Justice BLACKMUN delivered the opinion of the Court.

Appellant San Diego Gas & Electric Company, a California corporation, asks this Court to rule that a State must provide a monetary remedy to a landowner whose property allegedly has been "taken" by a regulatory ordinance claimed to violate the Just Compensation Clause of the Fifth Amendment. This question was left open last Term in Agins v. City of Tiburon, 447 U.S. 255, 263 (1980). Because we conclude that we lack jurisdiction in this case, we again must leave the issue undecided. . . .

Justice BRENNAN, with whom Justice STEWART, Justice MAR-SHALL, and Justice POWELL join, dissenting.

Title 28 U.S.C. §1257 limits this Court's jurisdiction to review judgments of state courts to "[f]inal judgments or decrees rendered by the highest court of a State in which a decision could be had." The Court today dismisses this appeal on the ground that the Court of Appeal of California, Fourth District, failed to decide the federal question whether a "taking" of appellant's property had occurred, and therefore had not entered a final judgment or decree on that question appealable under §1257. Because the Court's conclusion fundamentally mischaracterizes the holding and judgment of the Court of Appeal, I respectfully dissent from the Court's dismissal and reach the merits of appellant's claim.

I

In 1966, appellant assembled a 412-acre parcel of land as a potential site for a nuclear power plant. At that time, approximately 116 acres of the property were zoned for industrial use, with most of the balance zoned in an agricultural holding category. In 1967, appellee city of San Diego adopted its general plan, designating most of appellant's property for industrial use. In 1973, the city took three critical actions which together form the predicate of the instant litigation: it down-zoned some of appellant's property from industrial to agricultural; it incorporated a new open-space element in its plan that designated about 233 acres of appellant's land for open-space use; and it prepared a report mapping appellant's property for purchase by the city for open-space use, contingent on passage of a bond issue.

Appellant filed suit in California Superior Court alleging, inter alia, a "taking" of its property by "inverse condemnation" in violation of the United States and California Constitutions, and seeking compensation of over $6 million. After a nonjury trial on liability, the court held that appellee city had taken a portion of appellant's property without just compensation, thereby violating the United States and California Constitutions. A subsequent jury trial on damages resulted in a judgment of over $3 million, plus interest as of the date of the "taking," and appraisal, engineering, and attorney's fees. . . .

. . . In faithful compliance with the instructions of the California Supreme Court's opinion in Agins v. City of Tiburon, the Court of Appeal held that the city's exercise of its police power, however arbitrary or excessive, could not *as a matter of federal constitutional law* constitute a "taking" under the Fifth and Fourteenth Amendments, and therefore that there was no "taking" without just compensation in the instant case. [Justice Brennan concluded that the California Court of Appeal had entered a Final judgment on the taking issue.]

IV

Having determined that property may be "taken for public use" by police power regulation within the meaning of the Just Compensation Clause of the Fifth Amendment, the question remains whether a government entity may constitutionally deny payment of just compensation to the property owner and limit his remedy to mere invalidation of the regulation instead. Appellant argues that it is entitled to the full fair market value of the property. Appellees argue that invalidation of the regulation is sufficient without payment of monetary compensation. In my view, once a court establishes that there was a regulatory "taking," the Constitution demands that the government entity pay just compensation for the period commencing on the date the regulation first effected the "taking," and ending on the date the government entity chooses to rescind or otherwise amend[19] the regulation. This interpretation, I believe, is supported by the express words and purpose of the Just Compensation Clause, as well as by cases of this Court construing it.

. . . Invalidation unaccompanied by payment of damages would hardly compensate the landowner for any economic loss suffered during the time his property was taken.[22] Moreover, mere invalidation would fall

19. Under this rule, a government entity is entitled to amend the offending regulation so that it no longer effects a "taking." It may also choose formally to condemn the property.

22. The instant litigation is a good case in point. The trial court, on April 9, 1976, found that the city's actions effected a "taking" of appellant's property on June 19, 1973. If true, then appellant has been deprived of all beneficial use of its property in violation of the Just Compensation Clause for the past seven years.

far short of fulfilling the fundamental purpose of the Just Compensation Clause. That guarantee was designed to bar the government from forcing some individuals to bear burdens which, in all fairness, should be borne by the public as a whole. Armstrong v. United States, 364 U.S. 40, 49 (1960). When one person is asked to assume more than a fair share of the public burden, the payment of just compensation operates to redistribute that economic cost from the individual to the public at large. See United States v. Willow River Co., 324 U.S. 499, 502 (1945); Monongahela Navigation Co. v. United States, 148 U.S. 312, 325 (1893). Because police power regulations must be substantially related to the advancement of the public health, safety, morals, or general welfare, see Village of Euclid v. Ambler Realty Co., 272 U.S. 365, 395 (1926), it is axiomatic that the public receives a benefit while the offending regulation is in effect.[23] If the regulation denies the private property owner the use and enjoyment of his land and is found to effect a "taking," it is only fair that the public bear the cost of benefits received during the interim period between application of the regulation and the government entity's rescission of it. The payment of just compensation serves to place the landowner in the same position monetarily as he would have occupied if his property had not been taken. Almota Farmers Elevator & Warehouse Co. v. United States, 409 U.S. 470, 473-474 (1973); United States v. Reynolds, 397 U.S. 14, 16 (1970). . . .

Invalidation hardly prevents enactment of subsequent unconstitutional regulations by the government entity. At the 1974 annual conference of the National Institute of Municipal Law Officers in California, a California City Attorney gave fellow City Attorneys the following advice:

"IF ALL ELSE FAILS, MERELY AMEND THE REGULATION AND START OVER AGAIN.

"If legal preventive maintenance does not work, and you still receive a claim attacking the land use regulation, or if you try the case and lose, don't worry about it. All is not lost. One of the extra 'goodies' contained in the recent [California] Supreme Court case of Selby v. City of San Buenaventura, 10 C.3d 110, appears to allow the City to change the regulation in question, even after trial and judgment, make it more reasonable, more restrictive, or whatever, and everybody starts over again. . . .

"See how easy it is to be a City Attorney. Sometimes you can lose the battle and still win the war. Good luck." Longtin, Avoiding and Defending Constitutional Attacks on Land Use Regulations (Including Inverse Condemnation), in 38B NIMLO Municipal Law Review 192-193 (1975) (emphasis in original).

23. A different case may arise where a police power regulation is not enacted in furtherance of the public health, safety, morals, or general welfare so that there may be no "public use." Although the government entity may not be forced to pay just compensation under the Fifth Amendment, the landowner may nevertheless have a damages cause of action under 42 U.S.C. §1983 for a Fourteenth Amendment due process violation.

V

In Agins v. City of Tiburon, 24 Cal. 3d, at 275, the California Supreme Court was "persuaded by various policy considerations to the view that inverse condemnation is an inappropriate and undesirable remedy in cases in which unconstitutional regulation is alleged." In particular, the court cited "the need for preserving a degree of freedom in land-use planning function, and the inhibiting financial force which inheres in the inverse condemnation remedy," in reaching its conclusion. Id., at 276. But the applicability of express constitutional guarantees is not a matter to be determined on the basis of policy judgments made by the legislative, executive, or judicial branches.[26] Nor can the vindication of those rights depend on the expense in doing so. See Watson v. Memphis, 373 U.S. 526, 537-538 (1963).

Because I believe that the Just Compensation Clause requires the constitutional rule outlined supra, I would vacate the judgment of the California Court of Appeal, Fourth District, and remand for further proceedings not inconsistent with this opinion.[27]

NOTE ON STATE-COURT RESPONSES TO SAN DIEGO GAS

Justice Brennan's interpretation of the federal Takings Clause of course did not bind state courts engaged in interpreting the takings clauses in their state constitutions. Yet within a few years of the *San Diego Gas* decision several state supreme courts had openly applied Brennan's rea-

---

26. Even if I were to concede a role for policy considerations, I am not so sure that they would militate against requiring payment of just compensation. Indeed, land-use planning commentators have suggested that the threat of financial liability for unconstitutional police power regulations would help to produce a more rational basis of decisionmaking that weighs the costs of restrictions against their benefits. Dunham, From Rural Enclosure to Re-Enclosure of Urban Land, 35 N.Y.U.L. Rev. 1238, 1253-1254 (1960). Such liability might also encourage municipalities to err on the constitutional side of police power regulations, and to develop internal rules and operating procedures to minimize overzealous regulatory attempts. Cf. Owen v. City of Independence, 445 U.S. 622, 651-652 (1980). After all, a policeman must know the Constitution, then why not a planner? In any event, one may wonder as an empirical matter whether the threat of just compensation will greatly impede the efforts of planners. Cf. id., at 656.

27. Because the California Court of Appeal, Fourth District, followed the instructions of the California Supreme Court and held that the city's regulation, however arbitrary or excessive, could not effect a "taking," the Court of Appeal did not address the issue whether San Diego's course of conduct *in fact* effected a "taking" of appellant's property. I would not reach that issue here, but leave it open for the Court of Appeal on remand initially to decide that question on its review of the Superior Court's judgment.

soning to hold that a regulatory taking in violation of the state takings clause entitles a victim to recover interim damages. Corrigan v. City of Scottsdale, 149 Ariz. 538, 720 P.2d 513 (1986); Burrows v. City of Keene, 121 N.H. 590, 432 A.2d 15 (1981); Rippley v. City of Lincoln, 330 N.W.2d 505 (N.D. 1983) (Brennan's dissent is "legally correct" and provides "a practical and fair solution" to the remedy question); Zinn v. State, 112 Wis. 2d 417, 334 N.W.2d 67 (1983). The decision that follows may enhance this trend.

FIRST ENGLISH EVANGELICAL LUTHERAN CHURCH OF GLENDALE v. COUNTY OF LOS ANGELES

—U.S.—, 107 S. Ct. 2378, 96 L. Ed. 2d 250 (1987)

Chief Justice REHNQUIST delivered the opinion of the Court.

In this case the California Court of Appeal held that a landowner who claims that his property has been "taken" by a land-use regulation may not recover damages for the time before it is finally determined that the regulation constitutes a "taking" of his property. We disagree, and conclude that in these circumstances the Fifth and Fourteenth Amendments to the United States Constitution would require compensation for that period.

In 1957, appellant First English Evangelical Lutheran Church purchased a 21-acre parcel of land in a canyon along the banks of the Middle Fork of Mill Creek in the Angeles National Forest. The Middle Fork is the natural drainage channel for a watershed area owned by the National Forest Service. Twelve of the acres owned by the church are flat land, and contained a dining hall, two bunkhouses, a caretaker's lodge, an outdoor chapel, and a footbridge across the creek. The church operated on the site a campground, known as "Lutherglen," as a retreat center and a recreational area for handicapped children.

In July 1977, a forest fire denuded the hills upstream from Lutherglen, destroying approximately 3,860 acres of the watershed area and creating a serious flood hazard. Such flooding occurred on February 9 and 10, 1978, when a storm dropped 11 inches of rain in the watershed. The runoff from the storm overflowed the banks of the Mill Creek, flooding Lutherglen and destroying its buildings.

In response to the flooding of the canyon, appellee County of Los Angeles adopted Interim Ordinance No. 11,855 in January 1979. The ordinance provided that "[a] person shall not construct, reconstruct, place or enlarge any building or structure, any portion of which is, or will be, located within the outer boundary lines of the interim flood protection area located in Mill Creek Canyon. . . ." The ordinance was effective immediately because the county determined that it was "required for the immediate preservation of the public health and safety. . . ." The interim flood protection area described by the ordinance included the flat areas on either side of Mill Creek on which Lutherglen had stood.

The church filed a complaint in the Superior Court of California a little more than a month after the ordinance was adopted. As subsequently amended, the complaint alleged two claims against the county and the Los Angeles County Flood Control District. The first alleged that the defendants were liable under Cal. Govt. Code Ann. §835 (West 1980)[1] for dangerous conditions on their upstream properties that contributed to the flooding of Lutherglen. As a part of this claim, appellant also alleged that "Ordinance No. 11,855 denies [appellant] all use of Lutherglen." The second claim sought to recover from the Flood District in inverse condemnation and in tort for engaging in cloud seeding during the storm that flooded Lutherglen. Appellant sought damages under each count for loss of use of Lutherglen. The defendants moved to strike the portions of the complaint alleging that the county's ordinance denied all use of Lutherglen, on the view that the California Supreme Court's decision in Agins v. Tiburon, 24 Cal. 3d 266 (1979), aff'd on other grounds, 447 U.S. 255 (1980), rendered the allegation "entirely immaterial and irrelevant[, with] no bearing upon any conceivable cause of action herein." See Cal. Civ. Proc. Code Ann. §436 (West Supp. 1987) ("The court may . . . strike out any irrelevant, false, or improper matter inserted in any pleading").

In *Agins v. Tiburon*, supra, the Supreme Court of California decided that a landowner may not maintain an inverse condemnation suit in the courts of that State based upon a "regulatory" taking. In the court's view, maintenance of such a suit would allow a landowner to force the legislature to exercise its power of eminent domain. Under this decision, then, compensation is not required until the challenged regulation or ordinance has been held excessive in an action for declaratory relief or a writ of mandamus and the government has nevertheless decided to continue the regulation in effect. Based on this decision, the trial court in the present case granted the motion to strike the allegation that the church had been denied all use of Lutherglen. It explained that "a careful re-reading of the *Agins* case persuades the Court that when an ordinance, even a non-zoning ordinance, deprives a person of the total use of his

1. Section 835 of the California Government Code establishes conditions under which a public entity may be liable "for injury caused by a dangerous condition of its property. . . ."

lands, his challenge to the ordinance is by way of declaratory relief or possibly mandamus." Because the appellant alleged a regulatory taking and sought only damages, the allegation that the ordinance denied all use of Lutherglen was deemed irrelevant.[2]

On appeal, the California Court of Appeal read the complaint as one seeking "damages for the uncompensated taking of all use of Lutherglen by County Ordinance No. 11,855. . . ." It too relied on the California Supreme Court's decision in *Agins* in rejecting the cause of action, declining appellant's invitation to reevaluate *Agins* in light of this Court's opinions in San Diego Gas & Electric Co. v. San Diego, 450 U.S. 621 (1981). The court found itself obligated to follow *Agins* "because the United States Supreme Court has not yet ruled on the question of whether a state may constitutionally limit the remedy for a taking to nonmonetary relief. . . ." It accordingly affirmed the trial court's decision to strike the allegations concerning appellee's ordinance. The Supreme Court of California denied review.

This appeal followed. . . . Appellant asks us to hold that the Supreme Court of California erred in *Agins v. Tiburon* in determining that the Fifth Amendment, as made applicable to the States through the Fourteenth Amendment, does not require compensation as a remedy for "temporary" regulatory takings—those regulatory takings which are ultimately invalidated by the courts. Four times this decade, we have considered similar claims and have found ourselves for one reason or another unable to consider the merits of the *Agins* rule. See MacDonald, Sommer & Frates v. Yolo County, 106 S. Ct. 2561 (1986); Williamson County Regional Planning Commn. v. Hamilton Bank, 473 U.S. 172 (1985); San Diego Gas & Electric Co., supra; *Agins v. Tiburon*, supra. For the reasons explained below, however, we find the constitutional claim properly presented in this case, and hold that on these facts the California courts have decided the compensation question inconsistently with the requirements of the Fifth Amendment.

I

Concerns with finality left us unable to reach the remedial question in the earlier cases where we have been asked to consider the rule of *Agins*. In each of these cases, we concluded either that regulations considered to be in issue by the state court did not effect a taking, *Agins v.*

---

2. The trial court also granted defendants' motion for judgment on the pleadings on the second cause of action, based on cloud seeding. It limited trial on the first cause of action for damages under Cal. Govt. Code Ann. §835 (West 1980), rejecting the inverse condemnation claim. At the close of plaintiff's evidence, the trial court granted a nonsuit on behalf of defendants, dismissing the entire complaint.

Tiburon, supra, 24 Cal. 3d at 263, or that the factual disputes yet to be resolved by state authorities might still lead to the conclusion that no taking had occurred. *MacDonald, Sommer & Frates,* supra; *Williamson County,* supra; *San Diego Gas & Electric Co.,* supra. Consideration of the remedial question in those circumstances, we concluded, would be premature.

The posture of the present case is quite different. Appellant's complaint alleged that "Ordinance No. 11,855 denies [it] all use of Lutherglen," and sought damages for this deprivation. In affirming the decision to strike this allegation, the Court of Appeal assumed that the complaint sought "damages for the uncompensated *taking* of all use of Lutherglen by County Ordinance No. 11,855." (Emphasis added.) It relied on the California Supreme Court's *Agins* decision for the conclusion that "the remedy for a *taking* [is limited] to nonmonetary relief. . . ." (Emphasis added.) The disposition of the case on these grounds isolates the remedial question for our consideration. The rejection of appellant's allegations did not rest on the view that they were false. Cf. *MacDonald, Sommer & Frates,* supra, 106 S. Ct., at 2568, n.8 (California court rejected allegation in the complaint that appellant was deprived of all beneficial use of its property); Agins v. Tiburon, 447 U.S., at 259, n.6 (same). Nor did the court rely on the theory that regulatory measures such as Ordinance No. 11,855 may never constitute a taking in the constitutional sense. Instead, the claims were deemed irrelevant solely because of the California Supreme Court's decision in *Agins* that damages are unavailable to redress a "temporary" regulatory taking. The California Court of Appeal has thus held that regardless of the correctness of appellants' claim that the challenged ordinance denies it "all use of Lutherglen" appellant may not recover damages until the ordinance is finally declared unconstitutional, and then only for any period after that declaration for which the county seeks to enforce it. The constitutional question pretermitted in our earlier cases is therefore squarely presented here.[6]

We reject appellee's suggestion that, regardless of the state court's treatment of the question, we must independently evaluate the adequacy of the complaint and resolve the takings claim on the merits before we can reach the remedial question. However "cryptic"—to use appellee's description—the allegations with respect to the taking were, the California courts deemed them sufficient to present the issue. We accord-

6. Our cases have also required that one seeking compensation must "seek compensation through the procedures the State has provided for doing so" before the claim is ripe for review. Williamson County Regional Planning Commn. v. Hamilton Bank, 473 U.S. 172, 194 (1985). It is clear that appellant met this requirement. Having assumed that a taking occurred, the California court's dismissal of the action establishes that "the inverse condemnation procedure is unavailable. . . ." Id., at 197. The compensation claim is accordingly ripe for our consideration.

ingly have no occasion to decide whether the ordinance at issue actually denied appellant all use of its property or whether the county might avoid the conclusion that a compensable taking had occurred by establishing that the denial of all use was insulated as a part of the State's authority to enact safety regulations. See e.g., Goldblatt v. Hempstead, 369 U.S. 590 (1962); Hadacheck v. Sebastian, 239 U.S. 394 (1915); Mugler v. Kansas, 123 U.S. 623 (1887). These questions, of course, remain open for decision on the remand we direct today. We now turn to the question of whether the Just Compensation Clause requires the government to pay for "temporary" regulatory takings.

II

Consideration of the compensation question must begin with direct reference to the language of the Fifth Amendment, which provides in relevant part that "private property [shall not] be taken for public use, without just compensation. . . ."

We have recognized that a landowner is entitled to bring an action in inverse condemnation as a result of " 'the self-executing character of the constitutional provision with respect to compensation. . . .' " United States v. Clarke, 445 U.S. 253, 257 (1980), quoting 6 P. Nichols, Eminent Domain §25.41 (3d rev. ed. 1972). As noted in Justice BRENNAN's dissent in *San Diego Gas & Electric Co.*, 450 U.S., at 654-655, it has been established at least since Jacobs v. United States, 290 U.S. 13 (1933), that claims for just compensation are grounded in the Constitution itself:

> The suits were based on the right to recover just compensation for property taken by the United States for public use in the exercise of its power of eminent domain. *That right was guaranteed by the Constitution.* The fact that condemnation proceedings were not instituted and that the right was asserted in suits by the owners did not change the essential nature of the claim. The form of the remedy did not qualify the right. It rested upon the Fifth Amendment. Statutory recognition was not necessary. A promise to pay was not necessary. Such a promise was implied because of the duty imposed by the Amendment. *The suits were thus founded upon the Constitution of the United States.* Id., at 16. (Emphasis added.)

Jacobs, moreover, does not stand alone, for the Court has frequently repeated the view that, in the event of a taking, the compensation remedy is required by the Constitution. See e.g., Kirby Forest Industries, Inc. v. United States, 467 U.S. 1, 5 (1984); United States v. Causby, 328 U.S. 256, 267 (1946); Seaboard Air Line R. Co. v. United States, 261 U.S. 299, 304-306 (1923); *Monongahela Navigation,* supra, 148 U.S., at 327.

It has also been established doctrine at least since Justice Holmes' opinion for the Court in Pennsylvania Coal Co. v. Mahon, 260 U.S. 393

(1922) that "[t]he general rule at least is, that while property may be regulated to a certain extent, if regulation goes too far it will be recognized as a taking." Id., at 415. While the typical taking occurs when the government acts to condemn property in the exercise of its power of eminent domain, the entire doctrine of inverse condemnation is predicated on the proposition that a taking may occur without such formal proceedings. In Pumpelly v. Green Bay Co., 13 Wall. 166, 177-178 (1872), construing a provision in the Wisconsin Constitution identical to the Just Compensation Clause, this Court said:

> It would be a very curious and unsatisfactory result if . . . it shall be held that if the government refrains from the absolute conversion of real property to the uses of the public it can destroy its value entirely, can inflict irreparable and permanent injury to any extent, can, in effect, subject it to total destruction without making any compensation, because, in the narrowest sense of that word, it is not *taken* for the public use.

Later cases have unhesitatingly applied this principle. See, e.g., Kaiser Aetna v. United States, 444 U.S. 164 (1979); United States v. Dickinson, 331 U.S. 745, 750 (1947); United States v. Causby, 328 U.S. 256 (1946).

While the Supreme Court of California may not have actually disavowed this general rule in *Agins*, we believe that it has truncated the rule by disallowing damages that occurred prior to the ultimate invalidation of the challenged regulation. The Supreme Court of California justified its conclusion at length in the *Agins* opinion, concluding that:

> In combination, the need for preserving a degree of freedom in the land-use planning function, and the inhibiting financial force which inheres in the inverse condemnation remedy, persuade us that on balance mandamus or declaratory relief rather than inverse condemnation is the appropriate relief under the circumstances. Agins v. Tiburon, 24 Cal. 3d, at 276-277.

We, of course, are not unmindful of these considerations, but they must be evaluated in the light of the command of the Just Compensation Clause of the Fifth Amendment. The Court has recognized in more than one case that the government may elect to abandon its intrusion or discontinue regulations. See, e.g., Kirby Forest Industries, Inc. v. United States, 467 U.S. 1 (1984); United States v. Dow, 357 U.S. 17, 26 (1958). Similarly, a governmental body may acquiesce in a judicial declaration that one of its ordinances has affected an unconstitutional taking of property; the landowner has no right under the Just Compensation Clause to insist that a "temporary" taking be deemed a permanent taking. But we have not resolved whether abandonment by the government requires payment of compensation for the period of time during which regulations deny a landowner all use of his land.

In considering this question, we find substantial guidance in cases where the government has only temporarily exercised its right to use private property. In *United States v. Dow*, supra, at 26, though rejecting a claim that the Government may not abandon condemnation proceedings, the Court observed that abandonment "results in an alteration in the property interest taken — from [one of] full ownership to one of temporary use and occupation. . . . In such cases compensation would be measured by the principles normally governing the taking of a right to use property temporarily. See Kimball Laundry Co. v. United States, 338 U.S. 1 [1949]; United States v. Petty Motor Co., 327 U.S. 372 [1946]; United States v. General Motors Corp., 323 U.S. 373 [1945]." Each of the cases cited by the *Dow* Court involved appropriation of private property by the United States for use during World War II. Though the takings were in fact "temporary," see *Petty Motor Co.*, supra, 327 U.S., at 375, there was no question that compensation would be required for the Government's interference with the use of the property; the Court was concerned in each case with determining the proper measure of the monetary relief to which the property holders were entitled. See *Kimball Laundry Co.*, supra, 338 U.S., at 4-21; *Petty Motor Co.*, supra, 327 U.S., at 377-381; *General Motors*, supra, 323 U.S., at 379-384.

These cases reflect the fact that "temporary" takings which, as here, deny a landowner all use of his property, are not different in kind from permanent takings, for which the Constitution clearly requires compensation. Cf. *San Diego Gas & Electric Co.*, 450 U.S., at 657 (BRENNAN, J., dissenting) ("Nothing in the Just Compensation Clause suggests that 'takings' must be permanent and irrevocable"). It is axiomatic that the Fifth Amendment's just compensation provision is "designed to bar Government from forcing some people alone to bear public burdens which, in all fairness and justice, should be borne by the public as a whole." Armstrong v. United States, 364 U.S., at 49. See also Penn Central Transportation Co. v. New York City, 438 U.S., at 123-125; Monongahela Navigation Co. v. United States, 148 U.S., at 325. In the present case the interim ordinance was adopted by the county of Los Angeles in January 1979, and became effective immediately. Appellant filed suit within a month after the effective date of the ordinance and yet when the Supreme Court of California denied a hearing in the case on October 17, 1985, the merits of appellant's claim had yet to be determined. The United States has been required to pay compensation for leasehold interests of shorter duration than this. The value of a leasehold interest in property for a period of years may be substantial, and the burden on the property owner in extinguishing such an interest for a period of years may be great indeed. See, e.g., *United States v. General Motors*, supra. Where this burden results from governmental action that amounted to a taking, the Just Compensation Clause of the Fifth Amendment requires that the government pay the landowner for the value of the use of the land during this period. Cf. United States v. Causby, 328 U.S., at 261 ("It is the owner's loss, not the taker's gain, which is the measure of the value of the property taken"). Invalidation of the ordinance or its successor ordinance after this period of time, though converting the taking into a "temporary" one, is not a sufficient remedy to meet the demands of the Just Compensation Clause. . . .

Nothing we say today is intended to abrogate the principle that the decision to exercise the power of eminent domain is a legislative function, " 'for Congress and Congress alone to determine.' " Hawaii Housing Authority v. Midkiff, 467 U.S. 229, 240 (1984), quoting Berman v. Parker, 348 U.S. 26, 33 (1954). Once a court determines that a taking has occurred, the government retains the whole range of options already available—amendment of the regulation, withdrawal of the invalidated regulation, or exercise of eminent domain. Thus we do not, as the Solicitor General suggests, "permit a court, at the behest of a private person, to require the . . . Government to exercise the power of eminent domain. . . ." Brief for United States as Amicus Curiae 22. We merely hold that where the government's activities have already worked a taking of all use of property, no subsequent action by the government can relieve it of the duty to provide compensation for the period during which the taking was effective.

We also point out that the allegation of the complaint which we treat as true for purposes of our decision was that the ordinance in question denied appellant all use of its property. We limit our holding to the facts presented, and of course do not deal with the quite different questions that would arise in the case of normal delays in obtaining building permits, changes in zoning ordinances, variances, and the like which are not before us. We realize that even our present holding will undoubtedly lessen to some extent the freedom and flexibility of land-use planners and governing bodies of municipal corporations when enacting land-use regulations. But such consequences necessarily flow from any decision upholding a claim of constitutional right; many of the provisions of the Constitution are designed to limit the flexibility and freedom of governmental authorities and the Just Compensation Clause of the Fifth Amendment is one of them. As Justice Holmes aptly noted more than 50 years ago, "a strong public desire to improve the public condition is not enough to warrant achieving the desire by a shorter cut than the constitutional way of paying for the change." Pennsylvania Coal Co. v. Mahon, 260 U.S., at 416.

Here we must assume that the Los Angeles County ordinances have denied appellant all use of its property for a considerable period of years, and we hold that invalidation of the ordinance without payment of fair value for the use of the property during this period of time would be a constitutionally insufficient remedy. The judgment of the California Court of Appeals is therefore reversed, and the case is remanded for further proceedings not inconsistent with this opinion.

It is so ordered.

Justice STEVENS, with whom Justice BLACKMUN and Justice O'CONNOR join as to Parts I and III, dissenting.

One thing is certain. The Court's decision today will generate a great deal of litigation. Most of it, I believe, will be unproductive. But the mere duty to defend the actions that today's decision will spawn will undoubtedly have a significant adverse impact on the land-use regulatory process. The Court has reached out to address an issue not actually presented in this case, and has then answered that self-imposed question in a superficial and, I believe, dangerous way.

Four flaws in the Court's analysis merit special comment. First, the Court unnecessarily and imprudently assumes that appellant's complaint alleges an unconstitutional taking of Lutherglen. Second, the Court distorts our precedents in the area of regulatory takings when it concludes that all ordinances which would constitute takings if allowed to remain in effect permanently, necessarily also constitute takings if they are in effect for only a limited period of time. Third, the Court incorrectly assumes that the California Supreme Court has already decided that it will never allow a state court to grant monetary relief for a temporary regulatory taking, and then uses that conclusion to reverse a judgment which is correct under the Court's own theories. Finally, the Court errs in concluding that it is the Takings Clause, rather than the Due Process Clause, which is the primary constraint on the use of unfair and dilatory procedures in the land-use area. . . .

The cases that the Court relies upon for the proposition that there is no distinction between temporary and permanent takings are inapposite, for they all deal with physical takings—where the diminution of value test is inapplicable.[8] None of those cases is controversial; the state certainly may not occupy an individual's home for a month and then escape compensation by leaving and declaring the occupation "temporary." But what does that have to do with the proper inquiry for regulatory takings?

---

8. In United States v. Dow, 357 U.S. 17 (1958), the United States had "entered into physical possession and began laying the pipe line through the tract." Id., at 19. In Kimball Laundry Co. v. United States, 338 U.S. 1 (1949), the United States Army had taken possession of the laundry plant including all "the facilities of the company, except delivery equipment." 7a., at 3. In United States v. Petty Motor Co., 327 U.S. 372 (1946), the United States acquired by condemnation a building occupied by tenants and ordered the tenants to vacate. In United States v. General Motors Corp., 323 U.S. 373 (1945), the Government occupied a portion of a leased building.

Why should there be a constitutional distinction between a permanent restriction that only reduces the economic value of the property by a fraction — perhaps one-third — and a restriction that merely postpones the development of a property for a fraction of its useful life — presumably far less than a third? In the former instance, no taking has occurred; in the latter case, the Court now proclaims that compensation for a taking must be provided. The Court makes no effort to explain these irreconcilable results. Instead, without any attempt to fit its proclamation into our regulatory takings cases, the Court boldly announces that once a property owner makes out a claim that a regulation would constitute a taking if allowed to stand, then he or she is entitled to damages for the period of time between its enactment and its invalidation. . . .

The Court's reasoning also suffers from severe internal inconsistency. Although it purports to put to one side "normal delays in obtaining building permits, changes in zoning ordinances, variances and the like," ante, at 2389, the Court does not explain why there is a constitutional distinction between a total denial of all use of property during such "normal delays" and an equally total denial for the same length of time in order to determine whether a regulation has "gone too far" to be sustained unless the Government is prepared to condemn the property. Precisely the same interference with a real estate developer's plans may be occasioned by protracted proceedings which terminate with a zoning board's decision that the public interest would be served by modification of its regulation and equally protracted litigation which ends with a judicial determination that the existing zoning restraint has "gone too far," and that the board must therefore grant the developer a variance. The Court's analysis takes no cognizance of these realities. Instead, it appears to erect an artificial distinction between "normal delays" and the delays involved in obtaining a court declaration that the regulation constitutes a taking. . . .

IV

There is, of course, a possibility that land-use planning, like other forms of regulation, will unfairly deprive a citizen of the right to develop his property at the time and in the manner that will best serve his economic interests. The "regulatory taking" doctrine announced in *Pennsylvania Coal* places a limit on the permissible scope of land-use restrictions. In my opinion, however, it is the Due Process Clause rather than that doctrine that protects the property owner from improperly motivated, unfairly conducted, or unnecessarily protracted governmental decision-making. Violation of the procedural safeguards mandated by the Due Process Clause will give rise to actions for damages under 42 U.S.C.

§1983, but I am not persuaded that delays in the development of property that are occasioned by fairly conducted administrative or judicial
proceedings are compensable, except perhaps in the most unusual circumstances. On the contrary, I am convinced that the public interest in
having important governmental decisions made in an orderly, fully informed way amply justifies the temporary burden on the citizen that is
the inevitable by-product of democratic government.

As I recently wrote:

> The Due Process Clause of the Fourteenth Amendment requires a State
> to employ fair procedures in the administration and enforcement of all kinds
> of regulations. It does not, however, impose the utopian requirement that
> enforcement action may not impose any cost upon the citizen unless the
> government's position is completely vindicated. We must presume that reg-
> ulatory bodies such as zoning boards, school boards, and health boards, gen-
> erally make a good-faith effort to advance the public interest when they are
> performing their official duties, but we must also recognize that they will
> often become involved in controversies that they will ultimately lose. Even
> though these controversies are costly and temporarily harmful to the private
> citizen, as long as fair procedures are followed, I do not believe there is any
> basis in the Constitution for characterizing the inevitable by-product of every
> such dispute as a 'taking' of private property. *Williamson,* supra, 473 U.S., at
> 205 (opinion concurring in judgment).

The policy implications of today's decision are obvious and, I fear, far
reaching. Cautious local officials and land-use planners may avoid taking
any action that might later be challenged and thus give rise to a damage
action. Much important regulation will never be enacted,[17] even perhaps
in the health and safety area. Were this result mandated by the Constitution, these serious implications would have to be ignored. But the loose
cannon the Court fires today is not only unattached to the Constitution,

---

17. It is no answer to say that "[a]fter all, if a policeman must know the Constitution,
then why not a planner?" San Diego Gas & Electric Co. v. San Diego, 450 U.S. 621, 661,
n.26 (1981) (BRENNAN, J., dissenting). To begin with, the Court has repeatedly recognized that it itself cannot establish any objective rules to assess when a regulation becomes
a taking. See Hodel v. Irving, 107 S. Ct. 2076 (1987); Andrus v. Allard, 444 U.S. 51, 65
(1979); *Penn Central,* 438 U.S., at 123-124. How then can it demand that land planners
do any better? However confusing some of our criminal procedure cases may be, I do not
believe they have been as open-ended and standardless as our regulatory takings cases
are. As one commentator concluded: "The chaotic state of taking law makes it especially
likely that availability of the damages remedy will induce land-use planning officials to
stay well back of the invisible line that they dare not cross." Johnson, Compensation for
Invalid Land-Use Regulations, 15 Ga. L. Rev. 559, 594 (1981); see also Sallet, The Problem
of Municipal Liability for Zoning and Land-Use Regulation, 31 Cath. U.L. Rev. 465, 478
(1982); Charles v. Diamond, 41 N.Y.2d 318, 331-332 (1977); Allen v. City and County of
Honolulu, 58 Haw. 432, 439, 571 P.2d 328, 331 (1977)....

but it also takes aim at a long line of precedents in the regulatory takings area. It would be the better part of valor simply to decide the case at hand instead of igniting the kind of litigation explosion that this decision will undoubtedly touch off.

I respectfully dissent.

Page 184.   After the third full paragraph, insert:

The Supreme Court has held that municipalities are immune from liability for *punitive* damages when they violate §1983. City of Newport v. Fact Concerts, Inc., 453 U.S. 247 (1981). It has also revised the test for the qualified (good faith) immunity of a public official. Overruling one prong of Wood v. Strickland (U.S. 1975), the Court has ruled that an official need only prove that his actions were *objectively* in good faith. Harlow v. Fitzgerald, 457 U.S. 800 (1982). The majority eliminated the *Wood* requirement that an official also prove his subjective good faith (lack of impermissible intentions) because that requirement had made it difficult for trial courts to weed out frivolous §1983 claims.

Legislative officials risk losing their absolute official immunity from §1983 liability when they act in nonlegislative roles. Hernandez v. City of Lafayette, 643 F.2d 1188 (5th Cir. 1981), *cert. denied*, 455 U.S. 907 (1982), held that a mayor who vetoed a rezoning ordinance was performing a legislative function and was thus entitled to absolute immunity. But in Scott v. Greenville County, 716 F.2d 1409 (4th Cir. 1983), elected county council members who blocked issuance of a building permit for the plaintiff developer's proposed low-income apartment project were held to have been acting in a nonlegislative capacity and thus to be only entitled to qualified immunity. A closer case, perhaps, was Altaire Builders, Inc. v. Village of Horseheads, 551 F. Supp. 1066 (W.D.N.Y. 1982). There the local governing body had denied the plaintiff's application for approval of a planned-unit-development (PUD) project in a zone where the local governing body could authorize PUDs. The District Court held that this decision was nonlegislative and that the officials had to prove good faith to be immune.

Are local governments bound to defray the litigation expenses of officials who successfully defend themselves against §1983 damage actions? In a case where there was no statute or contract providing for reimbursement, the New York Court of Appeals held in a 4-3 decision that an official had no right to make the village pay defense costs. Corning v. Village of Laurel Hollow, 48 N.Y.2d 348, 398 N.E.2d 537, 422 N.Y.S.2d 932 (1979). The dissenters argued that the decision would chill citizen interest in holding public office. When, if ever, should a municipality voluntarily finance the defense costs of its officials?

Bennett v. City of Slidell, 697 F.2d 657 (5th Cir. 1983), affirmed a §1983 judgment awarding the victim of a wrongfully withheld occupancy permit recoveries of $20,000 against the city and $1,000 against the city attorney. Should the city be entitled to shift, on an indemnification theory, both the $20,000 and its defense costs to the individual officials who wrongfully withheld the permit?

On the evolving law of §1983 damage actions, see Bley, Use of the Civil Rights Acts to Recover Money Damages for the Overregulation of Land, 14 Urb. Law. 223 (1982); Cass, Damage Suits Against Public Officers, 129 U. Pa. L. Rev. 1110 (1981).

Page 206. Before Note 2, insert:

A developer's plans to build a major beach hotel complex on Kauai, one of the Hawaiian islands, provoked a widely publicized vested-rights controversy. In February 1979 the County of Kauai approved the developer's application to have its tract rezoned to allow construction of the hotel complex. The developer had spent $158,000 on prepermit expenses by January 1980, at which time a grass-roots referendum to repeal the 1979 rezoning qualified for the ballot. In November 1980 Kauai voters approved the repeal measure by a margin of 10,800 to 5,600.

The County then brought a declaratory action to determine whether the developer had a vested right to proceed with the construction of the resort. The Hawaii Supreme Court held that any expenditures the developer had made *after* the repeal measure had qualified for the ballot had not been in good faith and that the $158,000 paid out before the referendum had qualified for the ballot were not sufficient, under Hawaii law, to estop the County from repealing the rezoning. County of Kauai v. Pacific Standard Life Ins. Co., 65 Hawaii 318, 653 P.2d 766 (1982). The developer then provided financial support for a second referendum campaign aimed at reversing the results of the first referendum. In February 1984 Kauai voters voted 8,500 to 5,900 to annul the prior referendum, thereby enabling construction of the hotel to proceed. N.Y. Times, Feb. 6, 1984, p.8, col. 6.

Page 211. At the end of the last full paragraph, insert:

The Washington Supreme Court has held that a local government may be liable in damages to a developer who relies to his detriment on a wrongly issued building permit. In J & B Dev. Co. v. King County, 100 Wash. 2d 299, 669 P.2d 468 (1983), the county had granted a permit for the construction of a single-family dwelling in a location that violated an unusual frontyard setback requirement. The landowner was framing the house when the County discovered its mistake and issued a stop work order. In the ensuing litigation, the Washington Supreme Court held that the landowner had stated a cause of action that the County was liable for damages under comparative negligence principles.

Chapter Three
Zoning Changes and the Rights of Neighbors

Page 228. Before *Minnetonka Congregation*, insert:

A study by the late Donald Hagman and a group of collaborators found that the success of a party involved in a land-use case before the Supreme Court of California seems primarily to be determined by the interest that the party represents. During the 1962-1966 period—what the study calls the "deferential era"—the court sided with government in 87.5 percent of the land-use cases it decided. Then its overarching principle apparently was that a local government should be free to choose between promoting and inhibiting development activity.

The California Supreme Court had a different attitude during the 1967-1977 period—what the Hagman study calls its "preservation era." Then the court sided with the party representing the antidevelopment interest "almost as if nothing else in a case mattered." Government won 53.7 percent of the cases in this later era, but its success rate was 84 percent when it sided with the preservationist (neighbor) interest, and only 6 percent when, as in *Topanga*, it sided with the development interest. See DiMento, Dozier, Emmons, Hagman, Kim, Greenfield-Sanders, Waldau & Woollacott, Land Development Control in the California Supreme Court, 27 U.C.L.A.L. Rev. 859 (1980). What result in *Topanga* if Los Angeles County were to have denied the variance and the applicant were to have challenged the adequacy of the findings upon which the County had based its denial?

Page 253.   After the heading "b. Stage Two: Judicial Acceptance of Dealmaking," add:

COLLARD v. INCORPORATED VILLAGE OF FLOWER HILL

52 N.Y.2d 598, 421 N.E.2d 818, 439 N.Y.S.2d 326 (1981)

[In 1976 the owners of a private sanitarium that had fallen into disuse applied to the Village of Flower Hill for a rezoning that would permit them to use the land for business purposes. The village board granted the application subject to the condition that the owner record a declaration of covenants providing, among other things, that "[n]o building or structure situated on the Subject Premises on the date of this Declaration of Covenants will be altered, extended, rebuilt, renovated or enlarged without the prior consent of the Board of Trustees of the Village." The owners recorded the declaration, and later sold the premises to appellants.]

JONES, Judge. . . .

Appellants, after acquiring title, made application in late 1978 to the village board for approval to enlarge and extend the existing structure on the premises. Without any reason being given that application was denied. Appellants then commenced this action to have the board's determination declared arbitrary, capricious, unreasonable, and unconstitutional and sought by way of ultimate relief an order directing the board to issue the necessary building permits.

[The trial court denied the Village's motion to dismiss. The Appellate Division reversed.] We now affirm.

At the outset this case involves the question of the permissibility of municipal rezoning conditioned on the execution of a private declaration of covenants restricting the use to which the parcel sought to be rezoned may be put. Prior to our decision in Church v. Town of Islip, 8 N.Y.2d 254, in which we upheld rezoning of property subject to reasonable conditions, conditional rezoning had been almost uniformly condemned by courts of all jurisdictions—a position to which a majority of States appear to continue to adhere. Since *Church*, however, the practice of conditional zoning has become increasingly widespread in this State, as well as having gained popularity in other jurisdictions (see, e.g., Scrutton v. County of Sacramento, 275 Cal. App. 2d 412, 79 Cal. Rptr. 872; Goffinet v. County of Christian, 30 Ill. App. 3d 1089, 333 N.E.2d 731; City of Greenbelt v. Bresler, 248 Md. 210, 236 A.2d 1; Sylvania Elec. Prods. v. City of Newton, 344 Mass. 428, 183 N.E.2d 118; Gladwyne Colony v. Lower Merion Twp., 409 Pa. 441, 187 A.2d 549).

Because much criticism has been mounted against this practice, both by commentators and the courts of some of our sister States,[3] further exposition is in order.

Probably the principal objection to conditional rezoning is that it constitutes illegal spot zoning, thus violating the legislative mandate requiring that there be a comprehensive plan for, and that all conditions be uniform within, a given zoning district. When courts have considered the issue (see, e.g., Baylis v. City of Baltimore, 219 Md. 164, 148 A.2d 429; Houston Petroleum Co. v. Automotive Prods. Credit Assn., 9 N.J. 122, 87 A.2d 319; Hausmann & Johnson v. Berea Bd. of Appeals, 40 Ohio App. 2d 432, 320 N.E.2d 685), the assumptions have been made that conditional zoning benefits particular landowners rather than the community as a whole and that it undermines the foundation upon which comprehensive zoning depends by destroying uniformity within use districts. Such unexamined assumptions are questionable. First, it is a downward change to a less restrictive zoning classification that benefits the property rezoned and not the opposite imposition of greater restrictions on land use. Indeed, imposing limiting conditions, while benefiting surrounding properties, normally adversely affects the premises on which the conditions are imposed. Second, zoning is not invalid per se merely because only a single parcel is involved or benefited (Matter of Mahoney v. O'Shea Funeral Homes, 45 N.Y.2d 719); the real test for spot zoning is whether the change is other than part of a well-considered and comprehensive plan calculated to serve the general welfare of the community (Rodgers v. Village of Tarrytown, 302 N.Y. 115, 96 N.E.2d 731). Such a determination, in turn, depends on the reasonableness of the rezoning in relation to neighboring uses—an inquiry required regardless of whether the change in zone is conditional in form. Third, if it is initially proper to change a zoning classification without the imposition of restrictive conditions not withstanding that such change may depart from uni-

---

3. See, e.g., Babcock, The Zoning Game, chs. 1, 3; Basset, Zoning, ch. 9; Crolly, The Rezoning of Properties Conditioned on Agreements with Property Owners—Zoning by Contract, N.Y.L.J., March 9, 1961, p.4, col. 1; Scott, Toward a Strategy for Utilization of Contract and Conditional Zoning, 51 J. Urban L. 94; Trager, Contract Zoning, 23 Md. L. Rev. 121; Note, Three Aspects of Zoning: Unincorporated Areas—Exclusionary Zoning—Conditional Zoning, 6 Real Prop., Prob. & Tr. J. 178 (1971); Comment, The Use and Abuse of Contract Zoning, 12 U.C.L.A.L. Rev. 897. For judicial criticism, see, e.g., Allred v. City of Raleigh, 277 N.C. 530, 178 S.E.2d 432; Baylis v. City of Baltimore, 219 Md. 164, 148 A.2d 429; City of Farmers Branch v. Hawnco, Inc., 435 S.W.2d 288 [Tex. Civ. App.]; Ford Leasing Dev. Co. v. Board of County Comrs., 186 Colo. 418, 528 P.2d 237; Hartnett v. Austin, 93 So. 2d 86 [Fla.]; Haymon v. City of Chattanooga, 513 S.W.2d 185 [Tenn. App.]; Houston Petroleum Co. v. Automotive Prods. Credit Assn., 9 N.J. 122, 87 A.2d 319; Sandenburgh v. Michigamme Oil Co., 249 Mich. 372, 228 N.W. 707; Ziemer v. County of Peoria, 33 Ill. App. 3d 612, 338 N.E.2d 145.

formity, then no reason exists why accomplishing that change subject to condition should automatically be classified as impermissible spot zoning.

Both conditional and unconditional rezoning involve essentially the same legislative act—an amendment of the zoning ordinance. The standards for judging the validity of conditional rezoning are no different from the standards used to judge whether unconditional rezoning is illegal. If modification to a less restrictive zoning classification is warranted, then a fortiori conditions imposed by a local legislature to minimize conflicts among districts should not in and of themselves violate any prohibition against spot zoning.

Another fault commonly voiced in disapproval of conditional zoning is that it constitutes an illegal bargaining away of a local government's police power (see, e.g., Hartnett v. Austin, 93 So. 2d 86 [Fla.], supra; Baylis v. City of Baltimore, 219 Md. 164, 148 A.2d 429, supra; Ziemer v. County of Peoria, 33 Ill. App. 3d 612, 338 N.E.2d 145, supra). Because no municipal government has the power to make contracts that control or limit it in the exercise of its legislative powers and duties, restrictive agreements made by a municipality in conjunction with a rezoning are sometimes said to violate public policy. While permitting citizens to be governed by the best bargain they can strike with a local legislature would not be consonant with notions of good government, absent proof of a contract purporting to bind the local legislature in advance to exercise its zoning authority in a bargained-for manner, a rule which would have the effect of forbidding a municipality from trying to protect landowners in the vicinity of a zoning change by imposing protective conditions based on the assertion that that body is bargaining away its discretion, would not be in the best interests of the public. The imposition of conditions on property sought to be rezoned may not be classified as a prospective commitment on the part of the municipality to zone as requested if the conditions are met; nor would the municipality necessarily be precluded on this account from later reversing or altering its decision (cf. Matter of Grimpel Assoc. v. Cohalan, 41 N.Y.2d 431).

Yet another criticism leveled at conditional zoning is that the State enabling legislation does not confer on local authorities authorization to enact conditional zoning amendments (see, e.g., Houston Petroleum Co. v. Automotive Prods. Credit Assn., 9 N.J. 122, 87 A.2d 319, supra; Baylis v. City of Baltimore, 219 Md. 164, 148 A.2d 429, supra). On this view any such ordinance would be ultra vires. While it is accurate to say there exists no explicit authorization that a legislative body may attach conditions to zoning amendments (see, e.g., Village Law, §7-700 et seq.), neither is there any language which expressly forbids a local legislature to do so. Statutory silence is not necessarily a denial of the authority to engage in such a practice. Where in the face of nonaddress in the enabling legislation there exists independent justification for the practice as an appropriate exercise of municipal power, that power will be implied. Conditional rezoning is a means of achieving some degree of flexibility in land-use control by minimizing the potentially deleterious effect of a zoning change on neighboring properties; reasonably conceived conditions harmonize the landowner's need for rezoning with the public interest and certainly fall within the spirit of the enabling legislation (see Church v. Town of Islip, 8 N.Y.2d 254, supra).

One final concern of those reluctant to uphold the practice is that resort to conditional rezoning carries with it no inherent restrictions apart from the restrictive agreement itself. This fear, however, is justifiable only if conditional rezoning is considered a contractual relationship between municipality and private party, outside the scope of the zoning power—a view to which we do not subscribe. When conditions are incorporated in an amending ordinance, the result is as much a "zoning regulation" as an ordinance, adopted without conditions. Just as the scope of all zoning regulation is limited by the police power, and thus local legislative bodies must act reasonably and in the best interests of public safety, welfare and convenience (Village of Euclid v. Amber Realty Co., 272 U.S. 365, 387; Matter of New York Inst. of Technology v. Le Boutillier, 33 N.Y.2d 125), the scope of permissible conditions must of necessity be similarly limited. If, upon proper proof, the conditions imposed are found unreasonable, the rezoning amendment as well as the required conditions would have to be nullified, with the affected property reverting to the preamendment zoning classification.

Against this backdrop we proceed to consideration of the contentions advanced by appellants in the appeal now before us. It is first useful to delineate arguments which they do not advance. Thus, they do not challenge the conditional zoning change made in 1976 at the behest of their predecessors in title; no contention is made that the village board was not authorized to adopt the resolution of October 4, 1976, conditioned as it was on the execution and recording of the declaration of covenants, or that the provisions of that declaration were in 1976 arbitrary, capricious, unreasonable or unconstitutional. The reason may be what is apparent, namely, that any successful challenge to the adoption of the 1976 resolution would cause appellants' premises to revert to their pre-1976 zoning classification—a consequence clearly unwanted by them.

The focus of appellants' assault is the provision of the declaration of covenants that no structure may be extended or enlarged "without the prior consent of the Board of Trustees of the Village." Appellants would have us import the added substantive prescription—"which consent may not be unreasonably withheld." Their argument proceeds along two paths: first, that as a matter of construction the added prescription should be read into the provision; second, that because of limitations associated with the exercise of municipal zoning power the village board would have been required to include such a prescription.

Appellants' construction argument must fail. The terminology employed in the declaration is explicit. The concept that appellants would invoke is not obscure and language to give it effect was readily available had it been the intention of the parties to include this added stipulation. Appellants point to no canon of construction in the law of real property or of contracts which would call for judicial insertion of the missing clause. Where language has been chosen containing no inherent ambiguity or uncertainty, courts are properly hesitant, under the guise of judicial construction, to imply additional requirements to relieve a party from asserted disadvantage flowing from the terms actually used (cf. Dress Shirt Sales v. Martinque Assoc., 12 N.Y.2d 339).

The second path either leads nowhere or else goes too far. If it is appellants' assertion that the village board was legally required to insist on inclusion of the desired prescription, there is no authority in the court to reform the zoning enactment of 1976 retroactively to impose the omitted clause. Whether the village board at that time would have enacted a different resolution in the form now desired by appellants is open only to speculation; the certainty is that they did not then take such legislative action. On the other hand, acceptance of appellants' proposition would produce as the other possible consequence the conclusion that the 1976 enactment was illegal, throwing appellants unhappily back to the pre-1976 zoning of their premises, a destination which they assuredly wish to sidestep. . . .

For the reasons stated the Board of Trustees of the Incorporated Village of Flower Hill may not now be compelled to issue its consent to the proposed enlargement and extension of the existing structure on the premises or in the alternative give an acceptable reason for failing to do so. Accordingly, the order of the Appellate Division should be affirmed, with costs.

Page 280.   At the end of the page, add:

ARNEL DEVELOPMENT CO. v. CITY OF COSTA MESA

28 Cal. 3d 511, 620 P.2d 565, 169 Cal. Rptr. 904 (1980)

TOBRINER, Justice.

Plaintiff Arnel proposed to construct a 50-acre development consisting of 127 single-family residences and 539 apartment units. Objecting to this proposal, a neighborhood association circulated an initiative rezoning the Arnel property and two adjoining properties (68 acres in all) to single family residential use. When the voters approved the initiative, Arnel instituted the instant action. The superior court upheld the initiative: the Court of Appeal reversed. We transferred the cause here on our own motion to examine further the holding of the Court of Appeal that the rezoning of specific, relatively small parcels of privately owned property is essentially adjudicatory in nature, and thus cannot be enacted by initiative. . . .

Numerous California cases have settled that the enactment of a measure which zones or rezones property is a legislative act. California courts have so held in cases permitting zoning by initiative (Associated Home Builders, etc. Inc. v. City of Livermore (1976) 18 Cal. 3d 582; San Diego Bldg. Contractors Assn. v. City Council (1974) 13 Cal. 3d 205), in cases upholding zoning referendums (Johnston v. City of Claremont (1958) 49 Cal. 2d 826; Dwyer v. City Council (1927) 200 Cal. 505), and in cases involving other issues which distinguish between adjudicative and legislative acts (Lockard v. City of Los Angeles (1949) 33 Cal. 2d 453 (scope of judicial review)).

The cases draw no distinctions based on the size of the area or the number of owners. Some of the cases involved measures which rezoned a substantial part of the city (e.g., San Diego Bldg. Contractors Assn. v. City Council, supra); some rezoned areas roughly comparable to the 68 acres at issue here (e.g., Lockard v. City of Los Angeles, supra); many involved parcels much smaller than 68 acres (Dwyer v. City Council, supra (proposed site for poultry farm owned by University of California, said to constitute one five-hundred-fiftieth of the City of Berkeley)); . . . . Thus whatever the legal controversy and whatever the size or ownership of the land involved, every California decision on point (and there are many more than the few cited in this paragraph) has held that the enactment or amendment of a zoning ordinance is a legislative act. . . .

Neither San Diego Bldg. Contractors Assn. v. City Council, supra, 13 Cal. 3d 205, nor Horn v. County of Ventura (1979) 24 Cal. 3d 605, points to a departure from the settled rule that rezoning is a legislative act. San Diego held that establishment of a 30-foot height limitation on buildings within a coastal zone was a zoning ordinance, and consequently a legislative measure which could be enacted by initiative. Although our opinion described the initiative as a "general" legislative act (13 Cal. 3d at p.212), we did so to distinguish the great number of more limited " 'administrative' zoning decisions, such as the grant of a variance or the award of a conditional use permit, which are adjudicatory in nature." (Ibid.) The decision thus conforms to established rules that zoning amendments are legislative, but administrative decisions, such as variances and use permits, are adjudicative.

Horn v. County of Ventura, supra, held in conformity with prior decisions that approval of a tentative subdivision map was an adjudicative act.[8] We did not arrive at that decision or conclude that the particular subdivision approval at issue was adjudicatory in character by examining the size of the subdivision or the number of persons affected. Instead, we stated a generic rule that "[s]ubdivision approvals, like variances and conditional use permits . . . [are] 'adjudicatory' in nature." (24 Cal. 3d at p.614). *Horn* thus did not depart from the classification established by prior precedent. . . .

We can appreciate the view that in a case in which, unlike the present case, proposed legislation affects only a few persons, the legislative body should grant those persons a hearing if practicable. To elevate this precatory suggestion to a constitutional demand, however, would radically constrain the power of legislative bodies. The rationale of our decision could not be confined to zoning cases; in *San Diego* we expressly denounced the claim that the Constitution provides more complete protection to ownership and development of real property than it provides to other personal rights. (13 Cal. 3d at pp. 213-214.) Thus whenever a legislative body enacted legislation which affected relatively few persons, that legislation would be invalid unless the persons affected received notice and hearing before the enacting body. We find no warrant for such a radical curtailment of the authority traditionally enjoyed by legislatures.

We conclude that no constitutional requirement compels us to depart from the California doctrine that rezoning is a legislative act. We recognize, however, that the courts of some other states, basing their decisions on nonconstitutional grounds, have held that in some instances

---

8. Prior California decisions had distinguished from zoning legislation a variety of administrative land use decisions, including the granting of a variance (see Topanga Assn. for a Scenic Community v. County of Los Angeles (1974) 11 Cal. 3d 506, 517), the granting of a use permit (see Johnston v. City of Claremont, 49 Cal. 2d 826, 834), and the approval of a subdivision map (Woodland Hills Residents Assn., Inc. v. City Council (1975) 44 Cal. App. 3d 825, 837-838). In classifying such decisions as adjudicative, courts have emphasized that the decisions generally involved the application of standards established in the zoning ordinance to individual parcels and often require findings to comply with statutory requirements or to resolve factual disputes.

It is significant that the courts have not resolved the legislative or adjudicative character of administrative land use decisions on a case by case basis, but instead have established a generic rule that variances, use permits, subdivision maps, and similar proceedings are necessarily adjudicative. Thus, even when such actions involve a substantial area (see Youngblood v. Board of Supervisors (1978) 22 Cal. 3d 644 (subdivision map for 217 acres)) or affect the community as a whole (City of Fairfield v. Superior Court (1975) 14 Cal. 3d 768 (use permit for shopping center in small community)), the courts invariably treat them as adjudicative in nature.

a zoning ordinance is an adjudicative decision.[10] The Court of Appeal, as we noted earlier, adopted that view, holding specifically that the rezoning of relatively small parcels of land is adjudicative in character. We therefore explain our reasons for rejecting that view and adhering to the settled California position.

From the doctrine that zoning ordinances are legislative, but variances and similar administrative decisions are adjudicative,[11] derive a number of rules which facilitate the making of land use decisions and simplify litigation challenging those decisions. Among those rules are: (1) Zoning ordinances, but not administrative decisions, can be enacted by initiative (Associated Home Builders, etc. Inc. v. City of Livermore, supra, 18 Cal. 3d 582). (2) Zoning ordinances, but not administrative decisions, are subject to referendum (Dwyer v. City Council, supra, 200 Cal. 505). (3) A zoning ordinance is reviewable by ordinary mandamus (Code Civ. Proc., §1084); an administrative decision, by administrative mandamus (Code Civ. Proc., §1094.5). (4) A zoning ordinance, unlike an administrative decision, does not require explicit findings (Ensign Bickford Realty Corp. v. City Council, supra, 68 Cal. App. 3d 467, 473). (5) A zoning ordinance is valid if it is reasonably related to the public welfare (see Miller v. Board of Public Works (1925) 195 Cal. 477, 488); administrative decisions must implement established standards and rest upon findings supported by substantial evidence. (Code Civ. Proc., §1094.5). Under the views advanced by plaintiffs, however, the application of these rules is uncertain until a reviewing court finds whether the decision is legislative or an adjudicative act. Plaintiffs propose, however, no test to distinguish legislative and adjudicative actions with reasonable certainty.

The factual setting of the present case illustrates the problems courts will face if we abandoned past precedent and attempted to devise a new test distinguishing legislative and adjudicative decisions. The Court of Appeal, for example, found here that the instant initiative was an adjudicative act because it rezoned a "relatively small" parcel of land. It is not, however, self-evident that 68 acres is a "relatively small" parcel; some cities have entire zoning classifications which comprise less than 68 acres. The size of the parcel, moreover, has very little relationship to the theoretical basis of the Court of Appeal holding—the distinction between the making of land-use policy, a legislative act, and the asserted

10. See West v. City of Portage (Mich. 1974) 221 N.W.2d 303; Fasano v. Board of County Commissioners of Washington County (Or. 1973) 507 P.2d 23; Leonard v. City of Bothell (Wash. 1976) 557 P.2d 1306. . . .

11. A holding that rezoning of relatively small parcels is an adjudicative act would necessarily imply that decisions presently considered adjudicative, such as the grant of a use permit or the approval of a subdivision map, would henceforth be classified as legislative acts if they affected a relatively large parcel of property.

adjudicatory act of applying established policy. The rezoning of a "relatively small" parcel, especially when done by initiative, may well signify a fundamental change in city land use policy.

Plaintiffs alternatively urge that the present initiative is adjudicatory because it assertedly affects only three landowners. But this is a very myopic view of the matter; the proposed construction of housing for thousands of people affects the prospective tenants, the housing market, the residents living nearby, and the future characer of the community. The number of landowners whose property is actually rezoned is as unsuitable a test as the size of the property rezoned. Yet without some test which distinguishes legislative from adjudicative acts with clarity and reasonable certainty, municipal governments and voters will lack adequate guidance in enacting and evaluating land use decisions.

In summary, past California land-use cases have established generic classifications, viewing zoning ordinances as legislative and other decisions, such as variances and subdivision map approvals, as adjudicative. This method of classifying land-use decisions enjoys the obvious advantage of economy; the municipality, the proponents of a proposed measure, and the opponents of the measure can readily determine if notice, hearings, and findings are required, what form of judicial review is appropriate, and whether the measure can be enacted by initiative or overturned by referendum.

To depart from past precedent and embark upon a case by case determination, on the other hand, would incur substantial administrative cost. Such a rule would expose the municipality to the uncertainty of whether a proposed measure would be held to be legislative or adjudicative: it would entail cost to the litigants, and it would burden the courts with the resolution of these issues.

Plaintiffs argue, however, that the administrative cost which would be entailed by departure from precedent in this case is justified to protect the rights of landowners. We believe, however, that those rights are adequately protected under existing law. . . . [L]andowners retain constitutional protection against zoning which is arbitrary, unreasonable, or deprives them of substantially all use of their land. When zoning is enacted by the city council, landowners by statute are entitled to notice and hearing. (Gov. Code, §65856). When zoning is enacted by initiative, landowners have the same opportunity as their opponents to present their case to the electorate. (See Oran, The Initiative and Referendum's Use in Zoning (1976) 64 Cal. L. Rev. 74, 93.)

Although from the landowner's view a "hearing" before the electorate may be less satisfactory than a hearing before a planning commission or city council, as a practical matter the initiative is unlikely to be employed in matters which could fairly be characterized as adjudicative in character. An initiative petition requires valid signatures of 10 percent of the registered voters. (Elec. Code, §4011.) Having accomplished that feat, the proponents must then be prepared to wage an expensive campaign to persuade the majority of the voters to support the measure. In consequence of these requirements, the initiative can be and is employed to support or oppose major projects which affect hundreds or thousands of persons and often present questions of policy concerning the quality of life and the future development of the city; it is not likely to be employed in matters which affect only an individual landowner and raise no policy issues.

Neither do we believe departure from settled precedent is necessary to protect the public interest in rational and orderly land-use planning. Zoning changes must conform to the city's general plan (see Gov. Code, §65860), which must in turn conform to requirements established by state statute. Zoning changes must also meet the criteria established in Associated Home Builders, etc. Inc. v. City of Livermore, supra, 18 Cal. 3d 582, which requires such legislation to reasonably relate to the welfare of the region affected. The spectre of a few voters imposing their selfish interests upon an objecting city and region has no basis in reality.

In conclusion, the current California rule that rezoning is a legislative act is well settled by precedent and comports with both federal and state constitutional requirements. The cost of departing from settled precedent in this setting is apparent; the benefits questionable and perhaps nonexistent. We therefore adhere to the rule that a zoning ordinance is a legislative act and, as such, may be enacted by initiative.

Appellants Arnel and South Coast Plaza presented numerous other issues on appeal which the Court of Appeal, erroneously concluding that the initiative was not a legislative act, but did resolve. In order to assure that these issues are considered by the Court of Appeal, we retransfer this cause to that court. . . .

RICHARDSON, Justice, dissenting. . . .

. . . [T]he majority emphasizes the *form* of the administrative action, without considering either its *substance* or *effect.*

The result is to deny appellant property owners important due process protections to which they clearly should be entitled when their property is subjected to an adjudicative disposition. Approximately 12 percent of the registered voters of Costa Mesa, by approval of an initiative, are permitted to abort the construction of a carefully considered moderate income housing project without giving appellant owners any prior opportunity to express their opposition at a full public hearing. When measured against this sacrifice of fundamental constitutional rights and interests the majority's express concern for the saving of "administrative costs" is of substantially less importance.

I find merit in appellants' primary contention that the rezoning of a very small number of specific parcels of property privately owned by a few landowners is essentially an adjudicative action which constitutionally requires that the affected owners be afforded both notice and a reasonable opportunity for hearing which are not presently afforded by the initiative process. . . .

I would reverse the judgment and direct the trial court to declare invalid the subject initiative ordinance.

CLARK, Justice, concurs.

NOTE ON ARNEL

1. *Subsequent history.* After the California Supreme Court had transferred the case back to it, the Court of Appeal held that the initiative measure was "arbitrary and discriminatory rezoning in excess of the city's police power." Arnel Development Co. v. City of Costa Mesa, 126 Cal. App. 3d 330, 178 Cal. Rptr. 723 (1981). The Court of Appeal relied heavily on Associated Home Builders v. City of Livermore (Cal. 1976), infra Casebook p.836, which requires that local land-use controls reasonably accommodate competing *regional* interests. The initiative measure failed that test, according to the court, because it gave inadequate weight to the regional shortage of low- and moderate-income housing.

2. *Fasano's fall from fashion.* Recent academic writings have been highly critical of the *Fasano* approach. Professor Jan Krasnowiecki, *in* Abolish Zoning, 31 Syracuse L. Rev. 719 (1980), has concluded that the advance planning and zoning of developing communities is impossible. He proposes that local governments have the authority to make case-by-case decisions on proposed projects, with "a statutory presumption that any housing project must be approved unless the approving agency gives persuasive reasons why it should not." A state statute would list the only harmful spillovers with which an agency could be concerned. Krasnowiecki thinks the *Fasano* court was right to regard zoning amendments as being quasi-judicial in character. Yet he concludes that it then erred when it embraced "the old concept of the comprehensive plan, thus transforming what should have been the beginning of a flexible zoning system into one of the most powerful antigrowth weapons ever devised in zoning history." Id. at 748-749.

Professor Carol Rose, *in* Planning and Dealing: Piecemeal Land Controls as a Problem of Local Legitimacy, 71 Cal. L. Rev. 839 (1983), describes the *Fasano* approach as "plan jurisprudence." Rose asserts that modern planning theory and actual local planning practice both deny that the comprehensive plan can play the role that *Fasano* asks it to play.

(For more on planning, see infra Casebook, Chapter Four.) Rose suggests that the legitimacy of a local land-use decision be judged not according to its consistency with a comprehensive plan, but rather according to whether the local agency mediated and accommodated conflicting local interests. Thus, while most commentators have deplored the "lawless" state of variance administration (see supra Casebook, p.220, Note 2), Rose applauds the tendency of members of variance boards to mediate informally the disputes that come before them.

Page 299. At the end of the page, add:

LARKIN v. GRENDEL'S DEN, INC.

454 U.S. 116, 103 S. Ct. 505, 74 L. Ed. 2d 297 (1982)

Chief Justice BURGER delivered the opinion of the Court.

The question presented by this appeal is whether a Massachusetts statute, which vests in the governing bodies of churches and schools the power effectively to veto applications for liquor licenses within a five hundred foot radius of the church or school, violates the Establishment Clause of the First Amendment or the Due Process Clause of the Fourteenth Amendment.

I

Appellee operates a restaurant located in the Harvard Square area of Cambridge, Massachusetts. The Holy Cross Armenian Catholic Parish is located adjacent to the restaurant; the back walls of the two buildings are ten feet apart. In 1977, appellee applied to the Cambridge License Commission for approval of an alcoholic beverages license for the restaurant.

Section 16C of Chapter 138 of the Massachusetts General Laws provides: "Premises . . . located within a radius of five hundred feet of a church or school shall not be licensed for the sale of alcoholic beverages if the governing body of such church or school files written objection thereto."[1]

Holy Cross Church objected to appellee's application, expressing con-

---

1. . . .
Section 16C originally was enacted in 1954 as an absolute ban on liquor licenses within 500 feet of a church or school, 1954 Mass. Acts, ch. 569, §1. A 1968 amendment modified the absolute prohibition, permitting licenses within the 500-foot radius "if the governing body of such church assents in writing," 1968 Mass. Acts, ch. 435. In 1970, the statute was amended to its present form, 1970 Mass. Acts, ch. 192.

cern over "having so many licenses *so* near" (emphasis in original).[2] The License Commission voted to deny the application, citing only the objection of Holy Cross Church and noting that the church "is within 10 feet of the proposed location."

On appeal, the Massachusetts Alcoholic Beverages Control Commission upheld the License Commission's action. The Beverages Control Commission found that "the church's objection under Section 16C was the only basis on which the [license] was denied."

Appellee then sued the License Commission and the Beverages Control Commission in United States District Court. [The District Court held that §16C violated the Establishment Clause and was void on its face. The First Circuit affirmed *en banc*.]

II

A

Appellants contend that the State may, without impinging on the Establishment Clause of the First Amendment, enforce what it describes as a "zoning" law in order to shield schools and places of divine worship from the presence nearby of liquor dispensing establishments. It is also contended that a zone of protection around churches and schools is essential to protect diverse centers of spiritual, educational and cultural enrichment. It is to that end that the State has vested in the governing bodies of all schools, public or private, and all churches, the power to prevent the issuance of liquor licenses for any premises within 500 feet of their institutions.

Plainly schools and churches have a valid interest in being insulated from certain kinds of commercial establishments, including those dispensing liquor. Zoning laws have long been employed to this end, and there can be little doubt about the power of a state to regulate the environment in the vicinity of schools, churches, hospitals and the like by exercise of reasonable zoning laws. . . .

. . . Given the broad powers of states under the Twenty-First Amendment, judicial deference to the legislative exercise of zoning powers by a city council or other legislative zoning body is especially appropriate in the area of liquor regulation. See, e.g., California v. Larue, 409 U.S. 109 (1972); California Retail Liquor Dealers Association v. Midcal Aluminum, Inc., 445 U.S. 97, 106-110 (1980).

However, §16C is not simply a legislative exercise of zoning power.

2. In 1979, there were 26 liquor licensees in Harvard Square and within a 500-foot radius of Holy Cross Church; 25 of these were in existence at the time Holy Cross Church objected to appellee's application. See App. 69-72.

As the Massachusetts Supreme Judicial Court concluded, §16C delegates to private, nongovernmental entities power to veto certain liquor license applications, Arno v. Alcoholic Beverages Control Commission, supra, 377 Mass., at 89, 384 N.E.2d 1223. This is a power ordinarily vested in agencies of government. See, e.g., California v. LaRue, supra, 409 U.S., at 116, commenting that a "state agency . . . is itself the repository of the State's power under the Twenty-First Amendment." We need not decide whether, or upon what conditions, such power may ever be delegated to nongovernmental entities; here, of two classes of institutions to which the legislature has delegated this important decision-making power, one is secular, but one is religious. Under these circumstances, the deference normally due a legislative zoning judgment is not merited.[5]

B

The purposes of the First Amendment guarantees relating to religion were twofold: to foreclose state interference with the practice of religious faiths, and to foreclose the establishment of a state religion familiar in other Eighteenth Century systems. Religion and government, each insulated from the other, could then coexist. Jefferson's idea of a "wall," see Reynolds v. United States, 98 U.S. (8 Otto) 145, 164 (1878), *quoting* Reply from Thomas Jefferson to an address by a committee of the Danbury Baptist Association (January 1, 1802), *reprinted in* 8 Works of Thomas Jefferson 113 (Washington ed. 1861), was a useful figurative illustration to emphasize the concept of separateness. Some limited and incidental entanglement between church and state authority is inevitable in a complex modern society, see, e.g., Lemon v. Kurtzman, 403 U.S. 602, 614 (1971); Walz v. Tax Commission, 397 U.S. 664, 670 (1970), but the concept of a "wall" of separation is a useful signpost. Here that "wall" is substantially breached by vesting discretionary governmental powers in religious bodies.

This Court has consistently held that a statute must satisfy three criteria to pass muster under the Establishment Clause: "First, the statute must have a secular legislative purpose; second, its principal or primary effect must be one that neither advances nor inhibits religion . . . ; finally, the statute must not foster "an excessive government entanglement with religion." Lemon v. Kurtzman, supra, 403 U.S., at 612-613, *quoting* Walz v. Tax Commission, supra, 397 U.S., at 674. Independent of the first of those criteria, the statute, by delegating a governmental power to religious institutions, inescapably implicates the Establishment Clause.

---

5. For similar reasons, the 21st Amendment does not justify §16C. The 21st Amendment reserves power to states, yet here the State has delegated to churches a power relating to liquor sales. The State may not exercise its power under the 21st Amendment in a way which impinges upon the Establishment Clause of the First Amendment.

The purpose of §16C, as described by the District Court, is to "protect[ ] spiritual, cultural, and educational centers from the 'hurly-burly' associated with liquor outlets." 495 F. Supp., at 766. There can be little doubt that this embraces valid secular legislative purposes.[6] However, these valid secular objectives can be readily accomplished by other means—either through an absolute legislative ban on liquor outlets within reasonable prescribed distances from churches, schools, hospitals and like institutions,[7] or by ensuring a hearing for the views of affected institutions at licensing proceedings where, without question, such views would be entitled to substantial weight.[8]

Appellants argue that §16C has only a remote and incidental effect on the advancement of religion. The highest court in Massachusetts, however, has construed the statute as conferring upon churches a veto power over governmental licensing authority. Section 16C gives churches the right to determine whether a particular applicant will be granted a liquor license, or even which one of several competing applicants will receive a license.

The churches' power under the statute is standardless, calling for no reasons, findings, or reasoned conclusions. That power may therefore be used by churches to promote goals beyond insulating the church from undesirable neighbors; it could be employed for explicitly religious goals, for exmaple, favoring liquor licenses for members of that congregation or adherents of that faith. We can assume that churches would act in good faith in their exercise of the statutory power, see Lemon v. Kurtzman, supra, 403 U.S., at 618-619, yet §16C does not by its terms require that churches' power be used in a religiously neutral way. "[T]he potential for conflict inheres in the situation," Levitt v. Committee for Public Education, 413 U.S. 472, 480 (1973); and appellants have not suggested any "effective means of guaranteeing" that the delegated power "will be used exclusively for secular, neutral, and nonideological purposes." Committee for Public Education v. Nyquist, supra, 413 U.S., at 780. In addition, the mere appearance of a joint exercise of legislative authority

6. In this facial attack, the Court assumes that §16C actually effectuates the secular goal of protecting churches and schools from the disruption associated with liquor serving establishments. The fact that Holy Cross Church is already surrounded by 26 liquor outlets casts some doubt on the effectiveness of the protection granted, however.

7. See California v. Larue, 409 U.S. 109, 120 (Stewart, J., concurring).

Section 16C, as originally enacted, consisted of an absolute ban on liquor licenses within 500 feet of a church or school, see note I supra; and 27 states continue to prohibit liquor outlets within a prescribed distance of various categories of protected institutions with certain exceptions and variations. [Citations to 27 state statutes omitted.]

8. Eleven states have statutes directing the licensing authority to consider the proximity of the proposed liquor outlet to schools or other institutions in deciding whether to grant a liquor license. [Citations omitted.]

by Church and State provides a significant symbolic benefit to religion in the minds of some by reason of the power conferred. It does not strain our prior holdings to say that the statute can be seen as having a "primary" and "principal" effect of advancing religion.

Turning to the third phase of the inquiry called for by Lemon v. Kurtzman, supra, we see that we have not previously had occasion to consider the entanglement implications of a statute vesting significant governmental authority in churches. This statute enmeshes churches in the exercise of substantial governmental powers contrary to our consistent interpretation of the Establishment Clause; "[t]he objective is to prevent, as far as possible, the intrusion of either [Church or State] into the precincts of the other." Lemon v. Kurtzman, supra, 403 U.S., at 614. We went on in that case to state: "Under our system the choice has been made that government is to be entirely excluded from the area of religious instruction *and churches excluded from the affairs of government.* The Constitution decrees that religion must be a private matter for the individual, the family, and the institutions of private choice, and that while some involvement and entanglement are inevitable, lines must be drawn." 403 U.S., at 625 (emphasis added). . . .

Section 16C substitutes the unilateral and absolute power of a church for the reasoned decisionmaking of a public legislative body acting on evidence and guided by standards, on issues with significant economic and political implications. The challenged statute thus enmeshes churches in the processes of government and creates the danger of "[p]olitical fragmentation and divisiveness along religious lines," Lemon v. Kurtzman, supra, 403 U.S., at 623. Ordinary human experience and a long line of cases teach that few entanglements could be more offensive to the spirit of the Constitution.[11]

The judgment of the Court of Appeals is affirmed.

Justice REHNQUIST, dissenting. . . .

In its original form, §16C imposed a flat ban on the grant of an alcoholic beverages license to any establishment located within 500 feet of a church or a school. 1954 Mass. Acts c. 569, §1. . . .

Over time, the legislature found that it could meet its goal of protecting people engaged in religious activities from liquor-related disruption with a less absolute prohibition. Rather than set out elaborate formulae or require an administrative agency to make findings of fact, the legislature settled on the simple expedient of asking churches to object if a proposed liquor outlet would disturb them. Thus, under the present version of §16C, a liquor outlet within 500 feet of a church or school can be licensed

11. Appellee also challenges the statute as a violation of due process. In light of our analysis we need not and do not reach that claim.

unless the affected institution objects. The flat ban, which the majority concedes is valid, is more protective of churches and more restrictive of liquor sales than the present §16C.

The evolving treatment of the grant of liquor licenses to outlets located within 500 feet of a church or a school seems to me to be the sort of legislative refinement that we should encourage, not forbid in the name of the First Amendment. If a particular church or a paticular school located within the 500 foot radius chooses not to object, the state has quite sensibly concluded that there is no reason to prohibit the issuance of the license. Nothing in the Court's opinion persuades me why the more rigid prohibition would be constitutional, but the more flexible not. . . .

The Court is apparently concerned for fear that churches might object to the issuance of a license for "explicitly religious" reasons, such as "favoring liquor licenses for members of that congregation or adherents of that faith." If a church were to seek to advance the interests of its members in this way, there would be an occasion to determine whether it had violated any right of an unsuccessful applicant for a liquor license. But our ability to discern a risk of such abuse does not render §16C violative of the Establishment Clause. . . .

NOTE ON LARKIN

Harvard Law Professor Laurence H. Tribe represented the owners of Grendel's Den in the *Larkin* litigation. After his victory in the Supreme Court, Tribe, invoking the Civil Rights Attorney's Fees Awards Act of 1976, 42 U.S.C. 1988 (1976), submitted to the Commonwealth of Massachusetts a bill of $332,441.68 for the work that he and two associates had performed. Francis X. Bellotti, the state's Attorney General, refused to pay the bill. Litigation ensued. Tribe's team was eventually awarded only $113,640.85, in part because team members had failed to keep contemporaneous records of time spent on the case. See Grendel's Den, Inc. v. Larkin, 749 F.2d 945 (1st Cir. 1984).

Page 307.   Before the last paragraph in Note 3, insert:

Arnel Development Co. v. City of Costa Mesa (Cal. 1980) is reprinted supra Supplement p. 54. The Supreme Court of Florida reached a like result in Florida Land Co. v. City of Winter Springs, 427 So. 2d 170 (Fla. 1983), where the plaintiff landowner unsuccessfully asserted that an ordinance that rezoned only the landowner's property could not become the subject of a referendum. Colorado has joined the trend toward permissive use of popular votes on land-use issues. Margolis v. District Court, 638 P.2d 297, 305 (Colo. 1981), holds that the rezoning of a small tract of land is a "legislative" act when the issue is the availability of an initiative or referendum. The Colorado court took pains to emphasize, however, that the same small-scale rezoning would be considered "quasi-judicial" if the issue were to be the standard of review that a court should apply. Should a court be able to call an event "legislative" in one context and "quasi-judicial" in another? Does the evolution of Colorado law illustrate the unhelpfulness of the legislative/quasi-judicial distinction?

Page 320.   At the beginning of the Note, insert:

0. *West Side Story.* Occidental Petroleum persevered and prepared an EIR for its exploratory drilling program. Its opponents also persevered, and continued to use CEQA-based challenges to delay Occidental's drilling. The subsequent history is reviewed in No Oil, Inc. v. City of Los Angeles, 196 Cal. App. 3d 223, 242 Cal. Rptr. 37 (1987) (rejecting No Oil's "adequacy" challenge to Occidental's final EIR).

Page 323.   At the beginning of the Note, insert:

0. *Round two.* The next draft of the City of Los Angeles's EIR fared no better. The California Court of Appeal held that the revised version remained inadequate because it also failed to include a genuine no project alternative and because the alternatives discussed were not tied to a consistently viewed project. County of Inyo v. City of Los Angeles, 124 Cal. App. 3d 1, 177 Cal. Rptr. 479 (1981).

Page 329.   Before "e. Assessment," add:

SEPA-based litigation predictably has begun to flower in both Massachusetts and New York. See Boston Preservation Alliance, Inc. v. Secretary of Environmental Affairs, 396 Mass. 489, 487 N.E.2d 197 (1986) (rejecting challenge to "scope" (adequacy) of EIR for redevelopment project in Boston's financial district); Chinese Staff & Workers Assn. v. City of New York, 68 N.Y.2d 359, 502 N.E.2d 176, 509 N.Y.S.2d 499 (1986) (SEPA EIS for high-rise luxury condominium project planned for vacant lot in Chinatown section of Manhattan held inadequate for failing to consider impact of project on neighborhood character); Jackson v. New York State Urban Dev. Corp., 67 N.Y.2d 400, 494 N.E.2d 429, 503 N.Y.S.2d 298 (1986) (rejecting SEPA-based attack on state agency's plan to redevelop Times Square area of Manhattan).

Minnesota and Michigan have environmental statutes that have more substantive bite than the usual SEPA has. See State by Powderly v. Erickson (Minn. 1979), infra Casebook p. 534, and the following case:

KIMBERLY HILLS NEIGHBORHOOD ASSOCIATION v. DION
114 Mich. App. 495, 320 N.W.2d 668 (1982)

MacKENZIE, Judge.

Plaintiffs brought this action to obtain equitable relief under the Michigan Environmental Protection Act (hereinafter MEPA), M.C.L. §691.1201 et seq.; M.S.A. §14.528(201) et seq. In such an action plaintiff must make a prima facie case by showing "that the conduct of the defendant has, or is likely to, pollute, impair or destroy the air, water or other natural resources or the public trust therein". M.C.L. §691.1203; M.S.A. §14.528(203). We hold that plaintiffs here failed to make out such a prima facie case. The trial court's decision is, therefore, reversed.

Defendants are owners of an 18-acre site in southeast Ann Arbor on which they planned to construct single family homes. The property was used for farming from the mid-19th century until the 1920's and is now covered with second growth trees and brush. When defendants purchased the property on November 7, 1977, it was located in Pittsfield Township and zoned to permit construction of single family homes on lots with an area of at least 10,000 square feet. The City of Ann Arbor annexed the property on August 17, 1978. The property was subsequently rezoned to permit construction of single family homes on lots with an area of at least 7,200 square feet. Plaintiffs are the Kimberly Hills Neighborhood Association, a voluntary association of about 110 residents of the area, and various individual residents. Plaintiffs' complaint sought an injunction against construction or development on the northerly 9.2 acres of defendants' land.

After suit was commenced on February 6, 1979, the trial court signed an ex parte interim restraining order prohibiting construction on the property during the pendency of the suit. Following a hearing on the temporary restraining order, the court modified the order to permit construction of four homes on a portion of the property. On March 28, 1979, after an evidentiary hearing on the request for a permanent injunction, requiring that defendants set aside at least four acres in the northwesterly portion of the property for a nature preserve and as a mating and breeding ground for pheasants in order to protect natural resources. Defendants were permanently enjoined from filling in, building upon, disturbing, polluting, impairing, or destroying a seasonal pond on the premises and defendants were also permanently enjoined from building upon or changing the natural characteristics of a specific area of the premises in the vicinity of the pond. In addition, defendants were ordered to set aside a corridor approximately 20 feet wide along the entire westerly border of the land in order to provide an access way for animal life. Further, defendants were ordered to provide two corridors approximately 40 feet wide for use by wildlife in an east-west direction, with one such corridor leading into the ordered nature preserve. . . .

Testimony indicated defendants' land included a diverse wetland, containing an intermittent pond providing a wildlife habitat for a number of species, some of which might not continue to exist on the property if the land were developed. There was testimony that part of defendants' 9.2 acres acted as a corridor for wildlife to travel through the area to defendants' land and to other similarly undeveloped property in the area.

Donald Inman, an environmental specialist in the Environmental Enforcement Division of the Michigan Department of Natural Resources (hereinafter DNR), testified that the state did not intervene in this suit because it saw no biological uniqueness to the habitat existing on the property. Patrick Ross of the faculty of the Urban Environment Studies Program of Grand Valley State College testified that the subject land would be an inappropriate place to establish a nature center. Terrence Pfeiffer, a consultant with an environmental consulting firm, testified that development of the property could result in the destruction of the habitat of those pheasants presently living there.

The standard in M.C.L. §691.1203; M.S.A. §14.528(203) for determining whether the defendants' development of the property will result in "pollution, impairment or destruction" of a natural resource within the meaning of the Act is derived from Const. 1963, art. 4, §52:

> The conservation and development of the natural resources of the state are hereby declared to be of paramount public concern in the interest of the health, safety and general welfare of the people. The legislature shall provide for the protection of the air, water and other natural resources of the state from pollution, impairment and destruction.

The operative provision granting the plaintiffs the right to maintain this action is M.C.L. §691.1202; M.S.A. §14.528(202), which provides:

> [Plaintiff] may maintain an action in the circuit court having jurisdiction where the alleged violation occurred or is likely to occur for declaratory and equitable relief . . . for the protection of the air, water and other natural resources and the public trust therein from pollution, impairment or destruction.

. . . The real question before us is whether the likely impact of defendants' proposed activities rises to the level of impairment or destruction. . . .

In West Michigan Environmental Action Council [v. Natural Resources Comm.], 405 Mich. at 760, 275 N.W.2d 538 [1979], the Court determined that the adverse impact amounted to an impairment as follows:

"In light of the limited number of the elk, the unique nature and location of this herd, and the apparently serious and lasting, though unquantifiable, damage that will result to the herd from the drilling of the ten exploratory wells, we conclude that defendants' conduct constitutes an impairment or destruction of a natural resource."

A close reading of the foregoing language shows that the Court balanced the rarity of the resources involved against the magnitude of the harm likely to result. Since elk are extremely rare in Michigan, destruction of a relatively small number of elk will amount to an impairment. Destruction of the same number of a more common species would not necessarily amount to an impairment. The magnitude of the harm likely to result from defendants' actions depends on the characteristics of the resources involved, the nature of defendants' actions, and the type of property involved.

When the evidence presented by plaintiffs here is measured against the foregoing standard, it does not appear that the impacts shown by plaintiffs amounted to the requisite statutory impairment. The trial court specifically found there was nothing unique in the way of clearings, growth, or species of animals on the 9.2 acres involved. If the property is developed, the intermittent pond may disappear, but there was no evidence that the disappearance of the pond is likely to have a significant effect on the drainage system as a whole, no evidence that the frogs and other amphibians who make the pond their home are particularly rare, and no evidence that disappearance of the pond is likely to have a significant impact on the population of those amphibians. Several old trees which provide nests for hawks and other birds will be cut down, but there was no evidence that those birds do not have ample nesting areas elsewhere. Similarly, although the brush areas on the property provide cover for rabbits, oppossum, and other small animals, and nesting areas for birds and insects, there was no showing that other suitable habitats are not available. Because the small animals, birds, and insects involved are all common, the disappearance of four acres of habitat will not have a significant impact on their population in Michigan or even in the Ann Arbor area. The four acres involved provided a poor habitat for one male pheasant, as each male pheasant requires 3 to 23 acres for territory. That this single male pheasant and his associated females will have to move elsewhere hardly amounts to an impairment of the Michigan pheasant population. In sum, it has not been shown, from a statewide perspective, that development will actually interfere with the maintenance of diversified natural areas for wildlife.

Development of defendants' property will undoubtedly change the character of the neighborhood. Such changes, however, are inevitable on the borderline between urban and rural areas. If the Michigan Environmental Protection Act is to be used as a tool to prevent such changes, the Act must be applied to an area broad enough to assure that the relief granted will have some effect. The relief the trial court granted here could be rendered useless by development of surrounding areas. The narrow local interests represented by plaintiffs here are not interests protected by the Act. . . .

Reversed. No costs, the matter involved being one of public concern.

Page 344. Before "3. Preliminary Injunctions and Bonds," insert:

A landowner who prevails in a §1983 case may seek to recover attorney's fees under the Civil Rights Attorney's Fees Act of 1976, 42 U.S.C. §1988 (1976). That Act authorizes a trial court, "in its discretion," to award reasonable fees to the party that prevails in certain Civil Rights Acts cases. In Entertainment Concepts, Inc., III v. Maciejewski, 631 F.2d 497 (7th Cir. 1980), this provision was construed to entitle the operator of an adult theater to recover from *local officials* the attorney's fees incurred in a successful challenge to an ordinance that unconstitutionally inhibited free expression.

The California Supreme Court has hinted that it will not be sympathetic to a landowner claim for attorney's fees under Cal. Civ. Proc. Code §1021.5, supra Casebook p.343. In Pacific Legal Foundation v. California Coastal Commission, 33 Cal. 3d 158, 655 P.2d 306, 188 Cal. Rptr. 104 (1982), the co-owners of a coastal single-family residence had added rock to a seawall to protect the residence from high waves caused by severe winter storms. The Coastal Commission later notified them that they needed a permit for these repairs. When the owners applied for a permit, the Commission granted it on condition that the owners dedicate a lateral easement of public access. This easement would encumber the lot's entire dry sand area, a strip with a width of over 100 feet. The landowners sought and won a court ruling that Commission's condition in this instance had violated applicable statutes. The Commission eventually dropped its appeal from this ruling, and the landowners sought to recover attorney's fees on the authority of §1021.5. The Supreme Court of California unanimously held that an award of attorney's fees should not be forthcoming. Mosk, J., writing for the court, said in part:

> Although we have no doubt that the right to be free from the deprivation of private property interests in an arbitrary manner may rise to the level of an "important right affecting the public interest," it is equally plain that the grant of administrative mandamus under the limited factual circumstances

shown here did not result in conferring a "significant benefit" on a "large class of persons." The decision vindicated only the rights of the owners of a single parcel of property. It in no way represents, for example, a ringing declaration of the rights of all or most landowners in the coastal zone, nor will it "certainly lead to the Commission's abandoning its prior unconstitutional practices of conditioning statutorily authorized permits upon an individual's surrender of his private property," as the plaintiffs contend. It is more likely that the Commission will heed the decision simply by striking conditions imposed under similar factual circumstances. We conclude that plaintiffs are not entitled to appellate attorney fees under section 1021.5.

188 Cal. Rptr. at 109.

There is increasing interest in the issue of the rights of unsuccessful environmental litigants to recover attorney's fees. In Ruckelshaus v. Sierra Club, 463 U.S. 680 (1983), the Supreme Court held in a 5-4 decision that to award fees to a wholly unsuccessful environmental litigant in a Clean Air Act case would violate the statutory requirement that fees be awarded only in "appropriate" instances. But compare Note, Awards of Attorneys' Fees to Unsuccessful Environmental Litigants, 96 Harv. L. Rev. 677 (1983), which reviews federal law and endorses the awarding of fees to losers in some instances.

Page 356.   At the end of the first paragraph, add:

The pretrial drama continued in Ernest W. Hahn, Inc. v. Codding, 501 F. Supp. 155 (N.D. Cal. 1980). Codding there argued that, because his suits against Hahn were couched as environmental and taxpayer actions, the *Noerr-Pennington* doctrine immunized him from antitrust liability. (The following case explains the scope of this doctrine.) The District Judge held otherwise. At the trial that followed Hahn introduced evidence that Codding's activities had delayed Hahn's completion of the Santa Rosa shopping center by four years. After one month of an expected nine-month trial, Hahn agreed to accept Codding's settlement offer of $24 million. San Francisco Chronicle, Dec. 13, 1983, p.6, col. 4.

Page 357.   Before "5. Settlements Between Developers and Neighbors," add:

LANDMARKS HOLDING CORP. v. BERMANT

664 F.2d 891 (2d Cir. 1981)

LUMBARD, Circuit Judge:
Plaintiffs, partners in a real estate development, appeal from an order entered in the District of Connecticut on January 19, 1981, granting

summary judgment to the defendants in an antitrust suit. The complaint alleged that the defendants, consisting of two existing shopping centers, individuals who were managers and/or part owners of those centers, and certain nearby property owners and residents, had conspired to prevent the plaintiffs from opening a competing shopping center by organizing protracted opposition before state administrative agencies, by litigating in the state courts in bad faith, and by soliciting and subsidizing others to bring baseless litigation in the state courts. Judge Eginton held that defendants' alleged actions were protected activity and dismissed the complaint. We disagree and we reverse.

I

As this case is before us on appeal from summary judgment, we must take as true the facts alleged in the complaint and as shown in affidavits and the discovery record. Hamden is a town of approximately 50,000 people situated in the Connecticut countryside six miles north of New Haven. In the 1960's, two shopping malls, Hamden Plaza and Hamden Mart, had the Hamden regional shopping market to themselves. Their freedom from competition was threatened, however, when in 1969 the plaintiffs proposed to build a modern, enclosed shopping mall in 104 acres of land that they owned on Evergreen Avenue in Hamden, less than one mile from Hamden Plaza. This case arises out of defendants' persistent, and ultimately successful, efforts to delay and block construction of that competing shopping center.

In 1969, the May Department Stores Co. signed a partnership agreement with plaintiffs to develop and operate a shopping center on the Evergreen Avenue site. The contract required plaintiffs to obtain the necessary zoning changes and provided that either party could terminate the agreement should the zoning reclassification not be forthcoming.

Upon learning of plaintiffs' plans, the owners of Hamden Mart and Hamden Plaza (the "Plaza defendants") decided to oppose the development. David Bermant, a co-owner of Hamden Plaza, conceded in a deposition taken on March 2, 1973: "We found out that this center is subject to rezoning by the Town, plus the expenditures of huge sums for new roads to serve the mall, also by the Town. . . . [I]t was decided to oppose this effort with every means, to either defeat or delay for as many years as possible, this proposed center." The defendants planned to litigate regardless of the merits, anticipating that even if they lost they "could delay the development of this property a minimum of three to five years. . . ." This delay, defendants hoped, would induce the May Department Stores Co. to abandon its plans and encourage prospective tenants to sign leases in Hamden Plaza or Hamden Mart rather than wait for the new center to be built.

Construction of the proposed mall required the plaintiffs to seek three separate rulings by the Hamden Planning and Zoning Commission ("HPZC"). First, plaintiffs had to apply to the HPZC to adopt regulations creating a zoning classification for shopping centers. Prior to 1970, Hamden had no such classification. Second, the plaintiffs needed to have the HPZC adopt street layout plans for access highways leading to the mall. Third, the plaintiffs needed a zoning change for their particular parcel from manufacturing classification to the newly created regional shopping classification.

The Plaza defendants appeared personally before the HPZC to oppose the changes sought by the plaintiffs. They appealed from each adverse decision of the HPZC to the Court of Common Pleas—knowing they lacked standing to do so—and from there to the Connecticut Supreme Court. They secretly funded a massive publicity campaign to arouse the citizenry of Hamden to oppose the development as a threat to the "quality of life." Finally, they solicited and subsidized opposition by residents of Hamden (the "landowner defendants") before the HPZC and in the Court of Common Pleas, although they knew many of the claims had no merit. . . .

Many of the appeals taken by the landowners were solicited and financed by the Plaza defendants. Three lawyers, who had already been retained by the Plaza defendants, offered to represent landowner residents in litigation against the proposed mall, free of charge. These lawyers never disclosed to their landowner-resident clients their simultaneous representation of the Plaza defendants, who were paying most of the legal fees. In the ensuing litigation, the Plaza defendants subsidized the lawyers and litigation expenses for the landowners without the knowledge or consent of those landowners. . . .

. . . The net result of the fourteen actions brought by the various defendants was that by 1975 the plaintiffs had succeeded in obtaining everything from HPZC that they needed. Every claim of the Plaza defendants and their straw litigants failed. . . . Yet the plaintiffs' courtroom victories proved Pyrrhic, for the protracted delays had by then forced them to abandon the development.

Plaintiffs brought this suit in 1971 to recoup their losses and later amended their complaint in 1977 and again in 1979 to include the obstructive and protracted litigation conducted by the defendants in opposition to plaintiffs' plans. . . .

II

The central issue on appeal is whether Plaza's conduct, as alleged in the complaint and revealed through discover, is immunized by the First

Amendment from antitrust liability under the *Noerr-Pennington* doctrine, Eastern Railroad Presidents Conference v. Noerr Motor Freight, Inc., 365 U.S. 127 (1961); United Mine Workers v. Pennington, 381 U.S. 657 (1965), or whether it falls within the "sham exception" to that doctrine as carved out by the Supreme Court in California Motor Transport Co. v. Trucking Unlimited, 404 U.S. 508 (1972), and in Otter Tail Power Co. v. United States, 410 U.S. 366 (1973), *affirmed after remand*, 417 U.S. 901 (1974).

In *Noerr* and *Pennington*, supra, the Supreme Court held that attempts to influence the legislative process, even though motivated by a desire to reduce or eliminate competition, were protected by the First Amendment. At the same time, however, the Court qualified this immunity by providing that such attempts would be actionable under the antitrust laws where they are a "mere sham to cover what is actually nothing more than an attempt to interfere directly with the business relations of a competitor." *Noerr*, supra, 365 U.S. at 144. California Motor Transport v. Trucking Unlimited, supra, expanded this "sham" exception, stating that "unethical conduct in the setting of the adjudicatory process" or the pursuit of "a pattern of baseless, repetitive claims" cannot seek refuge under the *Noerr-Pennington* doctrine since they constitute an abuse of process "effectively barring . . . access to the agencies and courts." 404 U.S. at 512-13. Accord, Otter Tail Power Co. v. United States, supra, 410 U.S. at 380, ("repetitive lawsuits carrying the hallmark of insubstantial claims" are unprotected); see generally R. Bork, The Antitrust Paradox 359 (1975); Fischel, Antitrust Liability for Attempts to Influence Government Action: the Bases and Limits of the *Noerr-Pennington* Doctrine, 45 U. Chi. L. Rev. 80 (1977). In short, abuse of the administrative and judicial process through unethical lawyer conduct and repetitive filing of insubstantial claims is unprotected by the *Noerr-Pennington* immunity. . . .

. . . We hold that [plaintiffs'] allegations state a cause of action under the antitrust laws. The right to petition the courts for the redress of grievances does not protect abuse of the judicial process through the institution and subsidization of baseless litigation and delay of its final resolution, solely to harass and hinder a competitor. Nothing in the First Amendment licenses the kinds of abuse of civil process that the record discloses here. We therefore reverse.

The district court's and defendants' reliance on Miracle Mile Associates v. City of Rochester, 617 F.2d 18 (2d Cir. 1980), is misplaced. . . .

In *Miracle Mile*, the City of Rochester opposed plaintiffs' plans to build a shopping center through proceedings instituted before various state and federal environmental agencies. Miracle Mile subsequently brought an action under the Sherman Act, charging that the City opposed the shopping center in bad faith and with the intent to suppress competition with commercial property owned by the City. In affirming the grant of summary judgment for the municipal defendant, the court found that the City had a "legitimate municipal interest in preserving the City from the adverse economic impact created by the suburban project," as distinguished from the "sham exception" cases "where the only motivation for resort to adjudicatory processes was the restraint or elimination of competition." 617 F.2d at 21. The State Environmental Quality Review Act, which the City invoked in the state proceedings, was intended to protect the interest of municipalities such as Rochester in preventing overdevelopment. That the City had a reasonable basis for invoking the Act was both conceded by the plaintiffs and evidenced by the City's success in the State Wetlands Proceedings. Having reasonably invoked administrative and judicial proceedings for the purpose for which they were intended, the City incurred no liability. Here, by contrast, the defendants had no reasonable basis for their appeals from the decision of the HPZC, which appeals were taken solely for anti-competitive purposes. . . .

Reversed and remanded.

VAN GRAAFEILAND, dissenting: . . .

I do not believe that the alleged improper conduct of defendants' attorneys rose, or perhaps "fell" is a better word, to the level of such "illegal and reprehensible" practices as perjury, fraud, and bribery, so as to corrupt and make illegal the entire judicial process in which defendants were engaged. See California Motor Transport Co. v. Trucking Unlimited, supra, 404 U.S. at 512-13. So far as appears, the administrative and judicial proceedings in Connecticut were fairly conducted. Plaintiffs had their day in court and prevailed. Plaintiffs' real complaint, one that is voiced all too often today, is that they had too many days in court. Relief from inordinate delay should have been sought in the Connecticut tribunals to which plaintiffs had ready access. While their plight merits sympathy, it does not merit invocation of the Sherman Act. . . .

NOTE ON NEIGHBORS' LIABILITIES FOR WRONGFUL OPPOSITION

The antitrust laws are not the only possible statutory basis for a landowner's action against harassing neighbors. In Bendetson v. Payson, 534 F. Supp. 539 (D. Mass. 1982), neighbors had fought a developer's attempts to build a low-income housing project. The neighbors had spoken out against the project at various administrative hearings and had filed lawsuits challenging the validity of administrative approvals the developer had received. The developer brought an action against the neighbors for damages and injunctive relief. The district judge held that the developer's complaint stated a cause of action under the federal Fair Housing Act, the federal Civil Rights Acts, and the common law doctrine of malicious prosecution.

Chapter Four
Planning, Planners, Plans

Page 406. Before "3. Why All This Matters: Barriers to Plan Amendments," insert:

J. DiMento, The Consistency Doctrine and the Limits of Planning (1980), is a sympathetic evaluation of recent planning legislation. *In California's Land Planning Requirements: The Case for Deregulation,* 54 S. Cal. L. Rev. 447 (1981), George Lefcoe, a law professor who has served for many years on the Los Angeles County Planning Commission, offers a different perspective. Lefcoe urges that the California legislature repeal all consistency requirements and also the statutory sections that require local governments to include open-space and housing elements in their general plans.

California's consistency statute withstood a constitutional challenge in City of Los Angeles v. State, 138 Cal. App. 3d 526, 187 Cal. Rptr. 893 (1982). Among their other arguments, the City of Los Angeles's attorneys asserted that the statute violated the state constitution's "home rule" provision that gives local government primacy in the governance of municipal affairs. The appellate court rejected this argument. "[I]n the absence of any evidence on the subject," it chose to defer to the Legislature's apparent conclusion that a consistency statute addresses problems of statewide concern.

Page 408. At the end of the page, insert:

The interpretation of Cal. Govt. Code §65300.5's internal consistency requirement was at issue in Sierra Club v. Kern County Board of Supervisors, 26 Cal. App. 698, 179 Cal. Rptr. 261 (1981). The County had rezoned the landowner's property from a light agricultural designation to a designation that permitted residential development at suburban densities. This rezoning was consistent with the *land-use element* of the County's plan but inconsistent with a map in the plan's *open-space conservation element.* When the Sierra Club attacked the validity of the zoning amendment on the ground that it was inconsistent with plan, the landowner emphasized a "precedence clause" in the land-use element that stated, "If any conflict exists between the adopted open space and conservation elements and this land use element, this element should take precedence. . . ."

The California Court of Appeal concluded that the issue of the validity of a precedence clause was moot in the case before it because Kern County had since deleted the clause from its plan. The court nevertheless decided to rule on the issue as one of broad public interest that would be likely to recur. It held that the legislature's intent in requiring an open-space element would be frustrated if a county could simply subordinate that element to other elements. It therefore held that any plan containing this sort of precedence clause would be internally inconsistent, and it held further that any zoning change adopted while the plan was internally inconsistent would be invalid. To support its conclusion the court cited an excerpt from the 300-page-long "general plan guidelines" published by the state Office of Planning and Research. This excerpt concluded that the internal consistency requirement "implies that all elements of the general plan have equal legal status." Does this mean that a local government cannot formally accord different weights to the verbal goals appearing in the various elements of its general plan?

Chapter Five

Subdivision Regulations, Building Codes, Aesthetic Controls

Page 421. At the end of the Note, add:

SUESS BUILDERS CO. v. CITY OF BEAVERTON

294 Or. 254, 656 P.2d 306 (1982)

LINDE, Justice.

Plaintiffs own 9.4 acres of land in the city of Beaverton. In a complaint against the city and the Tualatin Hills Park and Recreation District, plaintiffs allege that these governmental bodies temporarily deprived them of the rental value of the property and caused a permanent depression of its market value by designating the major part of the property as a future park site in the city's comprehensive land use plan, and that this constituted a compensable taking of their property for public use under Oregon Constitution article I, section 18 and the federal fifth and fourteenth amendments. . . . Upon the defendants' motion to dismiss the complaint, the trial court entered judgment for defendants. The Court of Appeals affirmed. . . .

. . . Except for the planned acquisition, the city's regulatory policy, in the form of its zoning ordinance, was to allow low density residential development of the land. According to this claim, the governmental bodies in effect told plaintiffs to hold parts of their land for the park district, subject to taxes and without an opportunity to make economic use of it or to place it on the market, until the district was politically and financially ready to buy it for the planned park.

If so, that would not be the equivalent of taking the property entirely when the comprehensive plan was adopted. Adoption of the plan would not mean that defendants were obligated to buy the land and plaintiffs could sue for the price. The governmental bodies could change their minds, as they in fact did, and the landowners would retain their property. Given that governments, like other buyers, do change their plans and that if they do not, they would eventually pay for the property, it cannot even be taken for granted that the property could not be sold in the interim. But adoption of a plan could be the equivalent of taking the use of the property until the government decided to buy it or to release it, if the legal effect of defendants' actions is to "freeze" the status of the land for that purpose without any possibility of an economic use. If that is the effect, it might be described as analogous to seizing from the landowner an option to buy the land during an indefinite term. As this case comes before us upon a judgment dismissing the complaint, the narrow issue is whether the plaintiffs sufficiently plead such action by the defendants to require them to answer. . . .

. . . The language [of the complaint] is broad enough to encompass a hypothetical claim that defendants told plaintiffs that the property was certain to be acquired, that it would be useless to pursue any proposals for private development, and that defendants began to acquire easements for certain facilities. If that were the case, and the defendants later abandoned their plans, a court could find that one or perhaps both of the governmental bodies had temporarily taken all economic use of plaintiffs' property. The complaint may, of course, not mean to claim so much, or the evidence may not support it. These are matters for an answer, motions, and subsequent procedures on summary judgment or trial. As the trial court dismissed the complaint, we judge it only on its face. It is to be "liberally construed." O.R.C.P. 12A. For the reasons stated, the complaint was sufficient to survive defendants' motion to dismiss. . . .

The decision of the Court of Appeals is reversed and the case is remanded to the circuit court for further proceedings.

Page 478.   Delete Adams v. State and substitute:

DINSKY v. TOWN OF FRAMINGHAM

386 Mass. 801, 438 N.E.2d 51 (1982)

NOLAN, Justice.

The plaintiffs brought this action against the town of Framingham (town) alleging negligence in the issuance of building and occupancy permits. After a trial in Superior Court, the judge granted the defendant's motion for a directed finding on the ground that the town owed the plaintiffs no duty of care beyond that owed to the public at large. We transferred the plaintiffs' appeal to this court on our own motion. We affirm the judgment for the town.

The judge made the following findings of fact in his memorandum of decision. The plaintiffs are the owners of a single family residence (the premises) on Badger Road in Framingham. By a letter dated February 13, 1974, the town's department of health authorized the town's building commissioner to issue a building permit for the construction of a one family residence on the premises on the "condition that the lots shall be graded as to prevent low spots that will not drain and create a public nuisance." In addition, the letter provided that "prior to issuance of an occupancy permit, inspection by your Department, or the Town Engineer, or the Board of Health, should be performed to insure compliance with the proposed grading." The building commissioner issued a building permit for the premises on February 15, 1974, and an occupancy permit was issued on December 18, 1975. The permits issued despite the fact that the requirements expressed in the department of health letter pertaining to the proposed grading and proper drainage were not met. On December 22, 1975, the builder conveyed the premises to the plaintiffs.

Beginning in March, 1978, the plaintiffs began experiencing serious flooding on the premises. The basement, garage, and driveway became flooded and large portions of their lawn were covered by water over one inch deep. Shortly afterward, large cracks developed in the foundation walls. The flooding condition has continued during periods of heavy precipitation. . . .

. . . [T]he plaintiffs argue that the building commissioner owed a specific, affirmative duty to them to enforce the building code and to issue building and occupancy permits in a nonnegligent manner. The town argues in response that the duty of the building commissioner, absent specific language to the contrary in the building code, is to ensure compliance with the building code for the benefit of the public generally and that the duty does not run to individuals in their private capacity.

The issue of whether a municipality's failure to enforce a building code gives rise to a private cause of action is one of first impression for this court. We shall, therefore, look to the decisions of other jurisdictions which have ruled on this point. We begin with the idea that the purpose of a building code has been considered traditionally to be the protection of the general public. This rule is well stated in 7 E. McQuillin, Municipal Corporations §24.507, at 479 (3d ed. 1981): "The enactment and enforcement of building codes and ordinances constitute a governmental function. The primary purpose of such codes and ordinances is to secure to the municipality as a whole the benefits of a well-ordered municipal government, or, as sometimes expressed, to protect the health and secure the safety of occupants of buildings, and not to protect the personal or property interests of individuals." The traditional rule, that a building code is enacted for the benefit of the public and therefore that its violation does not give rise to a private right of action, continues to be followed by the majority of the States that have considered the question. [Nolan, J., then reviewed many decisions supporting the traditional rule.]

Although the majority of jurisdictions that have addressed the issue adhere to the traditional public duty rule, two States, Louisiana and Wisconsin have rejected it, and Alaska has seriously questioned it. In Stewart v. Schmieder, 386 So. 2d 1351 (La. 1980), the applicable statute required the building inspector to examine detailed plans before issuing a building permit. The court held that the inspector's failure to perform this duty rendered the municipality liable for the injuries which resulted when the building collapsed. The Wisconsin court in Coffey v. Milwaukee, 74 Wis. 2d 526, 247 N.W.2d 132 (1976), held that a complaint alleging a building inspector's negligence in inspecting standpipes stated a cause of action against the municipality. The court rejected the traditional distinction between a public duty and a special duty as artificial, but also stated that the court would in certain circumstances decline to enforce a municipality's liability for public policy reasons. See also Hawes v. Germantown Mut. Ins. Co., 103 Wis. 2d 524, 309 N.W.2d 356 (1981); Adams v. State, 555 P.2d 235 (Alaska 1976).

We have examined the State Building Code and G.L. c. 143, §§3 and 3A, which impose obligations upon building commissioners. There does not appear to be any language in the enactments which would warrant a finding that the Legislature intended to create private causes of action for property owners on the facts of this case. The enactments confer no specific duties upon building commissioners or inspectors with regard to individual citizens or property owners. General Laws c. 143, §3A, *as amended through* St. 1979, c. 617, §2, describes the responsibilities of a building inspector in this way: "[T]he local inspector shall enforce the state building code as to any building or structure within the city or town from which he is appointed." The State Building Code speaks in terms of a public interest only. . . . We conclude that there is nothing in either the General Laws or in the State Building Code which shows a legislative intent to impose liability on a municipality to individual property owners for the negligent issuance of building permits or the nonenforcement of the State Building Code.

After a review of the pertinent legislation and the relevant cases of other jurisdictions, we conclude that we will not depart from the majority rule that in the absence of a special duty owed to the plaintiffs, different from that owed to the public at large, no cause of action for negligent inspection can be maintained. To hold otherwise would cause a municipality to become substantially an insurer of each and every construction project. The tremendous exposure to liability that could result from such a decision would likely dissuade municipalities from enacting regulations designed for the protection and welfare of the public. Accordingly, we affirm the judgment for the defendant.

Page 501. At the end of the Note, add:

A significant article on aesthetic regulation is Costonis, Law and Aesthetics: A Critique and a Reformulation of the Dilemmas, 80 Mich. L. Rev. 355 (1982). Costonis compares two rationales for aesthetic controls. The conventional one is "the visual beauty rationale." Costonis asserts that a "cultural stability rationale" more accurately identifies the impetus for aesthetic regulation. ". . . [T]he visual beauty interest, insofar as it has any discernible legal content, is subsumed under the stability interest. It is true, of course, that viewers respond affirmatively to particular visual configurations in the environment. Their responses, in fact, are often sufficiently patterned to refute the objection that aesthetics is too subjective to warrant legal protection. But these configurations are compelling because they signify values that stabilize cultural, group, or individual identity, not because their visual qualities conform to the canons of one or another school of aesthetic formalism." Id. at 357-358. Costonis goes on to consider the constitutional problems — for example, First Amendment issues — that government programs to stabilize cultural values are apt to pose.

Page 512. At the end of Note 2, insert:

In State v. Jones, 305 N.C. 520, 290 S.E. 675 (1982), the Supreme Court of North Carolina half-heartedly joined the judicial trend toward permitting a government to pursue exclusively aesthetic objectives. In the course of sustaining the validity of a junkyard-control ordinance against the assertions that it violated both the Due Process Clause of the Fourteenth Amendment and an analogous provision of the state constitution, Branch, C.J., wrote in part:

> . . . [W]e expressly overrule our previous cases to the extent that they prohibited regulation based upon aesthetic considerations alone. We do not grant blanket approval of all regulatory schemes based upon aesthetic considerations. Rather, we adopt the test . . . that the diminution in value of an individual's property should be balanced against the corresponding gain to the public from such regulation. Some of the factors which should be considered and weighed in applying such a balancing test include such private concerns such as whether the regulation results in confiscation of the most substantial part of the value of the property or deprives the property owner of the property's reasonable use, and such public concerns as the purpose of the regulation and the manner in achieving a permitted purpose. 1 A. Rathkopf, The Law of Zoning and Planning §4.02, at 4-3 (4th ed. 1982). Aesthetic

regulation may provide corollary benefits to the general community such as protection of property values, promotion of tourism, indirect protection of health and safety, preservation of the character and integrity of the community, and promotion of the comfort, happiness, and emotional stability of area residents. See, Rowlett, Aesthetic Regulation Under the Police Power: The New General Welfare and the Presumption of Constitutionality, 34 Vand. L. Rev. 603 (1981). Such corollary community benefits would be factors to be considered in balancing the public interests in regulation against the individual property owner's interest in the use of his property free from regulation. The test focuses on the reasonableness of the regulation by determining whether the aesthetic purpose to which the regulation is reasonably related outweighs the burdens imposed on the private property owner by the regulation. Id. at 649. See e.g., Berg Agency v. Township of Maplewood, 163 N.J. Super. 542, 559, 395 A.2d 261, 270 (1978). We therefore hold that reasonable regulation based on aesthetic considerations may constitute a valid basis for the exercise of the police power depending on the facts and circumstances of each case. We feel compelled to caution the local legislative bodies charged with the responsibility for and the exercise of the police power in the promulgation of regulations based *solely* upon aesthetic considerations that this a matter which should not be delegated by them to subordinate groups or organizations which are not authorized to exercise the police power by the General Assembly.

290 S.E.2d at 681. Is the court's balancing test stiffer than the usual Due Process standard of review? Should it be?

Page 514.   Delete People v. Mobil Oil Corp. and substitute:

METROMEDIA, INC. v. CITY OF SAN DIEGO

453 U.S. 490, 101 S. Ct. 2882, 69 L. Ed. 2d 800 (1981)

[The facts of this case appear in Metromedia, Inc. v. City of San Diego (Cal. 1980), supra Casebook p.502. There the Supreme Court of California rejected a variety of constitutional challenges to a San Diego ordinance that regulated billboards. The billboard companies appealed. The case elicited five opinions from the Justices of the Supreme Court. Although no opinion commanded a majority, the Court held that certain features of the ordinance violated the First Amendment.]

Justice WHITE announced the judgment of the Court and delivered an opinion, in which Justice STEWART, Justice MARSHALL, and Justice POWELL, joined. . . .

Billboards are a well-established medium of communication, used to convey a broad range of different kinds of messages. As Justice Clark noted in his dissent below:

"The outdoor sign or symbol is a venerable medium for expressing political, social and commercial ideas. From the poster or 'broadside' to the billboard, outdoor signs have played a prominent role throughout American history, rallying support for political and social causes." 26 Cal. 3d, at 888. The record in this case indicates that besides the typical commercial uses, San Diego billboards have been used "to publicize the 'City in motion' campaign of the City of San Diego, to communicate meassages from candidates for municipal, state and national offices, including candidates for judicial office, to propose marriage, to seek employment, to encourage the use of seat belts, to denounce the United Nations, to seek support for Prisoners of War and Missing in Action, to promote the United Crusade and a variety of other charitable and socially related endeavors and to provide directions to the traveling public."[10]

But whatever its communicative function, the billboard remains a "large, immobile, and permanent structure which like other structures is subject to . . . regulation." Id., at 870. Moreoever, because it is designed to stand out and apart from its surroundings, the billboard creates a unique set of problems for land-use planning and development.

Billboards, then, like other media of communication, combine communicative and noncommunicative aspects. As with other media, the government has legitimate interests in controlling the noncommunicative aspects of the medium, but the First and Fourteenth Amendments foreclose a similar interest in controlling the communicative aspects. Because regulation of the noncommunicative aspects of a medium often impinges to some degree on the communicative aspects, it has been necessary for the courts to reconcile the government's regulatory interests with the individual's right to expression. . . .

As construed by the California Supreme Court, the ordinance restricts the use of certain kinds of outdoor signs. . . .

. . . [U]nder the ordinance (1) a sign advertising goods or services available on the property where the sign is located is allowed; (2) a sign on a building or other property advertising goods or services produced or offered elsewhere is barred; (3) noncommercial advertising, unless within one of the specific exceptions, is everywhere prohibited. The occupant of property may advertise his own goods or services; he may not advertise the goods or services of others, nor may he display most noncommercial messages.

IV

Appellants' principal submission is that enforcement of the ordinance will eliminate the outdoor advertising business in San Diego and that

10. Joint Stipulation of Facts No. 23, App. 46a-47a.

the First and Fourteenth Amendments prohibit the elimination of this medium of communication. Appellants contend that the city may bar neither all offsite commercial signs nor all noncommercial advertisements and that even if it may bar the former, it may not bar the latter. Appellants may raise both arguments in their own right because, although the bulk of their business consists of offsite signs carying commercial advertisements, their billboards also convey a substantial amount of noncommercial advertising. Because our cases have consistently distinguished between the constitutional protection afforded commercial as opposed to noncommercial speech, in evaluating appellants' contention we consider separately the effect of the ordinance on commercial and noncommercial speech. . . .

. . . [I]n Central Hudson Gas & Electric Corp. v. Public Service Comm'n, 447 U.S. 557 (1980), we held: "The Constitution . . . accords a lesser protection to commercial speech than to other constitutionally guaranteed expression. The protection available for a particular commercial expression turns on the nature both of the expression and of the governmental interests served by its regulation." Id., at 562-563. We then adopted a four-part test for determining the validity of government restrictions on commercial speech as distinguished from more fully protected speech. (1) The First Amendment protects commercial speech only if that speech concerns lawful activity and is not misleading. A restriction on otherwise protected commercial speech is valid only if it (2) seeks to implement a substantial governmental interest, (3) directly advances that interest, and (4) reaches no further than necessary to accomplish the given objective. Id., at 563-566.

Appellants agree that the proper approach to be taken in determining the validity of the restrictions on commercial speech is that which was articulated in *Central Hudson*, but assert that the San Diego ordinance fails that test. We do not agree.

There can be little controversy over the application of the first, second, and fourth criteria. There is no suggestion that the commercial advertising at issue here involves unlawful activity or is misleading. Nor can there be substantial doubt that the twin goals that the ordinance seeks to further — traffic safety and the appearance of the city — are substantial governmental goals. It is far too late to contend otherwise with respect to either traffic safety, Railway Express Agency, Inc. v. New York, 336 U.S. 106 (1949), or esthetics, see Penn Central Transportation Co. v. New York City, 438 U.S. 104 (1978); Village of Belle Terre v. Boraas, 416 U.S. 1 (1974); Berman v. Parker, 348 U.S. 26, 33 (1954). Similarly, we reject appellants' claim that the ordinance is broader than necessary and, therefore, fails the fourth part of the *Central Hudson* test. If the city has a sufficient basis for believing that billboards are traffic hazards and are unattractive, then obviously the most direct and perhaps the only effective approach to solving the problems they create is to prohibit them. The city has gone no further than necessary in seeking to meet its ends. Indeed, it has stopped short of fully accomplishing its ends: It has not prohibited all billboards, but allows onsite advertising and some other specifically exempted signs.

The more serious question, then, concerns the third of the *Central Hudson* criteria: Does the ordinance "directly advance" governmental interests in traffic safety and in the appearance of the city? . . .

It is . . . argued that the city denigrates its interest in traffic safety and beauty and defeats its own case by permitting onsite advertising and other specified signs. Appellants question whether the distinction between onsite and offsite advertising on the same property is justifiable in terms of either esthetics or traffic safety. The ordinance permits the occupant of property to use billboards located on that property to advertise goods and services offered at that location; identical billboards, equally distracting and unattractive, that advertise goods or services available elsewhere are prohibited even if permitting the latter would not multiply the number of billboards. . . .

. . . San Diego has obviously chosen to value one kind of commercial speech — onsite advertising — more than another kind of commercial speech — offsite advertising. The ordinance reflects a decision by the city that the former interest, but not the latter, is stronger than the city's interests in traffic safety and esthetics. The city has decided that in a limited instance — onsite commercial advertising — its interest should yield. We do not reject that judgment. As we see it, the city could reasonably conclude that a commercial enterprise — as well as the interested public — has a stronger interest in identifying its place of business and advertising the products or services available there than it has in using or leasing its available space for the purpose of advertising commercial enterprises located elsewhere. It does not follow from the fact that the city has concluded that some commercial interests outweigh its municipal interests in this context that it must give similar weight to all other commercial advertising. Thus, offsite commercial billboards may be prohibited while onsite commercial billboards are permitted.

The constitutional problem in this area requires resolution of the conflict between the city's land-use interests and the commercial interests of those seeking to purvey goods and services within the city. In light of the above analysis, we cannot conclude that the city has drawn an ordinance broader than is necessary to meet its interests, or that it fails directly to advance substantial government interests. In sum, insofar as it regulates commercial speech the San Diego ordinance meets the constitutional requirements of *Central Hudson*, supra.

V

It does not follow, however, that San Diego's general ban on signs carrying noncommercial advertising is also valid under the First and Fourteenth Amendments. The fact that the city may value commercial messages relating to onsite goods and services more than it values commercial communications relating to offsite goods and services does not justify prohibiting an occupant from displaying its own ideas or those of others.

As indicated above, our recent commercial speech cases have consistently accorded noncommercial speech a greater degree of protection than commercial speech. San Diego effectively inverts this judgment, by affording a greater degree of protection to commercial than to noncommercial speech. There is a broad exception for onsite commercial advertisements, but there is no similar exception for noncommercial speech. The use of onsite billboards to carry commercial messages related to the commercial use of the premises is freely permitted, but the use of otherwise identical billboards to carry noncommercial messages is generally prohibited. The city does not explain how or why noncommercial billboards located in places where commercial billboards are permitted would be more threatening to safe driving or would detract more from the beauty of the city. Insofar as the city tolerates billboards at all, it cannot choose to limit their content to commercial messages; the city may not conclude that the communication of commercial information concerning goods and services connected with a particular site is of greater value than the communication of noncommercial messages.

Furthermore, the ordinance contains exceptions that permit various kinds of noncommercial signs, whether on property where goods and services are offered or not, that would otherwise be within the general ban. A fixed sign may be used to identify any piece of property and its owner. Any piece of property may carry or display religious symbols, commemorative plaques of recognized historical societies and organizations, signs carrying news items or telling the time or temperature, signs erected in discharge of any governmental function, or temporary political campaign signs. No other noncommercial or ideological signs meeting the structural definition are permitted, regardless of their effect on traffic safety or esthetics.

Although the city may distinguish between the relative value of different categories of commercial speech, the city does not have the same range of choice in the area of noncommercial speech to evaluate the strength of, or distinguish between, various communicative interests. See Carey v. Brown, 447 U.S., at 462. Because some noncommercial messages may be conveyed on billboards throughout the commercial and industrial zones, San Diego must similarly allow billboards conveying other noncommercial messages throughout those zones.[20] . . .

VII

Because the San Diego ordinance reaches too far into the realm of protected speech, we conclude that it is unconstitutional on its face. The judgment of the California Supreme Court is reversed, and the case is remanded to that court.[26]

Justice BRENNAN, with whom Justice BLACKMUN joins, concurring in the judgment. . . .

Where the plurality and I disagree is in the characterization of the San Diego ordinance and thus in the appropriate analytical framework to apply. The plurality believes that the question of a total ban is not presented in this case, ante, n.20, because the ordinance contains exceptions to its general prohibition. In contrast, my view is that the *practical* effect of the San Diego ordinance is to eliminate the billboard as an effective medium of communication. . . . None of the exceptions provides a practical alternative for the general commercial or noncommercial billboard advertiser. Indeed, unless the advertiser chooses to buy or lease premises in the city, or unless his message falls within one of the narrow exempted categories, he is foreclosed from announcing either commercial or noncommercial ideas through a billboard.

The characterization of the San Diego regulation as a total ban of a medium of communication has more than semantic implications, for it suggests a First Amendment analysis quite different from the plurality's. Instead of relying on the exceptions to the ban to invalidate the ordinance, I would apply the tests this Court has developed to analyze content-neutral prohibitions of particular media of communication. . . .

. . . In the case of billboards, I would hold that a city may totally ban them if it can show that a sufficiently substantial governmental interest is directly furthered by the total ban, and that any more narrowly drawn restriction, i.e., anything less than a total ban, would promote less well the achievement of that goal.

20. Because a total prohibition of outdoor advertising is not before us, we do not indicate whether such a ban would be consistent with the First Amendment. But see Schad v. Mount Ephraim, 452 U.S. 61 (1981), on the constitutional problems created by a total prohibition of a particular expressive forum, live entertainment in that case. Despite Justice Stevens' insistence to the contrary, we do not imply that the ordinance is unconstitutional *because* it "does not abridge enough speech." . . .

26. . . . Since our judgment is based essentially on the inclusion of noncommercial speech within the prohibitions of the ordinance, the California courts may sustain the ordinance by limiting its reach to commercial speech, assuming the ordinance is susceptible to this treatment.

Applying that test to the instant case, I would invalidate the San Diego ordinance. The city has failed to provide adequate justification for its substantial restriction on protected activity. See Schad v. Mount Ephraim, [452 U.S.,] at 72. First, although I have no quarrel with the substantiality of the city's interest in traffic safety, the city has failed to come forward with evidence demonstrating that billboards actually impair traffic safety in San Diego. . . .

Second, I think that the city has failed to show that its asserted interest in aesthetics is su ficiently substantial in the commercial and industrial areas of San Diego. . . .

. . . A billboard is not *necessarily* inconsistent with oil storage tanks, blighted areas, or strip development. Of course, it is not for a court to impose its own notion of beauty on San Diego. But before deferring to a city's judgment, a court must be convinced that the city is seriously and comprehensively addressing aesthetic concerns with respect to its environment. Here, San Diego has failed to demonstrate a comprehensive coordinated effort in its commercial and industrial areas to address other obvious contributors to an unattractive environment. In this sense the ordinance is underinclusive. See Erznoznik v. City of Jacksonville, 422 U.S. 205, 214 (1975). Of course, this is not to say that the city must address all aesthetic problems at the same time, or none at all. Indeed, from a planning point of view, attacking the problem incrementally and sequentially may represent the most sensible solution. On the other hand, if billboards alone are banned and no further steps are contemplated or likely, the commitment of the city to improving its physical environment is placed in doubt. By showing a comprehensive commitment to making its physical environment in commercial and industrial areas more attractive, and by allowing only narrowly tailored exceptions, if any, San Diego could demonstrate that its interest in creating an aesthetically pleasing environment is genuine and substantial. This is a requirement where, as here, there is an infringement of important constitutional consequence.

I have little doubt that some jurisdictions will easily carry the burden of proving the substantiality of their interest in aesthetics. For example, the parties acknowledge that a historical community such as Williamsburg, Va. should be able to prove that its interest in aesthetics and historical authenticity are sufficiently important that the First Amendment value attached to billboards must yield. See Tr. of Oral Arg., 22-25. And I would be surprised if the Federal Government had much trouble making the argument that billboards could be entirely banned in Yellowstone National Park, where their very existence would so obviously be inconsistent with the surrounding landscape. I express no view on whether San Diego or other large urban areas will be able to meet the burden. But San Diego failed to do so here, and for that reason I would strike down its ordinance.

III . . .

. . . I cannot agree with the plurality's view that an ordinance totally banning commercial billboards but allowing noncommercial billboards would be constitutional. For me, such an ordinance raises First Amendment problems at least as serious as those raised by a total ban, for it gives city officials the right—before approving a billboard—to determine whether the proposed message is "commercial" or "noncommercial." . . .

. . . I would be unhappy to see city officials dealing with the following series of billboards and deciding which ones to permit: the first billboard contains the message "Visit Joe's Ice Cream Shoppe"; the second, "Joe's Ice Cream Shoppe uses only the highest quality dairy products"; the third, "Because Joe thinks that dairy products are good for you, please shop at Joe's Shoppe"; and the fourth, "Joe says to support dairy price supports; they mean lower prices for you at his Shoppe." Or how about some San Diego Padres baseball fans—with no connection to the team—who together rent a billboard and communicate the message "Support the San Diego Padres, a great baseball team." May the city decide that a United Automobile Workers billboard with the message "Be a patriot—do not buy Japanese-manufactured cars" is "commercial" and therefore forbid it? What if the same sign is placed by Chrysler?

I do not read our recent line of commercial cases as authorizing this sort of regular and immediate line-drawing by governmental entities. . . .

. . . I have no doubt that those who seek to convey commercial messages will engage in the most imaginative of exercises to place themselves within the safe haven of noncommercial speech, while at the same time conveying their commercial message. Encouraging such behavior can only make the job of city officials—who already are inclined to ban billboards—that much more difficult and potentially intrusive upon legitimate noncommercial expression.

Accordingly, I would reverse the decision of the California Supreme Court upholding the San Diego billboard ordinance.

Justice STEVENS, dissenting in part.

If enforced as written, the ordinance at issue in this case will eliminate the outdoor advertising business in the city of San Diego.[1] The principal

---

1. The parties so stipulated.

question presented is, therefore, whether a city may prohibit this medium of communication. Instead of answering that question, the plurality focuses its attention on the exceptions from the total ban and, somewhat ironically, concludes that the ordinance is an unconstitutional abridgment of speech because it does not abridge enough speech. . . .

Although it is possible that some future applications of the San Diego ordinance may violate the First Amendment, I am satisfied that the ordinance survives the challenges that these appellants have standing to raise. Unlike the plurality, I do not believe that this case requires us to decide any question concerning the kind of signs a property owner may display on his own premises. I do, however, believe that it is necessary to confront the important question, reserved by the plurality, whether a city may entirely ban one medium of communication. My affirmative answer to that question leads me to the conclusion that the San Diego ordinance should be upheld. . . .

Because the legitimacy of the interests supporting a city-wide zoning plan designed to improve the entire municipality are beyond dispute, in my judgment the constitutionality of the prohibition of outdoor advertising involves two separate questions. First, is there any reason to believe that the regulation is biased in favor of one point of view or another, or that it is a subtle method of regulating the controversial subjects that may be placed on the agenda for public debate? Second, is it fair to conclude that the market which remains open for the communication of both popular and unpopular ideas is ample and not threatened with gradually increasing restraints?

In this case, there is not even a hint of bias or censorship in the city's actions. Nor is there any reason to believe that the overall communications market in San Diego is inadequate. Indeed, it may well be true in San Diego as in other metropolitan areas that the volume of communication is excessive and that the public is presented with too many words and pictures to recognize those that are most worthy of attention. . . .

Chief Justice BURGER, dissenting.

Today the Court takes an extraordinary—even a bizarre—step by severely limiting the power of a city to act on risks it perceives to traffic safety and the environment posed by large, permanent billboards. Those joining the plurality opinion invalidate a city's effort to minimize these traffic hazards and eyesores simply because, in exercising rational legislative judgment, it has chosen to permit a narrow class of signs that serve special needs.

Relying on simplistic platitudes about content, subject matter, and the dearth of other means to communicate, the billboard industry attempts to escape the real and growing problems every municipality faces in protecting safety and preserving the environment in an urban area. The Court's disposition of the serious issues involved exhibits insensitivity to the impact of these billboards on those who must live with them and the delicacy of the legislative judgments involved in regulating them. American cities desiring to mitigate the dangers mentioned must, as a matter of *federal constitutional law*, elect between two unsatisfactory options: (a) allowing all "noncommercial" signs, no matter how many, how dangerous, or how damaging to the environment; or (b) forbidding signs altogether. Indeed, lurking in the recesses of today's opinions is a not-so-veiled threat that the second option, too, may soon be withdrawn. This is the long arm and voracious appetite of federal power—this time judicial power—with a vengeance, reaching and absorbing traditional concepts of local authority. . . .

In Kovacs v. Cooper, [336 U.S. 77 (1949),] the Court upheld a municipal ordinance that totally banned sound trucks from a town's borders; other media were available. The Court had no difficulty distinguishing *Saia v. New York*, 334 U.S. 558 (1948), decided seven months earlier, where the Court had invalidated an ordinance requiring a permit from the local police chief before using a sound truck. The danger seen in *Saia* was in allowing a single government official to regulate a medium of communication with the attendant risk that the decision would be based on the message, not the medium.

The ordinance in *Kovacs*, however, did not afford that kind of potential for censorship and was held not to violate the First Amendment. Justice Frankfurter, concurring, expressed this point more broadly: "So long as a legislature does not prescribe what ideas may be noisily expressed and what may not be, nor discriminate among those who would make inroads upon the public peace, it is not for us to supervise the limits the legislature may impose in safeguarding the steadily narrowing opportunities for serenity and reflection." Id., at 97. . . .

The means chosen to effectuate legitimate governmental interests are not for this Court to select. "These are matters for the legislative judgment controlled by public opinion." Kovacs v. Cooper, 336 U.S., at 96-97 (Frankfurter, J., concurring). The plurality ignores this Court's seminal opinions in *Kovacs* by substituting its judgment for that of city officials and disallowing a ban on one offensive and intrusive means of communication when other means are available. . . .

The messages conveyed on San Diego billboards—whether commercial, political, social, or religious—are not inseparable from the billboards that carry them. These same messages can reach an equally large audience through a variety of other media: newspapers, television, radio, magazines, direct mail, pamphlets, etc. True, these other methods may not be so "eye-catching"—or so cheap—as billboards,[5] but there has been no suggestion that billboards heretofore have advanced any particular viewpoint or issue disproportionately to advertising generally. . . .

The fatal flaw in the plurality's logic comes when it concludes that San Diego, by exempting on-site commercial signs, thereby has "afford[ed] a greater degree of protection to commercial than to noncommercial speech." The "greater degree of protection" our cases have given noncommercial speech establishes a narrow range of constitutionally permissible regulation. To say noncommercial speech receives a greater degree of *constitutional* protection, however, does not mean that a legislature is forbidden to afford differing degrees of *statutory* protection when the restrictions on each form of speech—commercial and noncommercial—otherwise pass constitutional muster under the standards respectively applicable. . . .

By allowing communication of certain commercial ideas via billboards, but forbidding noncommercial signs altogether, a city does not necessarily place a greater "value" on commercial speech. In these situations, the city is simply recognizing that it has greater latitude to distinguish among various forms of commercial communication when the same distinctions would be impermissible if undertaken with regard to noncommercial speech. Indeed, when adequate alternative channels of communication are readily available so that the message may be freely conveyed through other means, a city arguably is more faithful to the Constitution by treating all noncommercial speech the same than by attempting to impose the same classifications in noncommercial as it has in commercial areas. To undertake the same kind of balancing and content judgment with noncommercial speech that is permitted with commercial speech is far more likely to run afoul of the First Amendment. . . .

Justice REHNQUIST, dissenting.

I agree substantially with the views expressed in the dissenting opinions of The Chief Justice and Justice Stevens and make only these two additional observations: (1) In a case where city planning commissions and zoning boards must regularly confront constitutional claims of this sort, it is a genuine misfortune to have the Court's treatment of the subject be a virtual Tower of Babel, from which no definitive principles

---

5. Before trial, the parties stipulated: "Many businesses and politicians and other persons rely upon outdoor advertising because other forms of advertising are insufficient, inappropriate and prohibitively expensive." Joint Stipulation of Facts No. 28, App. 48a. This sweeping, conclusory, and rather vague generalization does nothing to explain how other media are insufficient, inappropriate, or too expensive. More important, the stipulation does not suggest that any particular point of view or issue will be suppressed by the elimination of billboards.

can be clearly drawn; and (2) I regret even more keenly my contribution to this judicial clangor, but find that none of the views expressed in the other opinions written in the case come close enough to mine to warrant the necessary compromise to obtain a Court opinion.

In my view, the aesthetic justification alone is sufficient to sustain a total prohibition of billboards within a community, see Berman v. Parker, 348 U.S. 26, 32-33 (1954), regardless of whether the particular community is "a historical community such as Williamsburg" or one as unsightly as the older parts of many of our major metropolitan areas. Such areas should not be prevented from taking steps to correct, as best they may, mistakes of their predecessors. Nor do I believe that the limited exceptions contained in the San Diego ordinance are the types which render this statute unconstitutional. The closest one is the exception permitting billboards during political campaigns, but I would treat this as a virtually self-limiting exception which will have an effect on the aesthetics of the city only during the periods immediately prior to a campaign. As such, it seems to me a reasonable outlet, limited as to time, for the free expression which the First and Fourteenth Amendments were designed to protect.

Unlike Justice Brennan, I do not think a city should be put to the task of convincing a local judge that the elimination of billboards would have more than a negligible impact on aesthetics. Nothing in my experience on the bench has led me to believe that a judge is in any better position than a city or county commission to make decisions in an area such as aesthetics. Therefore, little can be gained in the area of constitutional law, and much lost in the process of democratic decisionmaking, by allowing individual judges in city after city to second-guess such legislative or administrative determinations.

NOTE ON METROMEDIA

On remand the Supreme Court of California held that the San Diego ordinance could not be saved. Justice Broussard, writing for the majority, reasoned:

> [W]e can salvage the constitutionality of the ordinance only by limiting its scope to prohibit only commercial signs. Such a construction would be inconsistent with the language of the ordinance and the original intent of the city council at the time of enacting the ordinance. The resulting legislation would compel the city to distinguish between commercial and noncommercial speech, a task rife with constitutional enigmas, and might not effectively achieve the city's objective of promoting traffic safety and improving community appearance. We therefore conclude that the ordinance cannot fairly

and reasonably be construed in a manner that would preserve its constitutionality.

Metromedia, Inc. v. City of San Diego, 32 Cal. 3d 180, 649 P.2d 902, 185 Cal. Rptr. 260, 261 (1982). In a dissent Justice Kaus argued: "Since the city has made it clear that it prefers to retain this ordinance to the extent constitutionally permissible, I believe that we should construe the ordinance's prohibition on offsite billboards as applicable only to commercial billboards. As so interpreted, the ordinance is constitutional and should be upheld." 185 Cal. Rptr. at 270.

City of Lakewood v. Colfax Unlimited Assn., Inc., 634 P.2d 52 (Colo. 1981), decided a few months after the Supreme Court's decision in *Metromedia*, provides some indication of how lower courts have responded to the Court's "Tower of Babel." In *City of Lakewood* the owners of onsite commercial signs asserted that the City's sign ordinance infringed First Amendment freedoms. The Supreme Court of Colorado held that the City had failed to prove that the following provisions of its ordinance were sufficiently supportive of the City's legitimate interests in traffic safety and aesthetics:

1. limitations on the *content* of onsite commercial signs (for example, in some zones the City had prohibited mention of the prices of goods and services);
2. a ban on the *alteration* of any message conveyed by a noncomforming commercial sign;
3. the preferential treatment of specified types of commercial signs — for example, contractor signs and real estate "for sale" signs — over other onsite commercial messages;
4. the preferential treatment of specified subcategories of noncommercial speech (for example, religious and fraternal symbols, scoreboards at athletic fields) over other types of noncommercial speech; and
5. a ban on political advertisements on bus-stop benches.

Although the City's ordinance included a severability clause, the Colorado Supreme Court regarded the defects as so pervasive that it invalidated the sign ordinance in its entirety.

One observer has worried that the prohibition of offsite advertising on billboards will impede new firms from entering certain types of markets, and thereby enrich well-known established firms at the expense of consumers. Leffler, The Prohibition of Billboard Advertising: An Economic Analysis of the *Metromedia* Decision, 1 S. Ct. Econ. Rev. 113 (1983).

Page 521.   After the heading "Note on On-Site Advertising," insert:

0. *Sambo's: The story continues.* The District Court's decision was reversed in Sambo's Restaurants, Inc. v. City of Ann Arbor, 663 F.2d 686 (6th Cir. 1981). The Sixth Circuit disapproved the finding that the plaintiffs had waived their rights. It also held that the use of the "Sambo's" tradename was constitutionally protected commercial speech in this instance, in part because the city had not introduced evidence that use of the tradename would in fact threaten racial harmony in the city.

Page 533.   At the end of Note 1, insert:

In 1981 Congress considerably sweetened the Internal Revenue Code's already generous tax incentives for historic preservation. Perhaps as a result, preservation activity boomed. The Interior Department's National Park Service, which determines a rehabilitator's eligibility to receive these tax benefits, in the 1978-1987 period approved rehabilitation projects involving $11 billion of investment in 17,000 buildings. The Tax Reform Act of 1986 tightened up on this tax shelter. See infra Supplement p. 118. This led in the short run to a drop in rehabilitation activity. See Brooks, The Changes in Historic Rehabilitations, N.Y. Times, Aug. 23, 1987, Sec. 8, p.2, col. 1. The long-term effects are unclear because the tax changes in 1986 hit most other types of tax shelters even harder, leaving historic-rehabilitation projects as "one of the few big real-estate breaks left." Gottschalk, "Tax Changes for Historic Rehabilitation Lead Syndicators to Seek Smaller Investors," Wall St. J., Mar. 2, 1987, p.23, col. 4.

Professor Carol Rose believes that the underlying rationale of historic preservation is to strengthen the social ties that bind a community together. See Preservation and Community: New Directions in the Law of Historic Preservation, 33 Stan. L. Rev. 473 (1981). Her analysis seems to be in harmony with John Costonis's subsequent suggestion that all types of aesthetic regulation are designed to enhance cultural stability. Costonis, Law and Aesthetics, 80 Mich. L. Rev. 355 (1982).

Two controversies over historic landmark designations have involved structures that symbolize popular American culture. The California Historical Resources Commission nominated to the National Register of Historic Places the last surviving McDonald's restaurant built in the original "golden arches" design. The 30-year-old restaurant was located in a shopping center in Downey, a suburb of Los Angeles. The Commission staff's report asked rhetorically, "Are we then required to register the oldest Burger King, Shakey's Pizza Parlor or Bob's Big Boy Restaurant?

The answer is, probably not. The factor that sets this property apart from the rest, is that the McDonald brothers' concept revolutionized eating habits in America, creating the first sucessful franchising of an idea which has now become an American way of life." Soiffer, Beef over a Burger Stand, S.F. Chronicle, Nov. 28, 1983, p.5, col. 1.

In Boston preservationists lobbied to have the City's most conspicuous neon sign designated as an historic landmark. In 1965 the Cities Service Company erected a 3600-square foot sign to publicize its then-new Citgo name. Located high over Kenmore Square, the sign performed computer-synchronized light displays of the Citgo logo. Reacting in part to rising energy costs, company officials turned off the sign in 1979, and in 1982 began to talk of removing it. In response to an outpouring of public support for preservation of the sign, Citgo agreed in 1983 to operate it for at least three additional years. Luberoff, But Is It Art?, 86 Technology Rev. 76 (July 1983).

Do the McDonald's and Citgo controversies support Rose's and Costonis's perceptions of the wellspring of historic preservation efforts?

Chapter Six

Alternatives to Public Regulation: Nuisance Litigation, Covenants, and Government Incentives

Page 572. Before Powell v. Taylor, insert:

NOTE ON "RIGHT TO FARM" STATUTES

In 1979 North Carolina enacted the following statutory provision, which quickly became the model for so-called right-to-farm legislation:

North Carolina Gen. Stat. §106-701 (1985 Supp.)

> (a) No agricultural operation or any of its appurtenances shall be or become a nuisance, private or public, by changed conditions in or about the locality thereof after the same has been in operation for more than one year, when such operation was not a nuisance at the time the operation began; provided, that provisions of this subsection shall not apply whenever a nuisance results from the negligent or improper operation of such agricultural operation or its appurtenances. . . .

By 1983 some 37 states had adopted right-to-farm acts, many of which differ in some measure from the North Carolina model. See Grossman & Fischer, Protecting the Right to Farm: Statutory Limits on Nuisance Actions Against the Farmer, 1983 Wis. L. Rev. 95, 118 n.108. What justifications might there be for limiting the nuisance liabilities of certain enterprises? Are agricultural operations more deserving of favored treatment than, say, industrial or mining operations are? Did North Carolina confer on its farmers and ranchers the right quantum of protection from nuisance litigation? Cf. infra Casebook pp. 680-687 on the use of subsidies to preserve agricultural lands.

Page 579.   Before Falloon v. Schilling, add:

PRAH v. MARETTI

108 Wis. 2d 223, 321 N.W.2d 182 (1982)

ABRAHAMSON, Justice.

This appeal from a judgment of the circuit court for Waukesha county, Max Raskin, circuit judge, was certified to this court by the court of appeals, sec. (Rule) 809.61, Stats. 1979-80, as presenting an issue of first impression, namely, whether an owner of a solar-heated residence states a claim upon which relief can be granted when he asserts that his neighbor's proposed construction of a residence (which conforms to existing deed restrictions and local ordinances) interferes with his access to an unobstructed path for sunlight across the neighbor's property. This case thus involves a conflict between one landowner (Glenn Prah, the plaintiff) interested in unobstructed access to sunlight across adjoining property as a natural source of energy and an adjoining landowner (Richard D. Maretti, the defendant) interested in the development of his land.

The circuit court concluded that the plaintiff presented no claim upon which relief could be granted and granted summary judgment for the defendant. We reverse the judgment of the circuit court and remand the cause to the circuit court for further proceedings.

I

According to the complaint, the plaintiff is the owner of a residence which was constructed during the years 1978-1979. The complaint alleges that the residence has a solar system which includes collectors on the roof to supply energy for heat and hot water and that after the plaintiff built his solar-heated house, the defendant purchased the lot adjacent to and immediately to the south of the plaintiff's lot and commenced planning construction of a home. The complaint further states that when the plaintiff learned of defendant's plans to build the house he advised the defendant that if the house were built at the proposed location, defendant's house would substantially and adversely affect the integrity of plaintiff's solar system and could cause plaintiff other damage. Nevertheless, the defendant began construction. The complaint further alleges that the plaintiff is entitled to "unrestricted use of the sun and its solar power" and demands judgment for injunctive relief and damages.

After filing his complaint, the plaintiff moved for a temporary injunction to restrain and enjoin construction by the defendant. In ruling on that motion the circuit court heard testimony, received affidavits and viewed the site.

The record made on the motion reveals the following additional facts: Plaintiff's home was the first residence built in the subdivision, and although plaintiff did not build his house in the center of the lot it was built in accordance with applicable restrictions. Plaintiff advised defendant that if the defendant's home were built at the proposed site it would cause a shadowing effect on the solar collectors which would reduce the efficiency of the system and possibly damage the system. To avoid these adverse effects, plaintiff requested defendant to locate his home an additional several feet away from the plaintiff's lot line, the exact number being disputed. Plaintiff and defendant failed to reach an agreement on the location of defendant's home before defendant started construction. The Architectural Control Committee of the subdivision and the Planning Commission of the City of Muskego approved the defendant's plans for his home, including its location on the lot. After such approval, the defendant apparently changed the grade of the property without prior notice to the Architectural Control Committee. The problem with defendant's proposed construction, as far as the plaintiff's interests are concerned, arises from a combination of the grade and the distance of defendant's home from the defendant's lot line. . . .

III . . .

The plaintiff presents three legal theories to support his claim that the defendant's continued construction of a home justifies granting him relief: (1) the construction constitutes a common law private nuisance; (2) the construction is prohibited by sec. 844.01, Stats. 1979-80;[3] and

3. Sec. 844.01, Stats. 1979-80, provides:

"(1) Any person owning or claiming an interest in real property may bring an action claiming physical injury to, or interference with, the property or his interest therein; the action may be to redress past injury, to restrain further injury, to abate the source of injury, or for other appropriate relief.

"(2) Physical injury includes unprivileged intrusions and encroachments; the injury may be surface, subsurface or suprasurface; the injury may arise from activities on the plaintiff's property, or from activities outside the plaintiff's property which affect plaintiff's property.

"(3) Interference with an interest is any activity other than physical injury which lessens the possibility of use or enjoyment of the interest.

"(4) The lessening of a security interest without physical injury is not actionable unless such lessening constitutes waste."

We can find no reported cases in which sec. 844.01 has been interpreted and applied, and the parties do not cite any.

(3) the construction interferes with the solar easement plaintiff acquired under the doctrine of prior appropriation.[4]

As to the claim of private nuisance the circuit court concluded that the law of private nuisance requires the court to make "a comparative evaluation of the conflicting interests and to weigh the gravity of the harm to the plaintiff against the utility of the defendant's conduct." The circuit court concluded: "A comparative evaluation of the conflicting interests, keeping in mind the omissions and commissions of both Prah and Maretti, indicates that defendant's conduct does not cause the gravity of the harm which the plaintiff himself may well have avoided by proper planning." The circuit court also concluded that sec. 844.01 does not apply to a home constructed in accordance with deed and municipal ordinance requirements. Further, the circuit court rejected the prior appropriation doctrine as "an intrusion of judicial egoism over legislative passivity."

We consider first whether the complaint states a claim for relief based on common law private nuisance. . . .

. . . The Restatement defines private nuisance as "a nontrespassory invasion of another's interest in the private use and enjoyment of land." Restatement (Second) of Torts sec. 821D (1977). The phrase "interest in the private use and enjoyment of land" as used in sec. 821D is broadly defined to include any disturbance of the enjoyment of property. . . .

Although the defendant's obstruction of the plaintiff's access to sunlight appears to fall within the Restatement's broad concept of a private nuisance as a nontrespassory invasion of another's interest in the private use and enjoyment of land, the defendant asserts that he has a right to develop his property in compliance with statutes, ordinances and private covenants without regard to the effect of such development upon the plaintiff's access to sunlight. . . .

The defendant is not completely correct in asserting that the common law did not protect a landowner's access to sunlight across adjoining property. [The court then discussed the English doctrine of ancient lights and American decisions and statutes protecting landowners from spite fences.]

This court's reluctance in the nineteenth and early part of the twentieth century to provide broader protection for a landowner's access to

4. Under the doctrine of prior appropriation the first user to appropriate the resource has the right of continued use to the exclusion of others.

The doctrine of prior appropriation has been used by several western states to allocate water, Paug Vik v. Wards Cove, 633 P.2d 1015 (Alaska 1981), and by the New Mexico legislature to allocate solar access, secs. 47-3-1 to 47-3-5, N.M. Stats. 1978. See also Note, The Allocation of Sunlight: Solar Rights and the Prior Appropriation Doctrine, 47 Colo. L. Rev. 421 (1976).

sunlight was premised on three policy considerations. First, the right of landowners to use their property as they wished, as long as they did not cause physical damage to a neighbor, was jealously guarded. Metzger v. Hochrein, 107 Wis. 267, 272, 83 N.W. 308 (1900).

Second, sunlight was valued only for aesthetic enjoyment or as illumination. Since artificial light could be used for illumination, loss of sunlight was at most a personal annoyance which was given little, if any, weight by society.

Third, society had a significant interest in not restricting or impeding land development. Dillman v. Hoffman, 38 Wis. 559, 574 (1875). This court repeatedly emphasized that in the growth period of the nineteenth and early twentieth centuries change is to be expected and is essential to property and that recognition of a right to sunlight would hinder property development. The court expressed this concept as follows: "As the city grows, large grounds appurtenant to residences must be cut up to supply more residences. . . . The cistern, the outhouse, the cesspool, and the private drain must disappear in deference to the public waterworks and sewer; the terrace and the garden, to the need for more complete occupancy. . . . Strict limitation [on the recognition of easements of light and air over adjacent premises is] in accord with the popular conception upon which real estate has been and is daily being conveyed in Wisconsin and to be essential to easy and rapid development at least of our municipalities." Miller v. Hoeschler, 126 Wis. at 268, 270, 105 N.W. 790 [1905].

Considering these three policies, this court concluded that in the absence of an express agreement granting access to sunlight, a landowner's obstruction of another's access to sunlight was not actionable. Miller v. Hoeschler, supra, 126 Wis. at 271, 105 N.W. 709; Depner v. United States National Bank, 202 Wis. at 410, 232 N.W. 851. These three policies are no longer fully accepted or applicable. They reflect factual circumstances and social priorities that are now obsolete.

First, society has increasingly regulated the use of land by the landowner for the general welfare. Euclid v. Ambler Realty Co., 272 U.S. 365 (1926); Just v. Marinette, 56 Wis. 2d 7, 201 N.W.2d 761 (1972).

Second, access to sunlight has taken on a new significance in recent years. In this case the plaintiff seeks to protect access to sunlight, not for aesthetic reasons or as a source of illumination but as a source of energy. Access to sunlight as an energy source is of significance both to the landowner who invests in solar collectors and to a society which has an interest in developing alternative sources of energy.[11]

11. State and federal governments are encouraging the use of the sun as a significant source of energy. In this state the legislature has granted tax benefits to encourage the utilization of solar energy. See Ch. 349, 350, Laws of 1979. See also Ch. 354, Laws of 1981

Third, the policy of favoring unhindered private development in an expanding economy is no longer in harmony with the realities of our society. State v. Deetz, 66 Wis. 2d 1, 224 N.W.2d 407 (1974). The need for easy and rapid development is not as great today as it once was, while our perception of the value of sunlight as a source of energy has increased significantly.

Courts should not implement obsolete policies that have lost their vigor over the course of the years. The law of private nuisance is better suited to resolve landowners' disputes about property development in the 1980's than is a rigid rule which does not recognize a landowner's interest in access to sunlight. As we said in Ballstadt v. Pagel, 202 Wis. 484, 489, 232 N.W. 862 (1930), "What is regarded in law as constituting a nuisance in modern times would no doubt have been tolerated without question in former times." We read State v. Deetz, 66 Wis. 2d 1, 224 N.W.2d 407 (1974), as an endorsement of the application of common law nuisance to situations involving the conflicting interests of landowners and as rejecting per se exclusions to the nuisance law reasonable use doctrine.

In *Deetz* the court abandoned the rigid common law common enemy rule with respect to surface water and adopted the private nuisance reasonable use rule, namely that the landowner is subject to liability if his or her interference with the flow of surface waters unreasonably invades a neighbor's interest in the use and enjoyment of land. Restatement (Second) of Torts, sec. 822, 826, 829 (1977). This court concluded that the common enemy rule which served society "well in the days of burgeoning national expansion of the mid-nineteenth and early-twentieth centuries" should be abandoned because it was no longer "in harmony with the realities of our society." *Deetz*, supra, 66 Wis. 2d at 14-15, 224 N.W.2d 407. We recognized in *Deetz* that common law rules adapt to changing social values and conditions.

Yet the defendant would have us ignore the flexible private nuisance law as a means of resolving the dispute between the landowners in this case and would have us adopt an approach, already abandoned in *Deetz*, of favoring the unrestricted development of land and of applying a rigid and inflexible rule protecting his right to build on his land and disregarding any interest of the plaintiff in the use and enjoyment of his land. This we refuse to do.

Private nuisance law, the law traditionally used to adjudicate conflicts

---

(eff. May 7, 1982) enabling legislation providing for local ordinances guaranteeing access to sunlight.

The federal government has also recognized the importance of solar energy and currently encourages its utilization by means of tax benefits, direct subsidies and government loans for solar projects. . . .

between private landowners, has the flexibility to protect both a landowner's right of access to sunlight and another landowner's right to develop land. Private nuisance law is better suited to regulate access to sunlight in modern society and is more in harmony with legislative policy and the prior decisions of this court than is an inflexible doctrine of non-recognition of any interest in access to sunlight across adjoining land.

We therefore hold that private nuisance law, that is, the reasonable use doctrine as set forth in the Restatement, is applicable to the instant case. Recognition of a nuisance claim for unreasonable obstruction of access to sunlight will not prevent land development or unduly hinder the use of adjoining land. It will promote the reasonable use and enjoyment of land in a manner suitable to the 1980's. That obstruction of access to light might be found to constitute a nuisance in certain circumstances does not mean that it will be or must be found to constitute a nuisance under all circumstances. The result in each case depends on whether the conduct complained of is unreasonable.

Accordingly we hold that the plaintiff in this case has stated a claim under which relief can be granted. Nonetheless we do not determine whether the plaintiff in this case is entitled to relief. In order to be entitled to relief the plaintiff must prove the elements required to establish actionable nuisance, and the conduct of the defendant herein must be judged by the reasonable use doctrine.

IV

The defendant asserts that even if we hold that the private nuisance doctrine applies to obstruction of access to sunlight across adjoining land, the circuit court's granting of summary judgment should be affirmed.

Although the memorandum decision of the circuit court in the instant case is unclear, it appears that the circuit court recognized that the common law private nuisance doctrine was applicable but concluded that defendant's conduct was not unreasonable. The circuit court apparently attempted to balance the utility of the defendant's conduct with the gravity of the harm. Sec. 826, Restatement (Second) of Torts (1977).[16] The defendant urges us to accept the circuit court's balance as adequate. We decline to do so.

16. The factors involved in determining the gravity of the harm caused by the conduct complained of are set out in sec. 827 of the Restatement as follows:

"*Sec. 827. Gravity of Harm—Factors Involved.*

"In determining the gravity of the harm from an intentional invasion of another's interest in the use and enjoyment of land, the following factors are important:

The circuit court concluded that because the defendant's proposed house was in conformity with zoning regulations, building codes and deed restrictions, the defendant's use of the land was reasonable. This court has concluded that a landowner's compliance with zoning laws does not automatically bar a nuisance claim. Compliance with the law "is not the controlling factor, though it is, of course, entitled to some weight." Bie v. Ingersoll, 27 Wis. 2d 490, 495, 135 N.W.2d 250 (1965). The circuit court also concluded that the plaintiff could have avoided any harm by locating his own house in a better place. Again, plaintiff's ability to avoid the harm is a relevant but not a conclusive factor. See secs. 826, 827, 828, Restatement (Second) of Torts (1977).

Furthermore, our examination of the record leads us to conclude that the record does not furnish an adequate basis for the circuit court to apply the proper legal principles on summary judgment. The application of the reasonable use standard in nuisance cases normally requires a full exposition of all underlying facts and circumstances. Too little is known in this case of such matters as the extent of the harm to the plaintiff, the suitability of solar heat in that neighborhood, the availability of remedies to the plaintiff, and the costs to the defendant of avoiding the harm. Summary judgment is not an appropriate procedural vehicle in this case when the circuit court must weigh evidence which has not been presented at trial.

Because the plaintiff has stated a claim of common law private nuisance upon which relief can be granted, the judgment of the circuit court must be reversed. We need not, and do not, reach the question of whether the complaint states a claim under sec. 844.01, Stats. 1979-80, or under the doctrine of prior appropriation. . . .

The judgment of the circuit court is reversed and the cause remanded for proceedings not inconsistent with this opinion.

"(a) the extent of the harm involved;

"(b) the character of the harm involved;

"(c) the social value that the law attaches to the type of use or enjoyment invaded;

"(d) the suitability of the particular use or enjoyment invaded to the character of the locality; and

"(e) the burden on the person harmed of avoiding the harm."

"The factors involved in determining the utility of conduct complained of are set out in sec. 828 of the Restatement as follows:

"*Sec. 828. Utility of Conduct—Factors Involved.*

"In determining the utility of conduct that causes an intentional invasion of another's interest in the use and enjoyment of land, the following factors are important:

"(a) the social value that the law attaches to the primary purpose of the conduct;

"(b) the suitability of the conduct to the character of the locality; and

"(c) the impracticability of preventing or avoiding the invasion."

CALLOW, Justice (dissenting). . . .

The majority . . . concludes that this court's past reluctance to extend protection to a landowner's access to sunlight beyond the spite fence cases is based on obsolete policies which have lost their vigor over the course of the years. . . . The majority has failed to convince me that these policies are obsolete. . . .

. . . I firmly believe that a landowner's right to use his property within the limits of ordinances, statutes, and restrictions of record where such use is necessary to serve his legitimate needs is a fundamental precept of a free society which this court should strive to uphold.

As one commentator has suggested: "It is fashionable to dismiss such values as deriving from a bygone era in which people valued development as a 'goal in itself,' but current market prices for real estate, and more particularly the premiums paid for land whose zoning permits intensive use, suggest that people still place very high values on such rights." Williams, Solar Access and Property Rights: A Maverick Analysis, 11 Conn. L. Rev. 430, 443 (1979). . . .

The legislature has recently acted in this area. Chapter 354, Laws of 1981 (effective May 7, 1982), was enacted to provide the underlying legislation enabling local governments to enact ordinances establishing procedures for guaranteeing access to sunlight. This court's intrusion into an area where legislative action is being taken is unwarranted, and it may undermine a legislative scheme for orderly development not yet fully operational. . . .

I examine with interest the definition of nuisance as set out in the Restatement (Second) of Torts and adopted in the majority opinion: "A private nuisance is a nontrespassory *invasion* of another's interest in the private use and enjoyment of land." Restatement (Second) of Torts sec. 821D (1977) (emphasis added). The majority believes that the defendant's obstruction of the plaintiff's access to sunlight falls within the broad definition of "use and enjoyment of land." Supra, at 187-188. I do not believe the defendant's "obstruction" of the plaintiff's access to sunlight falls within the definition of "invasion," as it applies to the private use and enjoyment of land. Invasion is typically synonymous with "entry," "attack," "penetration," "hostile entrance," "the incoming or spread of something unusually hurtful." Webster's Third International Dictionary, 1188 (1966). Most of the nuisance cases arising under this definition involve noxious odors, smoke, blasting, flooding, or *excessive light* invading the plaintiff's right to the use or enjoyment of his property. *See* Prosser, Law of Torts, sec. 89, 591-92 (4th ed. 1971). See Williams, Solar Access and Property Rights: A Maverick Analysis, 11 Conn. L. Rev. at 441 (there are significant practical differences between dust and noise, on the one hand, and solar access blockage on the other). Clearly, an owner who merely builds his home in compliance with all building code and municipal regulations is not "invading" another's right to the use and enjoyment of his property. To say so is to acknowledge that all construction may be an "invasion" because all construction has some restrictive impact on adjacent land. A "view," for example, is modified by any construction simply because it is there.

In order for a nuisance to be actionable in the instant case, the defendant's conduct must be "intentional and unreasonable." It is impossible for me to accept the majority's conclusion that Mr. Maretti, in lawfully seeking to construct his home, may be intentionally and unreasonably interfering with the plaintiff's access to sunlight. In addressing the "unreasonableness" component of the actor's conduct, it is important to note that "[t]here is liability for a nuisance only to those to whom it causes significant harm, of a kind that would be suffered by a normal person in the community or by property in normal condition and used for a normal purpose." Restatement (Second) of Torts sec. 821F (1979). The comments to the Restatement further reveal that "[if] normal persons in that locality would not be substantially annoyed or disturbed by the situation, then the invasion is not a significant one, even though the idiosyncracies of the particular plaintiff may make it unendurable to him." Id. Comment d. See Bie v. Ingersoll, 27 Wis. 2d 490, 493, 135 N.W.2d 250 (1965); Belmar Drive-In Theatre Co. v. The Illinois State Toll Highway Commission et al., 34 Ill. 2d 544, 547-49, 216 N.E.2d 788 (1966).

I conclude that plaintiff's solar heating system is an unusually sensitive use. In other words, the defendant's proposed construction of his home, under ordinary circumstances, would not interfere with the use and enjoyment of the usual person's property. See W. Prosser, supra, sec. 87 at 578-79. "The plaintiff cannot, by devoting his own land to an unusually sensitive use, such as a drive-in motion picture theater easily affected by light, make a nuisance out of conduct of the adjoining defendant which would otherwise be harmless." Id. at 579. . . .

Because I do not believe that the facts of the present case give rise to a cause of action for private nuisance, I dissent.

NOTE ON PRAH

Compare Sher v. Liederman, 181 Cal. App. 3d 873, 226 Cal. Rptr. 698 (1986), review denied (Cal. Aug. 28, 1986), in which the defendant's trees had grown to impair the passive-solar features of the plaintiff's house. The California Court of Appeal explicitly rejected the Wisconsin Supreme Court's reasoning in *Prah* and held that the plaintiff's complaint did not state a cause of action for private nuisance.

Page 610.   Before Note on Age Restrictions, add:

O'CONNOR v. VILLAGE GREEN OWNERS ASSOCIATION
33 Cal. 3d 790, 662 P.2d 427, 191 Cal. Rptr. 320 (1983)

KAUS, Justice.

These consolidated appeals involve the validity and enforceability of an age restriction in the covenants, conditions and restrictions (CC & Rs) of a condominium development which limits residency to persons over the age of 18. In Marina Point, Ltd. v. Wolfson (1982) 30 Cal. 3d 721, we recently condemned such an age restriction in an apartment complex as violative of the Unruh Civil Rights Act (Civ. Code, §51). We conclude that the age restriction in the CC & Rs of a condominium development also violates the act.

The Village Green is a housing complex of 629 units in the Baldwin Hills area of Los Angeles. It was built in 1942 and was operated as an apartment complex until 1973 when it was converted to a condominium development. As part of the condominium conversion the developer drafted and recorded a declaration of CC & Rs which run with the property and which contain a prohibition against residency by anyone under the age of 18. The CC & Rs also establish the Village Green Owners Association (association) and authorize it to enforce the regulations set forth therein. The association is a nonprofit organization whose membership consists of all owners of units at Village Green.

John and Denise O'Connor bought a two-bedroom unit in Village Green in 1975. On July 4, 1979, their son Gavin was born. Shortly thereafter, the association gave them written notice that the presence of their son Gavin in the unit constituted a violation of the CC & Rs and directed them to discontinue having Gavin live there.

After making unsuccessful attempts to find other suitable housing, the O'Connors filed a complaint against the association seeking to have the age restriction declared invalid and to enjoin its enforcement. The first amended complaint alleged, inter alia, that the age restriction violated the Unruh Civil Rights Act (Civ. Code, §51).[2] The association filed a general demurrer which the trial court sustained without leave to amend. The action was dismissed and the O'Connors appealed. . . .

In Marina Point, Ltd. v. Wolfson, supra, 30 Cal. 3d 721, we considered the question of whether the Unruh Civil Rights Act (the act) prohibited

2. The complaint also alleged that the age restriction violated: (1) the Los Angeles City Ordinance which prohibits discrimination in rental housing on the basis of age, parenthood, or pregnancy; (2) the Fourteenth Amendment of the United States Constitution and article I, section 1, of the California Constitution; and (3) the California Fair Housing Law (Health & Saf. Code, §35700 et seq.).

an apartment owner's discrimination against children. We reviewed the history of the act—Civil Code section 51—and noted that it had emanated from earlier "public accommodation" legislation and had extended the reach of such statutes from common carriers and places of accommodation to cover "all business establishments of every kind whatsoever."[3] Relying on our interpretation of the act in In re Cox (1970) 3 Cal. 3d 205, we held that the act barred all types of arbitrary discrimination. The act's reference to particular bases of discrimination—"sex, color, race, religion, ancestry or national origin"—was illustrative rather than restrictive.

We noted, however, that although the act prohibits a business establishment from engaging in any form of arbitrary discrimination, it does not absolutely prohibit such an establishment from excluding a customer in all circumstances. "Clearly, an entrepreneur need not tolerate customers who damage property, injure others or otherwise disrupt his business. A business establishment may, of course, promulgate reasonable deportment regulations that are rationally related to the services performed and the facilities provided." (Marina Point, Ltd. v. Wolfson, supra, 30 Cal. 3d at p.737, quoting from In re Cox, supra, 3 Cal. 3d at p.217.) We rejected, however, the landlord's contention in *Marina Point* that the exclusion of children was such a reasonable restriction. It was not a sufficient justification to state that children are "rowdier, noisier, more mischievous and more boisterous than adults." (30 Cal. 3d at p.737.) Exclusion of persons based on a generalization about the class to which they belong is not permissible. (Id., at pp. 736-740.) Nor could exclusion of children from an ordinary apartment complex be justified on the basis that the presence of children does not accord with the nature of the business enterprise and of the facilities provided—as might be said of bars, adult book stores and senior citizens homes. (Id., at p.741.)

In sum, we held in *Marina Point* that the landlord's blanket exclusion of children from residency was prohibited by the act. It could not be justified by any claim about generalized characteristics of children or the nature of the apartment complex. Indeed, the claim that the facilities were incompatible with the presence of children was belied by the fact that children formerly had been permitted to reside in the complex. (30 Cal. 3d at p.744, fn. 13.)

3. Unless otherwise noted, all section references hereafter are to the Civil Code.

Section 51 provides in relevant part: "This section shall be known, and may be cited, as the Unruh Civil Rights Act.

"All persons within the jurisdiction of this state are free and equal, and no matter what their sex, race, color, religion, ancestry, or national origin are entitled to the full and equal accommodations, advantages, facilities, privileges, or services in all business establishments of every kind whatsoever."

In *Marina Point* there was no question that the apartment complex was a "business establishment" within the meaning of the act. The determinative question in that case was whether the act encompassed discrimination against children. Since that question was answered in *Marina Point*, the only question to be decided in the present case is whether the discriminatory policy against children is being invoked by a "business establishment" within the meaning of the act. . . .

. . . Although our cases so far have all dealt with profit-making entities, we see no reason to insist that profit-seeking be a sine qua non for coverage under the act. Nothing in the language or history of its enactment calls for excluding an organization from its scope simply because it is nonprofit. (See Horowitz, The 1959 California Equal Rights in "Business Establishments" Statute — A Problem in Statutory Application (1960) 33 S. Cal. L. Rev. 260, 290-291.) Indeed, hospitals are often nonprofit organizations, and they are clearly business establishments to the extent that they employ a vast array of persons, care for an extensive physical plant and charge substantial fees to those who use the facilities. The Village Green Owners Association has sufficient businesslike attributes to fall within the scope of the act's reference to "business establishments of every kind whatsoever." Contrary to the association's attempt to characterize itself as but an organization that "mows lawns" for owners, the association in reality has a far broader and more businesslike purpose. The association, through a board of directors, is charged with employing a professional property management firm, with obtaining insurance for the benefit of all owners and with maintaining and repairing all common areas and facilities of the 629-unit project. It is also charged with establishing and collecting assessments from all owners to pay for its undertakings and with adopting and enforcing rules and regulations for the common good. In brief, the association performs all the customary business functions which in the traditional landlord-tenant relationship rest on the landlord's shoulders. A theme running throughout the description of the association's powers and duties is that its overall function is to protect and enhance the project's economic value. Consistent with the Legislature's intent to use the term "business establishments" in the broadest sense reasonably possible (Burks v. Poppy Construction Co., 57 Cal. 2d at p.468 [1962]), we conclude that the Village Green Owners Association is a business establishment within the meaning of the act.

Anticipating that it might be found to be a business establishment for purposes of applicability of the act, the association attempts to distinguish its discriminatory policy from that in *Marina Point* on the ground that it has fewer effective remedies for abating a nuisance caused by a child. Although a landlord does have the summary remedy of unlawful detainer proceedings for dealing with a disruptive child, we are not persuaded that the association is so powerless to remedy any problems arising from particular conduct that it must be permitted to maintain a discriminatory policy based on generalized traits. The association could adopt deportment regulations and rely on its normal procedures to enforce them. No reason appears why that would be any less effective than other use and conduct regulations the association may have. Moreover, we note that the restrictive covenant against children is already invalid under *Marina Point* as to units held as income property and rented out by their owners. (See Swann v. Burkett (1962) 209 Cal. App. 2d 685, 694-695, 26 Cal. Rptr. 286.) The association therefore is already faced with the burden of planning for the presence of children.

[Reversed.]

MOSK, Justice, dissenting. . . .

The majority are in error on both issues involved in this case. First, age preference has consistently been recognized as valid rather than invidious discrimination, both by the federal government and by the Legislature of California. Second, an association of homeowners — whether their homes are separate premises, or part of one structure as in a condominium apartment — cannot by any stretch of judicial imagination be held to be a business.

On the first point it bears emphasis that the United States Congress has adopted a number of programs to provide housing exclusively for those over 62. (See generally 12 U.S.C. §1701 et seq., 42 U.S.C. §1485 et seq.) If an age restriction is valid at age 62, why cannot an age restriction be placed at age 18? Age preference is age preference, regardless of the precise chronological point at which it is placed.

Meanwhile our state Legislature, with knowledge that age preferences have been established in a number of housing developments, and that each was upheld whenever challenged in court (e.g., Ritchey v. Villa Nueva Condominium Ass'n (1978) 81 Cal. App. 3d 688, 146 Cal. Rptr. 695; Flowers v. John Burnham & Co. (1971) 21 Cal. App. 3d 700, 98 Cal. Rptr. 644), not only failed to add age to the other categories in Civil Code sections 51 and 53 which prohibit discrimination, but emphatically refused to do so whenever age was proposed as an addition to those sections. I fail to understand how my colleagues can arrogate to themselves the right to legislate in an area in which the Legislature has deliberately refused to do so. . . .

A homeowners association, the principal function of which is to perform or arrange for the services an owner of a single family dwelling would normally perform or arrange — such as mowing lawns, fixing defective plumbing, repairing roofs, cutting trees and watering gardens — does not come within the definition of the term "business establishment" as it is used throughout the decision in *Marina Point*. The association has no patrons, tenants or customers, only dues-paying members; it is in no way entrepreneurial in nature; and it is not open for public patronage. To consider the association a "business enterprise" under the Unruh Act would require the ludicrous holding that the owner-resident of a single family dwelling is engaged in a "business enterprise" when he or she hires a gardener or a plumber. . . .

The result in this case is disastrous for the many well-conceived, constructively operated developments in this state limited to persons over a prescribed age. They may not be a major factor in other jurisdictions, but they are particularly significant in California, which has the enticing environment and equable climate to attract many persons of middle and older age. These men and women, many of them having earned their right to retirement in other parts of the country, now make a major contribution to the economy of our state. Their comfort and peace of mind should not be deemed expendable on the altar of judicial creativity.

I would affirm the judgment.

RICHARDSON, Justice, concurs.

Page 612.   At the end of the carryover paragraph, insert:

In Taormina Theosophical Community, Inc. v. Silver, 140 Cal. App. 3d 964, 190 Cal. Rptr. 38 (1983), a nonprofit organization (Taormina) had acquired a tract of exurban land for the purpose of establishing a retirement community for Theosophists. Although Theosophists are not required to adhere to a particular religious creed, they are expected to promote the brotherhood of man, to study comparative religion and philosophy, and to explore "the psychical powers latent in man." Before subdividing the tract, Taormina recorded covenants that, among other things, restricted ownership and occupancy of lots to persons who were members of the Theosophical Society. Taormina brought this action to enforce these restrictions against the Silvers, a couple who had purchased a lot in violation of some of the covenants. (Some facts of the case suggest that this was a friendly lawsuit designed to clear title to the tract.)

The California Court of Appeal held that the restriction that limited *ownership* to Theosophists violated a state statute prohibiting unreasonable restraints on alienation. It found the quantum of the restraint to be "very great" because the Theosophical Society had only 6000 members nationwide. "While the gathering of like minded people may be a laudable goal, such purpose is not sufficient to sustain the heavy burden on alienability." The court also held that the provision limiting *occupancy* to Theosophists violated another statute that prohibited covenants restricting occupancy on the basis of a person's religion. Although the court did not characterize Theosophy as being a religion, it concluded that in enacting this statute "the Legislature indicated that it considered the manner in which a person approaches spiritual matters an improper and irrelevant criterion for denying access to land."

How might one advise the Jesuits and the Hare Krishnas, to pick two unrelated examples, to exclude nonbelievers from their communities?

Page 672.   Before "D. Land Use Without Public Regulation," insert:

4. *Sources.* Symposium, 56 S. Cal. L. Rev. 1177-1447 (1982), with nine articles on covenant law, is the most significant academic outpouring on this topic in recent memory. Most contributors to the symposium favored the unification and simplification of the law of real covenants, equitable servitudes, and easements. Selected issues in the law of homeowners associations are discussed in Ellickson, Cities and Homeowners Associations, 130 U. Pa. L. Rev. 1519 (1982).

Page 673.   Before the first full paragraph, insert:

Professor Kmiec assails current systems of zoning and subdivision regulation in Deregulating Land Use: An Alternative Free Enterprise Development System, 130 U. Pa. L. Rev. 28 (1981). He urges the abolition of these traditional regulatory systems, and their replacement with a more market-oriented system. Kmiec would entitle a local government to influence private development only by means of performance standards (his term is "intensity" regulations) and exactions.

Page 678.   Before "E. Government Tax and Spending Policies as Land-Use Controls," insert:

4. *Update on Houston.* Houston has added to its portfolio of land-use controls. In 1982 the city council adopted an ordinance that imposed standards for block length, streetfront setbacks, and offstreet parking. These regulations do not vary by district, however, and thus do not signify that Houston has finally embraced a system of zoning. See 34 Land Use L. & Zoning Dig. 3 (Aug. 1982).

Because of a shortage of sewer capacity, Houston in 1983 stopped issuing sewer hook-up permits in many areas. This moratorium led, with the city's blessing, to the emergence of an active market in existing sewer permits, which were reported to sell for $3,000 to $5,000 per dwelling unit. The sewer moratorium obviously functioned, if only temporarily, as a form of growth control. See King, Houston Spawns a Thriving Underground Market in Sewer Rights, N.Y. Times, Nov. 28, 1983, p.12, col. 1.

Billboards, prominent along Houston's freeways, have become a concern of city leaders. By 1987 Houston had an ordinance that limited the erection of new billboards, and was exerting informal pressure to encourage the removal of existing ones. "Freeway Billboards in Peril as Houston Seeks Recovery," N.Y. Times, June 15, 1987, p.8, col. 1.

Severe shocks to the Houston economy helped provoke these civic efforts to clean up the city's image. Prices in Houston's real estate markets dropped sharply after international oil prices plummeted in 1982. By 1983 vacancy rates approached 20 percent in both the commercial and residential rental sectors, and landlords began offering steep discounts to attract tenants. See King, Once-Booming Houston Real Estate Market Is in Deep Slump, N.Y. Times, June 5, 1983, p.12, col. 1. In the 1984-1987 period, prices in the overbuilt single-family house market collapsed by more than 50 percent in some suburban neighborhoods, leading to spates of foreclosures and abandoned houses. See Frazier, Housing-Market Bust in Houston Is Creating Rash of Instant Slums, Wall St. J., Feb. 5, 1987, p.1, col. 6.

In 1986 an intercity comparison of single-family house prices again placed Houston at the bottom of the list for cities of its size. A 2,000-square-foot house in an "upscale neighborhood" was estimated to cost $81,500 in Houston, compared to $140,000 in Dallas, and $210,000 in a New York City suburb. See S.F. Examiner, July 27, 1986, p.R-6, col. 3 (reporting estimates made by Coldwell Banker Residential Real Estate's Nationwide Relocation Service).

The Houston electorate's distaste for zoning is not unique. In November 1982 the voters of rural Tehama County in northern California narrowly approved an initiative measure designed to annul virtually all of the county's public land-use regulations. The central provisions of this measure were subsequently invalidated for violating the California statutory provisions that require local governments to prepare general plans. See Patterson v. County of Tehama, 184 Cal. App. 3d 1546, 229 Cal. Rptr. 696 (1986).

Page 687. Before Note 2, add:

The debate over farmland preservation was enlivened in 1981 with the publication of the Final Report of the National Agricultural Lands Study (NALS), a product of the Carter Administration's Department of Agriculture and Council on Environmental Quality. The NALS reported a sharp escalation in the rate at which agricultural land was being converted to urban uses. This trend, it concluded, ultimately posed a threat to the national and world food supply. It therefore recommended, with some equivocation, that governments adopt comprehensive growth management policies to curb the rate of farmland conversion. The NALS recommendation prompted Congress to enact the Farmland Protection Policy Act of 1981, 7 U.S.C. §§4201-4209 (Supp. 1987), which directs federal agencies to consider program alternatives that will minimize loss of agricultural lands.

Critics immediately attacked both the NALS's factual premises and its policy recommendations. They asserted that the NALS exaggerated the urbanization rate of agricultural land during the 1970s by a factor of at least two to three. See Simon, Are We Losing Our Farmland?, Pub. Interest, No. 67, at 49 (1982); Fischel, The Urbanization of Agricultural Land: A Review of the National Agricultural Lands Study, 58 Land Econ. 236 (1982). Professor Fischel also asserted that local antidevelopment interests were the main proponents of farmland preservation, because they saw it as a tool for intervening in the land-use decisions of pro-development communities in which they did not reside.

In 1982 the Report of the President's Commission on Housing (a Reagan Administration taskforce) cited Fischel's study and recommended that Congress repeal the Farmland Protection Policy Act of 1981 "because it could have a potentially serious and detrimental impact on the cost and availability of land for housing." Id. at 195.

Page 689.   Before Note 4, insert:

In 1981 Congress revamped and augmented the tax incentives available to taxpayers who renovate either historic structures or oldish structures located within historic districts. It repealed I.R.C. §191, and in its place authorized rehabilitators of eligible structures to receive tax credits ranging from 15 to 25 percent of qualifying rehabilitation expenses.

The Tax Reform Act of 1986 diminished the lure of historic-preservation activity for some investors. See I.R.C. §§46(b)(4), 48(g). It reduced the maximum tax credit available for certified historic structures from 25 percent to 20 percent. The 1986 Act called for those taking credits to remain in ownership for at least five years. It required that the amount of any credit be deducted from the building's basis, thus lowering the cost-recovery deductions that taxpayers had been able to take under the 1981 law. Perhaps most importantly, the 1986 Act in effect limited the maximum annual credit to $7,000, and allowed a taxpayer with income over $250,000 to take the credit only against tax due on *passive* income. The unsurprising upshots of these amendments are described in Gottschalk, Tax Changes for Historic Rehabilitations Lead Syndicators to Seek Smaller Investors, Wall St. J., March 2, 1987, p.23, col. 4.

Chapter Seven
Financing the Urban Infrastructure

Page 732. At the end of Note 2, add:

The Supreme Court of Utah reaffirmed its opposition of general taxes on development in Lafferty v. Payson City, 642 P.2d 376 (Utah 1982) (excerpted on another issue infra Supplement p. 119). In *Lafferty* the court struck down an "impact fee" of $1,000 per dwelling unit.

3. *Condominium taxes.* The City of Santa Monica, California, imposed a tax of $1,000 per salable unit on subdividers who either built new condominium projects or converted existing buildings to condominium ownership. The city ordinance stated that the tax was "imposed solely for revenue purposes." Condominium developers attacked the ordinance on the ground that it was inconsistent with, and preempted by, the state Subdivision Map Act. In Pines v. City of Santa Monica, 29 Cal. 3d 656, 630 P.2d 521, 175 Cal. Rptr. 336 (1981), the California Supreme Court found no legislative intent to preempt local subdivision taxes. It therefore rejected the developers' challenge.

Page 744. At the end of Note 2, add:

Section 1983 does not entitle a plaintiff to recover punitive damages from a municipality. See City of Newport v. Fact Concerts, Inc., 453 U.S. 247 (1981), analyzed in Ellis, Efficiency and Vicarious Liability for Punitive Damages, 1 S. Ct. Econ. Rev. 135 (1983).

Page 756. After the carryover paragraph, insert:

In Banberry Development Corp. v. South Jordan City, 631 P.2d 899 (Utah 1981), the Utah Supreme Court, spurning the mainstream position, embraced close judicial review of a local government's use of benefits financing. Oaks, J., summarized the *Banberry* doctrine in Lafferty v. Payson City, 642, P.2d 376 (Utah 1982), which involved a challenge to, among other things, the city's escalation of its hook-up charges:

> The *Banberry* opinion identifies seven important factors that should be considered "in determining the relative burden already borne and yet to be

borne by newly developed properties and other properties. . . ." 631 P.2d at 903-4. In brief, those factors are (1) the cost of existing capital facilities; (2) the means by which those facilities have been financed; (3) the extent to which the properties being charged the new fees have already contributed to the cost of the existing facilities; (4) the extent to which they will contribute to the cost of existing capital facilities in the future; (5) the extent to which they should be credited for providing common facilities that the municipality has provided without charge to other properties in its service area; (6) extraordinary costs, if any, in serving the new property; and (7) the time-price differential inherent in fair comparisons of amounts paid at different times. 631 P.2d at 904.

The objective of the complicated comparison in *Banberry* is to assure that municipal fees pertaining to newly developed properties do not require them to bear more than their equitable share of the capital costs (in comparison with other properties) in relation to benefits conferred. If properly applied, those seven factors should put the new homeowner on essentially the same basis as the average existing homeowner with respect to costs borne in the past and to be borne in the future, in comparison with benefits already received and yet to be received. The municipality has the burden of disclosing the basis of its calculations to whoever challenges the reasonableness of the fees, and its allocations need not achieve precise mathematical equality. *Banberry*, 631 P.2d at 904.

The City's brief in this case states that the increases in connection fees were based on the costs of expansion by future construction in the service areas involved. Thus, the expert evidence on the unit cost of water and sewer services was based on the 1979 cost of constructing the expansion facilities needed in those areas. That measure does not achieve the equitable allocation sought in *Banberry*, since it fixes the entire cost of new facilities on newly developed properties without assurance that these costs are equitable in relation to benefits conferred and in comparison with costs imposed on other property owners in the municipality. For example, if the costs of maintenance and repayment of bonded indebtedness for construction of the existing system are being financed by general tax revenues, service fees, or other payments collected from the entire municipality—including the newly constructed homes—the new homes will be burdened with all of the capital costs of expanding the service capacity plus a portion of the costs of the existing one. In an effort to avoid this kind of unfairness, the seven factors in *Banberry* require a different approach than imposing all costs of expansion of capacity on the newly developed properties.

642 P.2d at 379. The court remanded the *Lafferty* case to the trial court, which it asked to conduct further proceedings consistent with *Banberry*.

Page 759.   At the end of the second full paragraph, add:

The Michigan Court of Appeals' decision was reversed in Arrowhead Dev. Co. v. Livingston County Road Commn., 413 Mich. 505, 322 N.W.2d

702 (1982). The Michigan Supreme Court was reluctant to interpret ambiguous Michigan statutes as authorizing a road commission to exact the improvement of an off-site road because that sort of cost had not been "historically imposable" on subdividers.

Page 760. At the bottom of the page, add:

NOLLAN v. CALIFORNIA COASTAL COMMISSION

—U.S.—, 107 S. Ct. 3141, 97 L. Ed. 2d 677 (1987)

Justice SCALIA delivered the opinion of the Court.

James and Marilyn Nollan appeal from a decision of the California Court of Appeal ruling that the California Coastal Commission could condition its grant of permission to rebuild their house on their transfer to the public of an easement across their beachfront property. The California Court rejected their claim that imposition of that condition violates the Takings Clause of the Fifth Amendment, as incorporated against the States by the Fourteenth Amendment.

I

The Nollans own a beachfront lot in Ventura County, California. A quarter-mile north of their property is Faria County Park, an oceanside public park with a public beach and recreation area. Another public beach area, known locally as "the Cove," lies 1,800 feet south of their lot. A concrete seawall approximately eight feet high separates the beach portion of the Nollans' property from the rest of the lot. The historic mean high tide line determines the lot's oceanside boundary.

The Nollans originally leased their property with an option to buy. The building on the lot was a small bungalow, totaling 504 square feet, which for a time they rented to summer vacationers. After years of rental use, however, the building had fallen into disrepair, and could no longer be rented out.

The Nollans' option to purchase was conditioned on their promise to demolish the bungalow and replace it. In order to do so, under California Public Resources Code §§30106, 30212, and 30600 (West 1986), they were required to obtain a coastal development permit from the California Coastal Commission. On February 25, 1982, they submitted a permit application to the Commission in which they proposed to demolish the existing structure and replace it with a three-bedroom house in keeping with the rest of the neighborhood.

The Nollans were informed that their application had been placed on the administrative calendar, and that the Commission staff had recommended that the permit be granted subject to the condition that they allow the public an easement to pass across a portion of their property bounded by the mean high tide line on one side, and their seawall on the other side. This would make it easier for the public to get to Faria County Park and the Cove. The Nollans protested imposition of the condition, but the Commission overruled their objections and granted the permit subject to their recordation of a deed restriction granting the easement.

On June 3, 1982, the Nollans filed a petition for writ of administrative mandamus asking the Ventura County Superior Court to invalidate the access condition. They argued that the condition could not be imposed absent evidence that their proposed development would have a direct adverse impact on public access to the beach. The court agreed, and remanded the case to the Commission for a full evidentiary hearing on that issue.

On remand, the Commission held a public hearing, after which it made further factual findings and reaffirmed its imposition of the condition. It found that the new house would increase blockage of the view of the ocean, thus contributing to the development of "a 'wall' of residential structures" that would prevent the public "psychologically . . . from realizing a stretch of coastline exists nearby that they have every right to visit." The new house would also increase private use of the shorefront. These effects of construction of the house, along with other area development, would cumulatively "burden the public's ability to traverse to and along the shorefront." Therefore the Commission could properly require the Nollans to offset that burden by providing additional lateral access to the public beaches in the form of an easement across their property. The Commission also noted that it had similarly conditioned 43 out of 60 coastal development permits along the same tract of land, and that of the 17 not so conditioned, 14 had been approved when the Commission did not have administrative regulations in place allowing imposition of the condition, and the remaining 3 had not involved shorefront property.

The Nollans filed a supplemental petition for a writ of administrative mandamus with the Superior Court, in which they argued that imposition of the access condition violated the Takings Clause of the Fifth Amendment, as incorporated against the States by the Fourteenth Amendment. The Superior Court ruled in their favor on statutory grounds, finding, in part to avoid "issues of constitutionality," that the California Coastal Act of 1976, Cal. Pub. Res. Code Ann. §30000 et seq., authorized the Commission to impose public access conditions on coastal development permits for the replacement of an existing single-family home with a new one only where the proposed development would have an adverse impact on public access to the sea. App. 419. In the Court's view, the administrative record did not provide an adequate factual basis for concluding that replacement of the bungalow with the house would create a direct or cumulative burden on public access to the sea. Accordingly, the Superior Court granted the writ of mandamus and directed that the permit condition be struck.

The Commission appealed to the California Court of Appeal. While that appeal was pending, the Nollans satisfied the condition on their option to purchase by tearing down the bungalow and building the new house, and bought the property. They did not notify the Commission that they were taking that action.

The Court of Appeal reversed the Superior Court. 177 Cal. App. 3d 719, 223 Cal. Rptr. 28 (1986). It disagreed with the Superior Court's interpretation of the Coastal Act, finding that it required that a coastal permit for the construction of a new house whose floor area, height or bulk was more than 10% larger than that of the house it was replacing be conditioned on a grant of access. Id. at 723-724, 223 Cal. Rptr., at 31; see Cal. Pub. Res. Code §30212. It also ruled that the requirement did not violate the Constitution under the reasoning of an earlier case of the Court of Appeal, Grupe v. California Coastal Commn. 166 Cal. App. 3d 148, 212 Cal. Rptr. 578 (1985). In that case, the court had found that so long as a project contributed to the need for public access, even if the project standing alone had not created the need for access, and even if there was only an indirect relationship between the access exacted and the need to which the project contributed, imposition of an access condition on a development permit was sufficiently related to burdens created by the project to be constitutional. ... Since, in the Court of Appeal's view, there was no statutory or constitutional obstacle to imposition of the access condition, the Superior Court erred in granting the writ of mandamus. The Nollans appealed to this Court, raising only the constitutional question.

II

Had California simply required the Nollans to make an easement across their beachfront available to the public on a permanent basis in order to increase public access to the beach, rather than conditioning their permit to rebuild their house on their agreeing to do so, we have no doubt there would have been a taking. To say that the appropriation of a public easement across a landowner's premises does not constitute the taking of a property interest but rather, (as Justice BRENNAN contends) "a mere restriction on its use," post, n.3, is to use words in a manner that deprives them of all their ordinary meaning. Indeed, one of the principal uses of the eminent domain power is to assure that the government be able to require conveyance of just such interests, so long as it pays for them. J. Sackman, 1 Nichols on Eminent Domain §2.1[1] (Rev. 3d ed. 1985), 2 id., §5.01[5]; see 1 id., §1.42[9], 2 id., §6.14. Perhaps because the point is so obvious, we have never been confronted with a controversy that required us to rule upon it, but our cases' analysis of the effect of other governmental action leads to the same conclusion. We have repeatedly held that, as to property reserved by its owner for private use, "the right to exclude [others is] 'one of the most essential sticks in the bundle of rights that are commonly characterized as property.'" Loretto v. Teleprompter Manhattan CATV Corp., 458 U.S. 419, 433 (1982), quoting Kaiser Aetna v. United States, 444 U.S. 164, 176 (1979). In *Loretto* we observed that where governmental action results in "[a] permanent physical occupation" of the property, by the government itself or by others, see 458 U.S., at 432-433, n.9, "our cases uniformly have found a taking to the extent of the occupation, without regard to whether the action achieves an important public benefit or has only minimal economic impact on the owner," id. at 434-435. We think a "permanent physical occupation" has occurred, for purposes of that rule, where individuals are given a permanent and continuous right to pass to and fro, so that the real property may continuously be traversed, even though no particular individual is permitted to station himself permanently upon the premises.[2] . . .

Given, then, that requiring uncompensated conveyance of the easement outright would violate the Fourteenth Amendment, the question becomes whether requiring it to be conveyed as a condition for issuing a land use permit alters the outcome. We have long recognized that land use regulation does not effect a taking if it "substantially advance[s] legitimate state interests" and does not "den[y] an owner economically viable use of his land," Agins v. Tiburon, 447 U.S. 255, 260 (1980). See also Penn Central Transportation Co. v. New York City, 438 U.S. 104, 127 (1978) ("a use restriction may constitute a 'taking' if not reasonably necessary to the effectuation of a substantial government purpose"). Our cases have not elaborated on the standards for determining what constitutes a "legitimate state interest" or what type of connection between the regulation and the state interest satisfies the requirement that the

2. . . . Nor are the Nollans' rights altered because they acquired the land well after the Commission had begun to implement its policy. So long as the Commission could not have deprived the prior owners of the easement without compensating them, the prior owners must be understood to have transferred their full property rights in conveying the lot. [Footnote relocated. — Ed.]

former "substantially advance" the latter.[3] They have made clear, however, that a broad range of governmental purposes and regulations satisfies these requirements. See Agins v. Tiburon, supra, 447 U.S., at 260-262 (scenic zoning); Penn Central Transportation Co. v. New York City, supra (landmark preservation); Euclid v. Ambler Realty Co., 272 U.S. 365 (1926) (residential zoning); Laitos and Westfall, Government Interference with Private Interests in Public Resources, 11 Harv. Envtl. L. Rev. 1, 66 (1987). The Commission argues that among these permissible purposes are protecting the public's ability to see the beach, assisting the public in overcoming the "psychological barrier" to using the beach created by a developed shorefront, and preventing congestion on the public beaches. We assume, without deciding, that this is so—in which case the Commission unquestionably would be able to deny the Nollans their permit outright if their new house (alone, or by reason of the cumulative impact produced in conjunction with other construction)[4] would substantially impede these purposes, unless the denial would interfere so drastically with the Nollans' use of their property as to constitute a taking. See Penn Central Transportation Co. v. New York City, supra.

3. Contrary to Justice Brennan's claim, our opinions do not establish that these standards are the same as those applied to due process or equal-protection claims. To the contrary, our verbal formulations in the takings field have generally been quite different. We have required that the regulation "substantially advance" the "legitimate state interest" sought to be achieved, Agins v. Tiburon, 447 U.S. 255, 260 (1980), not that "the State 'could rationally have decided' the measure adopted might achieve the State's objective." Post, at ——, quoting Minnesota v. Clover Leaf Creamery Co., 449 U.S. 456, 466 (1981). Justice Brennan relies principally on an equal protection case, Minnesota v. Clover Leaf Creamery Co., supra, and two substantive due process cases, Williamson v. Lee Optical of Oklahoma, Inc., 348 U.S. 483, 487-488 (1955) and Day-Brite Lighting, Inc. v. Missouri, 342 U.S. 421, 423 (1952), in support of the standards he would adopt. But there is no reason to believe (and the language of our cases gives some reason to disbelieve) that so long as the regulation of property is at issue the standards for takings challenges, due process challenges, and equal protection challenges are identical; any more than there is any reason to believe that so long as the regulation of speech is at issue the standards for due process challenges, equal protection challenges, and First Amendment challenges are identical. Goldblatt v. Hempstead, 369 U.S. 590 (1962), does appear to assume that the inquiries are the same, but that assumption is inconsistent with the formulations of our later cases.

4. If the Nollans were being singled out to bear the burden of California's attempt to remedy these problems, although they had not contributed to it more than other coastal landowners, the State's action, even if otherwise valid, might violate either the incorporated Takings Clause or the Equal Protection Clause. One of the principal purposes of the Takings Clause is "to bar Government from forcing some people alone to bear public burdens which, in all fairness and justice, should be borne by the public as a whole." Armstrong v. United States, 364 U.S. 40, 49 (1960). But that is not the basis of the Nollans' challenge here.

The Commission argues that a permit condition that serves the same legitimate police-power purpose as a refusal to issue the permit should not be found to be a taking if the refusal to issue the permit would not constitute a taking. We agree. Thus, if the Commission attached to the permit some condition that would have protected the public's ability to see the beach notwithstanding construction of the new house—for example, a height limitation, a width restriction, or a ban on fences—so long as the Commission could have exercised its police power (as we have assumed it could) to forbid construction of the house altogether, imposition of the condition would also be constitutional. Moreover (and here we come closer to the facts of the present case), the condition would be constitutional even if it consisted of the requirement that the Nollans provide a viewing spot on their property for passersby with whose sighting of the ocean their new house would interfere. Although such a requirement, constituting a permanent grant of continuous access to the property, would have to be considered a taking if it were not attached to a development permit, the Commission's assumed power to forbid construction of the house in order to protect the public's view of the beach must surely include the power to condition construction upon some concession by the owner, even a concession of property rights, that serves the same end. If a prohibition designed to accomplish that purpose would be a legitimate exercise of the police power rather than a taking, it would be strange to conclude that providing the owner an alternative to that prohibition which accomplishes the same purpose is not.

The evident constitutional propriety disappears, however, if the condition substituted for the prohibition utterly fails to further the end advanced as the justification for the prohibition. When that essential nexus is eliminated, the situation becomes the same as if California law forbade shouting fire in a crowded theater, but granted dispensations to those willing to contribute $100 to the state treasury. While a ban on shouting fire can be a core exercise of the State's police power to protect the public safety, and can thus meet even our stringent standards for regulation of speech, adding the unrelated condition alters the purpose to one which, while it may be legitimate, is inadequate to sustain the ban. Therefore, even though, in a sense, requiring a $100 tax contribution in order to shout fire is a lesser restriction on speech than an outright ban, it would not pass constitutional muster. Similarly here, the lack of nexus between the condition and the original purpose of the building restriction converts that purpose to something other than what it was. The purpose then becomes, quite simply, the obtaining of an easement to serve some valid governmental purpose, but without payment of compensation. Whatever may be the outer limits of "legitimate state interests" in the takings and land use context, this is not one of

126

them. In short, unless the permit condition serves the same governmental purpose as the development ban, the building restriction is not a valid regulation of land use but "an out-and-out plan of extortion." J.E.D. Associates, Inc. v. Atkinson, 121 N.H. 581, 584, 432 A.2d 12, 14-15 (1981); see Brief for United States as Amicus Curiae 22, and n.20. See also Loretto v. Teleprompter Manhattan CATV Corp., 458 U.S., at 439, n.17.[5]

III

The Commission claims that it concedes as much, and that we may sustain the condition at issue here by finding that it is reasonably related to the public need or burden that the Nollans' new house creates or to which it contributes. We can accept, for purposes of discussion, the Commission's proposed test as to how close a "fit" between the condition and the burden is required, because we find that this case does not meet even the most untailored standards. The Commission's principal contention to the contrary essentially turns on a play on the word "access." The Nollans' new house, the Commission found, will interfere with "visual access" to the beach. That in turn (along with other shorefront development) will interfere with the desire of people who drive past the Nollans' house to use the beach, thus creating a "psychological barrier" to "access." The Nollans' new house will also, by a process not altogether clear from the Commission's opinion but presumably potent enough to more than offset the effects of the psychological barrier, increase the use of the public beaches, thus creating the need for more "access." These burdens on "access" would be alleviated by a requirement that the Nollans provide "lateral access" to the beach.

Rewriting the argument to eliminate the play on words makes clear that there is nothing to it. It is quite impossible to understand how a requirement that people already on the public beaches be able to walk across the Nollans' property reduces any obstacles to viewing the beach created by the new house. It is also impossible to understand how it lowers any "psychological barrier" to using the public beaches, or how it helps to remedy any additional congestion on them caused by construction of the Nollans' new house. We therefore find that the Com-

---

5. One would expect that a regime in which this kind of leveraging of the police power is allowed would produce stringent land-use regulation which the State then waives to accomplish other purposes, leading to lesser realization of the land-use goals purportedly sought to be served than would result from more lenient (but nontradeable) development restrictions. Thus, the importance of the purpose underlying the prohibition not only does not *justify* the imposition of unrelated conditions for eliminating the prohibition, but positively militates against the practice.

mission's imposition of the permit condition cannot be treated as an exercise of its land use power for any of these purposes. Our conclusion on this point is consistent with the approach taken by every other court that has considered the question, with the exception of the California state courts. See Parks v. Watson, 716 F.2d 646, 651-653 (CA9 1983); Bethlehem Evangelical Lutheran Church v. Lakewood, 626 P.2d 668, 671-674 (Colo. 1981); Aunt Hack Ridge Estates, Inc. v. Planning Commn., 160 Conn. 109, 117-120, 273 A.2d 880, 885 (1970); Longboat Key v. Lands End, Ltd., 433 So. 2d 574 (Fla. App. 1983); Pioneer Trust & Saving Bank v. Mount Prospect, 22 Ill. 2d 375, 380, 176 N.E.2d 799, 802 (1961); Lampton v. Pinaire, 610 S.W.2d 915, 918-919 (Ky. App. 1980); Schwing v. Baton Rouge, 249 So. 2d 304 (La. App. 1971); Howard County v. JJM, Inc., 301 Md. 256, 280-282, 482 A.2d 908, 920-921 (1984); Collis v. Bloomington, 310 Minn. 5, 246 N.W.2d 19 (1976); State ex rel. Noland v. St. Louis County, 478 S.W.2d 363 (Mo. 1972); Billings Properties, Inc. v. Yellowstone County, 144 Mont. 25, 33-36, 394 P.2d 182, 187-188 (1964); Simpson v. North Platte, 206 Neb. 240, 292 N.W.2d 297 (1980); Briar West, Inc. v. Lincoln, 206 Neb. 172, 291 N.W.2d 730 (1980); J.E.D. Associates v. Atkinson, supra; Longridge Builders, Inc. v. Planning Bd. of Princeton, 52 N.J. 348, 350-351, 245 A.2d 336, 337-338 (1968); Jenad, Inc. v. Scarsdale, 18 N.Y.2d 78 (1966); In re MacKall v. White, 85 App. Div. 2d 696, 445 N.Y.S.2d 486 (1981); Frank Ansuini, Inc. v. Cranston, 107 R.I. 63, 68-69, 71, 264 A.2d 910, 913, 914 (1970); College Station v. Turtle Rock Corp., 680 S.W.2d 802, 807 (Tex. 1984); Call v. West Jordan, 614 P.2d 1257, 1258-1259 (Utah 1980); Board of Supervisors of James County v. Rowe, 216 Va. 128, 136-139, 216 S.E.2d 199, 207-209 (1975); Jordan v. Menomonee Falls, 28 Wis. 2d 608, 617-618, 137 N.W.2d 442, 447-449 (1965).

Justice Brennan argues that imposition of the access requirement is not irrational. In his version of the Commission's argument, the reason for the requirement is that in its absence, a person looking toward the beach from the road will see a street of residential structures including the Nollans' new home and conclude that there is no public beach nearby. If, however, that person sees people passing and repassing along the dry sand behind the Nollans' home, he will realize that there is a public beach somewhere in the vicinity. The Commission's action, however, was based on the opposite factual finding that the wall of houses completely blocked the view of the beach and that a person looking from the road would not be able to see it at all.

Even if the Commission had made the finding that Justice Brennan proposes, however, it is not certain that it would suffice. We do not share Justice Brennan's confidence that the Commission "should have little difficulty in the future in utilizing its expertise to demonstrate a specific connection between provisions for access and burdens on access," that will avoid the effect of today's decision. We view the Fifth Amendment's property clause to be more than a pleading requirement, and compliance with it to be more than an exercise in cleverness and imagination. As indicated earlier, our cases describe the condition for abridgement of property rights through the police power as a "*substantial* advanc[ing]" of a legitimate State interest. We are inclined to be particularly careful about the adjective where the actual conveyance of property is made a condition to the lifting of a land use restriction, since in that context there is heightened risk that the purpose is avoidance of the compensation requirement, rather than the stated police power objective.

We are left, then, with the Commission's justification for the access requirement unrelated to land use regulation:

> Finally, the Commission notes that there are several existing provisions of pass and repass lateral access benefits already given by past Faria Beach Tract applicants as a result of prior coastal permit decisions. The access required as a condition of this permit is part of a comprehensive program to provide continuous public access along Faria Beach as the lots undergo development or redevelopment.

That is simply an expression of the Commission's belief that the public interest will be served by a continuous strip of publicly accessible beach along the coast. The Commission may well be right that it is a good idea, but that does not establish that the Nollans (and other coastal residents) alone can be compelled to contribute to its realization. Rather, California is free to advance its "comprehensive program," if it wishes, by using its power of eminent domain for this "public purpose," see U.S. Const., Amdt. V; but if it wants an easement across the Nollans' property, it must pay for it.

Reversed.

Justice BRENNAN, with whom Justice MARSHALL joins, dissenting. . . .

. . .The Court has thus struck down the Commission's reasonable effort to respond to intensified development along the California coast, on behalf of landowners who can make no claim that their reasonable expectations have been disrupted. The Court has, in short, given appellants a windfall at the expense of the public.

I

The Court's conclusion that the permit condition imposed on appellants is unreasonable cannot withstand analysis. First, the Court demands a degree of exactitude that is inconsistent with our standard for reviewing the rationality of a state's exercise of its police power for the welfare of its citizens. Second, even if the nature of the public access condition imposed must be identical to the precise burden on access created by appellants, this requirement is plainly satisfied.

A

There can be no dispute that the police power of the States encompasses the authority to impose conditions on private development. See, *e.g.*, Agins v. Tiburon, 447 U.S. 255 (1980); Penn Central Transportation Co. v. New York City, 438 U.S. 104 (1978); Gorieb v. Fox, 274 U.S. 603 (1927). It is also by now commonplace that this Court's review of the rationality of a State's exercise of its police power demands only that the State *"could rationally have decided"* that the measure adopted might achieve the State's objective. Minnesota v. Clover Leaf Creamery Co., 449 U.S. 456, 466 (1981) (emphasis in original). In this case, California has employed its police power in order to condition development upon preservation of public access to the ocean and tidelands. The Coastal Commission, if it had so chosen, could have denied the Nollans' request for a development permit, since the property would have remained economically viable without the requested new development. Instead, the State sought to accommodate the Nollans' desire for new development, on the condition that the development not diminish the overall amount of public access to the coastline. Appellants' proposed development would reduce public access by restricting visual access to the beach, by contributing to an increased need for community facilities, and by moving private development closer to public beach property. The Commission sought to offset this diminution in access, and thereby preserve the overall balance of access, by requesting a deed restriction that would ensure "lateral" access: the right of the public to pass and repass along the dry sand parallel to the shoreline in order to reach the tidelands and the ocean. In the expert opinion of the Coastal Commission, development conditioned on such a restriction would fairly attend to both public and private interests.

The Court finds fault with this measure because it regards the condition as insufficiently tailored to address the precise type of reduction in access produced by the new development. The Nollans' development blocks visual access, the Court tells us, while the Commission seeks to preserve lateral access along the coastline. Thus, it concludes, the State acted irrationally. Such a narrow conception of rationality, however, has long since been discredited as a judicial arrogation of legislative authority. "To make scientific precision a criterion of constitutional power would be to subject the State to an intolerable supervision hostile to the basic principles of our Government." Sproles v. Binford, 286 U.S. 374, 388 (1932). . . .

. . .The Commission has sought to discharge its responsibilities in a flexible manner. It has sought to balance private and public interests and to accept tradeoffs: to permit development that reduces access in some ways as long as other means of access are enhanced. In this case, it has determined that the Nollans' burden on access would be offset by a deed restriction that formalizes the public's right to pass along the shore. In its informed judgment, such a tradeoff would preserve the net amount of public access to the coastline. The Court's insistence on a precise fit between the forms of burden and condition on each individual parcel along the California coast would penalize the Commission for its flexibility, hampering the ability to fulfill its public trust mandate.[3] . . .

B

Even if we accept the Court's unusual demand for a precise match between the condition imposed and the specific type of burden on access created by the appellants, the State's action easily satisfies this requirement. First, the lateral access condition serves to dissipate the impression that the beach that lies behind the wall of homes along the shore is for private use only. It requires no exceptional imaginative powers to find plausible the Commission's point that the average person passing along the road in front of a phalanx of imposing permanent residences, including the appellants' new home, is likely to conclude that this particular portion of the shore is not open to the public. If, however, that person can see that numerous people are passing and repassing along the dry sand, this conveys the message that the beach is in fact open for use by the public. Furthermore, those persons who go down to the public beach a quarter-mile away will be able to look down the coastline and see that

3. The list of cases cited by the Court as support for its approach includes no instance in which the State sought to vindicate pre-existing rights of access to navigable water, and consists principally of cases involving a requirement of the dedication of land as a condition of subdivision approval. Dedication, of course, requires the surrender of ownership of property rather than, as in this case, a mere restriction on its use. The only case pertaining to beach access among those cited by the Court is Mackall v. White, 85 App. Div. 2d 696, 445 N.Y.S.2d 486 (1981). In that case, the court found that a subdivision application could not be conditioned upon a declaration that the landowner would not hinder the public from using a trail that had been used to gain access to a bay. The trail had been used despite posted warnings prohibiting passage, and despite the owner's resistance to such use. In that case, unlike this one, neither the state constitution, state statute, administrative practice, nor the conduct of the landowner operated to create reasonable expectation of a right of public access. [Footnote relocated. — Ed.]

persons have continuous access to the tidelands, and will observe signs that proclaim the public's right of access over the dry sand. The burden produced by the diminution in visual access—the impression that the beach is not open to the public—is thus directly alleviated by the provision for public access over the dry sand. The Court therefore has an unrealistically limited conception of what measures could reasonably be chosen to mitigate the burden produced by a diminution of visual access. . . .

II

The fact that the Commission's action is a legitimate exercise of the police power does not, of course, insulate it from a takings challenge, for when "regulation goes too far it will be recognized as a taking." Pennsylvania Coal Co. v. Mahon, 260 U.S. 393, 415 (1922). Conventional takings analysis underscores the implausibility of the Court's holding, for it demonstrates that this exercise of California's police power implicates none of the concerns that underlie our takings jurisprudence.

In reviewing a Takings Clause claim, we have regarded as particularly significant the nature of the governmental action and the economic impact of regulation, especially the extent to which regulation interferes with investment-backed expectations. *Penn Central*, 438 U.S., at 124. The character of the government action in this case is the imposition of a condition on permit approval, which allows the public to continue to have access to the coast. The physical intrusion permitted by the deed restriction is minimal. The public is permitted the right to pass and re-pass along the coast in an area from the seawall to the mean high tide mark. This area is at its *widest* 10 feet, which means that *even without the permit condition*, the public's right of access permits it to pass on average within a few feet of the seawall. Passage closer to the 8-foot high rocky seawall will make the appellants even less visible to the public than passage along the high tide area farther out on the beach. The intrusiveness of such passage is even less than the intrusion resulting from the required dedication of a sidewalk in front of private residences, exactions which are commonplace conditions on approval of development.[7] Furthermore, the high tide line shifts throughout the year, moving up to and beyond the seawall, so that public passage for a portion of the year would either be impossible or would not occur on appellant's property. Finally, although the Commission had the authority to provide for either passive

7. See, e.g., City of Bellefontaine Neighbors v. J.J. Kelley Realty & Bldg. Co., 460 S.W.2d 298 (Mo. Ct. App. 1970); Allen v. Stockwell, 210 Mich. 488, 178 N.W. 27 (1920). See generally Shultz & Kelley, Subdivision Improvement Requirements and Guarantees: A Primer, 28 Wash. U.J. Urban and Contemp. L. 3 (1985).

or active recreational use of the property, it chose the least intrusive alternative: a mere right to pass and repass.[8] As this Court made clear in PruneYard Shopping Center v. Robins, 447 U.S. 74, 83 (1980), physical access to private property in itself creates no takings problem if it does not "unreasonably impair the value or use of [the] property." Appellants can make no tenable claim that either their enjoyment of their property or its value is diminished by the public's ability merely to pass and re-pass a few feet closer to the seawall beyond which appellants' house is located. . . .

Examination of the economic impact of the Commission's action reinforces the conclusion that no taking has occurred. Allowing appellants to intensify development along the coast in exchange for ensuring public access to the ocean is a classic instance of government action that produces a "reciprocity of advantage." *Pennsylvania Coal*, supra, 260 U.S., at 415. Appellants have been allowed to replace a one-story 521-square-foot beach home with a two-story 1,674-square-foot residence and an attached two-car garage, resulting in development covering 2,464 square feet of the lot. Such development obviously significantly increases the value of appellants' property; appellants make no contention that this increase is offset by any diminution in value resulting from the deed restriction, much less that the restriction made the property less valuable than it would have been without the new construction. Furthermore, appellants gain an additional benefit from the Commission's permit condition program. They are able to walk along the beach beyond the confines of their own property only because the Commission has required deed restrictions as a condition of approving other new beach devel-

---

8. The Commission acted in accordance with its Guidelines both in determining the width of the area of passage, and in prohibiting any recreational use of the property. The Guidelines state that it may be necessary on occasion to provide for less than the normal 25-foot wide accessway along the dry sand when this may be necessary to "protect the privacy rights of adjacent property owners." They also provide this advice in selecting the type of public use that may be permitted:

> *Pass and Repass.* Where topographic constraints of the site make use of the beach dangerous, where habitat values of the shoreline would be adversely impacted by public use of the shoreline or where the accessway may encroach closer than 20 feet to a residential structure, the accessway may be limited to the right of the public to pass and repass along the access area. For the purposes of these guidelines, pass and repass is defined as the right to walk and run along the shoreline. This would provide for public access along the shoreline but would not allow for any additional use of the accessway. Because this severely limits the public's ability to enjoy the adjacent state owned tidelands by restricting the potential use of the access areas, this form of access dedication should be used only where necessary to protect the habitat values of the site, where topographic constraints warrant the restriction, or where it is necessary to protect the privacy of the landowner.

opments. Thus, appellants benefit both as private landowners and as members of the public from the fact that new development permit requests are conditioned on preservation of public access.

Ultimately, appellants' claim of economic injury is flawed because it rests on the assumption of entitlement to the full value of their new development. Appellants submitted a proposal for more intensive development of the coast, which the Commission was under no obligation to approve, and now argue that a regulation designed to ameliorate the impact of that development deprives them of the full value of their improvements. Even if this novel claim were somehow cognizable, it is not significant. "[T]he interest in anticipated gains has traditionally been viewed as less compelling than other property-related interests." Andrus v. Allard, 444 U.S. 51, 66 (1979).

With respect to appellants' investment-backed expectations, appellants can make no reasonable claim to any expectation of being able to exclude members of the public from crossing the edge of their property to gain access to the ocean. It is axiomatic, of course, that state law is the source of those strands that constitute a property owner's bundle of property rights. "[A]s a general proposition[,] the law of real property is, under our Constitution, left to the individual States to develop and administer." Hughes v. Washington, 389 U.S. 290, 295 (1967) (Stewart, J., concurring). See also Borax Consolidated v. Los Angeles, 296 U.S. 10, 22 (1935) ("Rights and interests in the tideland, which is subject to the sovereignty of the State, are matters of local law"). In this case, the state constitution explicitly states that no one possessing the "frontage" of any "navigable water in this State, shall be permitted to exclude the right of way to such water whenever it is required for any public purpose." Cal. Const., Art. X, §4. The state Code expressly provides that, save for exceptions not relevant here, "[p]ublic access from the nearest public roadway to the shoreline and along the coast shall be provided in new development projects." Cal. Pub. Res. Code Ann. §30212 (1986). The Coastal Commission Interpretative Guidelines make clear that fulfillment of the Commission's constitutional and statutory duty require that approval of new coastline development be conditioned upon provisions ensuring lateral public access to the ocean. At the time of appellants' permit request, the Commission had conditioned all 43 of the proposals for coastal new development in the Faria Family Beach Tract on the provision of deed restrictions ensuring lateral access along the shore. Finally, the Faria family had leased the beach property since the early part of this century, and "the Faria family and their lessees [including the Nollans] had not interfered with public use of the beachfront within the Tract, so long as public use was limited to pass and re-pass lateral access along the shore." California therefore has clearly established that the power of exclusion for which appellants seek compensation simply is not a strand in the bundle of appellants' property rights, and appellants have never acted as if it were. Given this state of affairs, appellants cannot claim that the deed restriction has deprived them of a reasonable expectation to exclude from their property persons desiring to gain access to the sea.

Even were we somehow to concede a pre-existing expectation of a right to exclude, appellants were clearly on notice when requesting a new development permit that a condition of approval would be a provision ensuring public lateral access to the shore. Thus, they surely could have had no expectation that they could obtain approval of their new development and exercise any right of exclusion afterward. . . .

III . . .

Fortunately, the Court's decision regarding this application of the Commission's permit program will probably have little ultimate impact either on this parcel in particular or the Commission program in general. A preliminary study by a Senior Lands Agent in the State Attorney General's Office indicates that the portion of the beach at issue in this case likely belongs to the public.[11] Since a full study had not been completed at the time of appellants' permit application, the deed restriction was requested "without regard to the possibility that the applicant is proposing development on public land." Furthermore, analysis by the same Land Agent also indicated that the public had obtained a prescriptive right to the use of Faria Beach from the seawall to the ocean.[12] The Superior Court explicitly stated in its ruling against the Commission on the permit condition issue that "no part of this opinion is intended to foreclose the public's opportunity to adjudicate the possibility that public rights in [appellants'] beach have been acquired through prescriptive use."

With respect to the permit condition program in general, the Commission should have little difficulty in the future in utilizing its expertise to demonstrate a specific connection between provisions for access and

---

11. The Senior Land Agent's report to the Commission states that "based on my observations, presently, most, if not all of Faria Beach waterward of the existing seawalls [lies] *below* the Mean High Tide Level, and would fall in public domain or sovereign category of ownership." (Emphasis added).

12. The report of the Senior Land Agent stated: "Based on my past experience and my investigation to date of this property it is my opinion that the area seaward of the revetment at 3822 Pacific Coast Highway, Faria Beach, as well as all the area seaward of the revetments built to protect the Faria Beach community, if not public owned, has been impliedly dedicated to the public for passive recreational use."

burdens on access produced by new development. Neither the Commission in its report nor the State in its briefs and at argument highlighted the particular threat to lateral access created by appellants' development project. In defending its action, the State emphasized the general point that *overall* access to the beach had been preserved, since the diminution of access created by the project had been offset by the gain in lateral access. This approach is understandable, given that the State relied on the reasonable assumption that its action was justified under the normal standard of review for determining legitimate exercises of a State's police power. In the future, alerted to the Court's apparently more demanding requirement, it need only make clear that a provision for public access directly responds to a particular type of burden on access created by a new development. Even if I did not believe that the record in this case satisfies this requirement, I would have to acknowledge that the record's documentation of the impact of coastal development indicates that the Commission should have little problem presenting its findings in a way that avoids a takings problem.

Nonetheless it is important to point out that the Court's insistence on a precise accounting system in this case is insensitive to the fact that increasing intensity of development in many areas calls for farsighted, comprehensive planning that takes into account both the interdependence of land uses and the cumulative impact of development. As one scholar has noted:

> Property does not exist in isolation. Particular parcels are tied to one another in complex ways, and property is more accurately described as being inextricably part of a network of relationships that is neither limited to, nor usefully defined by, the property boundaries with which the legal system is accustomed to dealing. Frequently, use of any given parcel of property is at the same time effectively a use of, or a demand upon, property beyond the border of the user. Sax, Takings, Private Property, and Public Rights, 81 Yale L.J. 149, 152 (1971) (footnote omitted).

As Congress has declared, "The key to more effective protection and use of the land and water resources [is for the states to] develo[p] land and water use programs for the coastal zone, including unified policies, criteria, standards, methods, and processes for dealing with land and water use decisions of more than local significance." 16 U.S.C. §1451(i). This is clearly a call for a focus on the overall impact of development on coastal areas. State agencies therefore require considerable flexibility in responding to private desires for development in a way that guarantees the preservation of public access to the coast. They should be encouraged to regulate development in the context of the overall balance of competing uses of the shoreline. The Court today does precisely the opposite,

overruling an eminently reasonable exercise of an expert state agency's judgment, substituting its own narrow view of how this balance should be struck. Its reasoning is hardly suited to the complex reality of natural resource protection in the twentieth century. I can only hope that today's decision is an aberration and that a broader vision ultimately prevails.[14]
I dissent.

Justice BLACKMUN, dissenting. . . .

I disagree with the Court's rigid interpretation of the necessary correlation between a burden created by development and a condition imposed pursuant to the State's police power to mitigate that burden. The land-use problems this country faces require creative solutions. These are not advanced by an "eye for an eye" mentality. The close nexus between benefits and burdens that the Court now imposes on permit conditions creates an anomaly in the ordinary requirement that a State's exercise of its police power need be no more than rationally based. See, e.g., Minnesota v. Clover Leaf Creamery Co., 449 U.S. 456, 466 (1981). In my view, the easement exacted from appellants and the problems their development created are adequately related to the governmental interest in providing public access to the beach. Coastal development by its very nature makes public access to the shore generally more difficult. Appellants' structure is part of that general development and, in particular, it diminishes the public's visual access to the ocean and decreases the public's sense that it may have physical access to the beach. These losses in access can be counteracted, at least in part, by the condition on appellants' construction permitting public passage that ensures access along the beach.

Traditional takings analysis compels the conclusion that there is no taking here. The governmental action is a valid exercise of the police power, and, so far as the record reveals, has a nonexistent economic effect on the value of appellants' property. No investment-backed expectations were diminished. It is significant that the Nollans had notice of the easement before they purchased the property and that public use of the beach had been permitted for decades.

For these reasons, I respectfully dissent.

---

14. I believe that States should be afforded considerable latitude in regulating private development, without fear that their regulatory efforts will often be found to constitute a taking. "If . . . regulation denies the property owner the use and enjoyment of his land and is found to effect a 'taking' ", however, I believe that compensation is the appropriate remedy for this constitutional violation. San Diego Gas & Electric Co. v. San Diego, 450 U.S. 621, 656 (1981) (BRENNAN, J., dissenting) (emphasis added). I therefore see my dissent here as completely consistent with my position in First English Evangelical Church v. Los Angeles County, 107 S. Ct. 2378 (1987).

Justice STEVENS, with whom Justice BLACKMUN joins, dissenting. . . .

In his dissent in San Diego Gas & Electric Co. v. San Diego, 450 U.S. 621 (1981), Justice Brennan proposed a brand new constitutional rule.* He argued that a mistake such as the one that a majority of the Court believes that the California Coastal Commission made in this case should automatically give rise to pecuniary liability for a "temporary taking." Id., at 653-661. Notwithstanding the unprecedented chilling effect that such a rule will obviously have on public officials charged with the responsibility for drafting and implementing regulations designed to protect the environment and the public welfare, six Members of the Court recently endorsed Justice BRENNAN's novel proposal. See *First English Evangelical Lutheran Church*, 107 S. Ct. 2378 (1987).

I write today to identify the severe tension between that dramatic development in the law and the view expressed by Justice Brennan's dissent in this case that the public interest is served by encouraging state agencies to exercise considerable flexibility in responding to private desires for development in a way that threatens the preservation of public resources. I like the hat that Justice Brennan has donned today better than the one he wore in *San Diego*, and I am persuaded that he has the better of the legal arguments here. Even if his position prevailed in this case, however, it would be of little solace to land-use planners who would still be left guessing about how the Court will react to the next case, and the one after that. As this case demonstrates, the rule of liability created by the Court in *First English* is a short-sighted one. Like Justice Brennan, I hope "that a broader vision ultimately prevails." . . .

Page 766.   At end of Note 1, add:

Federal judges have shown little sympathy when the alleged municipal discrimination is not along racial or other constitutionally suspect lines. See, for example, Mlikotin v. City of Los Angeles, 643 F.2d 652 (9th Cir. 1981), in which an owner of property situated in the Venice district of the City of Los Angeles brought a §1983 suit for damages. The plaintiff asserted that the city was providing inadequate services in the Venice district and that as a result the plaintiff's property had a lower market value than it otherwise would have. The Ninth Circuit affirmed the district court's decision to dismiss the suit for failing to state a claim upon which relief could be granted.

---

* "The constitutional rule I propose requires that, once a court finds that a police power regulation has effected a 'taking,' the government entity must pay just compensation for the period commencing on the date the regulation first effected the 'taking,' and ending on the date the government entity chooses to rescind or otherwise amend the regulation." 450 U.S., at 658. [Footnote in original.—Ed.]

Chapter Eight

The Regional Obligations of Municipalities

Page 816. **Delete** *Mount Laurel II* **(N.J. Super. 1978) and substitute:**

SOUTHERN BURLINGTON COUNTY NAACP v. TOWNSHIP OF MOUNT LAUREL [MOUNT LAUREL II]

92 N.J. 158, 456 A.2d 390 (1983)

[Argued in October and December 1980; decided on January 20, 1983. The Atlantic Reporter report of this decision is 120 pages long, contains 134 keynotes, and lists 28 different teams of attorneys. For some of the court's rulings the editors have deleted all discussion except what appears in the court's own "Summary of Rulings."]

WILENTZ, C.J.

This is the return, eight years later, of . . . *Mount Laurel I.* We set forth in that case, for the first time, the doctrine requiring that municipalities' land use regulations provide a realistic opportunity for low and moderate income housing. The doctrine has become famous. The *Mount Laurel* case itself threatens to become infamous. After all this time, ten years after the trial court's initial order invalidating its zoning ordinance, Mount Laurel remains afflicted with a blatantly exclusionary ordinance. Papered over with studies, rationalized by hired experts, the ordinance at its core is true to nothing but Mount Laurel's determination to exclude the poor. Mount Laurel is not alone; we believe that there is widespread non-compliance with the constitutional mandate of our original opinion in this case.

To the best of our ability, we shall not allow it to continue. This Court is more firmly committed to the original *Mount Laurel* doctrine than ever, and we are determined, within appropriate judicial bounds, to make it work. The obligation is to provide a realistic opportunity for housing, not litigation. We have learned from experience, however, that unless a strong judicial hand is used, *Mount Laurel* will not result in housing, but in paper, process, witnesses, trials and appeals. We intend by this decision to strengthen it, clarify it, and make it easier for public officials, including judges, to apply it.

This case is accompanied by five others, heard together and decided in this opinion. All involve questions arising from the *Mount Laurel* doctrine. They demonstrate the need to put some steel into that doctrine. The deficiencies in its application range from uncertainty and inconsistency at the trial level to inflexible review criteria at the appellate level. The waste of judicial energy involved at every level is substantial and is matched only by the often needless expenditure of talent on the part of lawyers and experts. The length and complexity of trials is often outrageous, and the expense of litigation is so high that a real question develops whether the municipality can afford to defend or the plaintiffs can afford to sue.

There is another side to the story. We believe, both through the representations of counsel and from our own research and experience, that the doctrine has done some good, indeed, perhaps substantial good. We have tried to make the doctrine clearer for we believe that most municipal officials will in good faith strive to fulfill their constitutional duty. There are a number of municipalities around the State that have responded to our decisions by amending their zoning ordinances to provide realistic opportunities for the construction of low and moderate income housing. Further, many other municipalities have at least recognized their obligation to provide such opportunities in their ordinances and master plans. Finally, state and county government agencies have responded by preparing regional housing plans that help both the courts and municipalities themselves carry out the *Mount Laurel* mandate. Still, we are far from where we had hoped to be and nowhere near where we should be with regard to the administration of the doctrine in our courts.

These six cases not only afford the opportunity for, but demonstrate the necessity of reexamining the *Mount Laurel* doctrine. We do so here. The doctrine is right but its administration has become ineffective.

A brief statement of the cases may be helpful at this point. *Mount Laurel II* results from the remand by this Court of the original *Mount Laurel* case. The municipality rezoned, purportedly pursuant to our instructions, a plenary trial was held, and the trial court found that the rezoning constituted a bona fide attempt by Mount Laurel to provide a realistic opportunity for the construction of its fair share of the regional lower income housing need. Reading our cases at that time (1978) as requiring no more, the trial court dismissed the complaint of the N.A.A.C.P. and other plaintiffs but granted relief in the form of a builder's remedy, to a developer intervenor who had attacked the total prohibition against mobile homes. Plaintiffs' appeal of the trial court's ruling sustaining the ordinance in all other respects was directly certified by this Court, as ultimately was defendant's appeal from the grant of a builder's remedy allowing construction of mobile homes. We reverse and remand to determine Mount Laurel's fair share of the regional need and for further proceedings to revise its ordinance; we affirm the grant of the builders' remedy. . . .

[The five other cases involved local governments other than Mount Laurel. Three were actions brought by landowners seeking a builder's remedy. In the remaining two cases local chapters of the Urban League were asking the court to order certain municipalities to revise their ordinances to comply with their fair-share obligations. In the interest of brevity the editors have deleted the New Jersey Supreme Court's discussion of these five cases.]

I. Background . . .

B. CONSTITUTIONAL BASIS FOR MOUNT LAUREL AND THE JUDICIAL ROLE . . .

. . .The basis for the constitutional obligation is simple: the State controls the use of land, *all* of the land. In exercising that control it cannot favor rich over poor. It cannot legislatively set aside dilapidated housing in urban ghettos for the poor and decent housing elsewhere for everyone else. The government that controls this land represents everyone. While the State may not have the ability to eliminate poverty, it cannot use that condition as the basis for imposing further disadvantages. And the same applies to the municipality, to which this control over land has been constitutionally delegated.

The clarity of the constitutional obligation is seen most simply by imagining what this state could be like were this claim never to be recognized and enforced: poor people forever zoned out of substantial areas of the state, not because housing could not be built for them but because they are not wanted; poor people forced to live in urban slums forever not because suburbia, developing rural areas, fully developed residential sections, seashore resorts, and other attractive locations could not accommodate them, but simply because they are not wanted. It is a vision not only at variance with the requirement that the zoning power be used for the general welfare but with all concepts of fundamental fairness and decency that underpin many constitutional obligations.

Subject to the clear obligation to preserve open space and prime agricultural land, a builder in New Jersey who finds it economically feasible to provide decent housing for lower income groups will no longer find it governmentally impossible. Builders may not be able to build just where they want—our parks, farms, and conservation areas are not a land bank for housing speculators. But if sound planning of an area

141

allows the rich and middle class to live there, it must also realistically and practically allow the poor. And if the area will accommodate factories, it must also find space for workers. The specific location of such housing will of course continue to depend on sound municipal land use planning.

While *Mount Laurel I* discussed the need for "an appropriate variety and choice of housing," 67 N.J. 179, 336 A.2d 713, the specific constitutional obligation addressed there, as well as in our opinion here, is that relating to low and moderate income housing. Id. All that we say here concerns that category alone; the doctrine as we interpret it has no present applicability to other kinds of housing. See *Pascack*, 74 N.J. at 480, 379 A.2d 6. It is obvious that eight years after *Mount Laurel I* the need for satisfaction of this doctrine is greater than ever. Upper and middle income groups may search with increasing difficulty for housing within their means; for low and moderate income people, there is nothing to search for.

No one has challenged the *Mount Laurel* doctrine on these appeals. Nevertheless, a brief reminder of the judicial role in this sensitive area is appropriate, since powerful reasons suggest, and we agree, that the matter is better left to the Legislature. We act first and foremost because the Constitution of our State requires protection of the interests involved and because the Legislature has not protected them. We recognize the social and economic controversy (and its political consequences) that has resulted in relatively little legislative action in this field. We understand the enormous difficulty of achieving a political consensus that might lead to significant legislation enforcing the constitutional mandate better than we can, legislation that might completely remove this Court from those controversies. But enforcement of constitutional rights cannot await a supporting political consensus. So while we have always preferred legislative to judicial action in this field, we shall continue—until the Legislature acts—to do our best to uphold the constitutional obligation that underlies the *Mount Laurel* doctrine. That is our duty. We may not build houses, but we do enforce the Constitution.

We note that there has been some legislative initiative in this field. We look forward to more. The new Municipal Land Use Law explicitly recognizes the obligation of municipalities to zone with regional consequences in mind, N.J.S.A. 40:55D-28(d); it also recognizes the work of the Division of State and Regional Planning in the Department of Community Affairs (DCA), in creating the State Development Guide Plan (1980) (SDGP), which plays an important part in our decisions today. Our deference to these legislative and executive initiatives can be regarded as a clear signal of our readiness to defer further to more substantial actions.

The judicial role, however, which could decrease as a result of legislative and executive action, necessarily will expand to the extent that we remain virtually alone in this field. In the absence of adequate legislative and executive help, we must give meaning to the constitutional doctrine in the cases before us through our own devices, even if they are relatively less suitable. That is the basic explanation of our decisions today.

C. SUMMARY OF RULINGS

Our rulings today have several purposes. First, we intend to encourage voluntary compliance with the constitutional obligation by defining it more clearly. We believe that the use of the State Development Guide Plan and the confinement of all *Mount Laurel* litigation to a small group of judges, selected by the Chief Justice with the approval of the Court, will tend to serve that purpose. Second, we hope to simplify litigation in this area. While we are not overly optimistic, we think that the remedial use of the SDGP may achieve that purpose, given the significance accorded it in this opinion. Third, the decisions are intended to increase substantially the effectiveness of the judicial remedy. In most cases, upon determination that the municipality has not fulfilled its constitutional obligation, the trial court will retain jurisdiction, order an immediate revision of the ordinance (including, if necessary, supervision of the revision through a court appointed master), and require the use of effective affirmative planning and zoning devices. The long delays of interminable appellate review will be discouraged, if not completely ended, and the opportunity for low and moderate income housing found in the new ordinance will be as realistic as judicial remedies can make it. We hope to achieve all of these purposes while preserving the fundamental legitimate control of municipalities over their own zoning and, indeed, their destiny.

The following is a summary of the more significant rulings of these cases:

(1) *Every* municipality's land use regulations should provide a realistic opportunity for decent housing for at least some part of its resident poor who now occupy dilapidated housing. The zoning power is no more abused by keeping out the region's poor than by forcing out the resident poor. In other words, each municipality must provide a realistic opportunity for decent housing for its indigenous poor except where they represent a disproportionately large segment of the population as compared with the rest of the region. This is the case in many of our urban areas.

(2) The existence of a municipal obligation to provide a realistic opportunity for a fair share of the region's present and prospective low and moderate income housing need will no longer be determined by

whether or not a municipality is "developing." The obligation extends, instead, to every municipality, any portion of which is designated by the State, through the SDGP as a "growth area." This obligation, imposed as a remedial measure, does not extend to those areas where the SDGP discourages growth — namely, open space, rural areas, prime farmland, conservation areas, limited growth areas, parts of the Pinelands and certain Coastal Zone areas. The SDGP represents conscious determination of the State, through the executive and legislative branches, on how best to plan its future. It appropriately serves as a judicial remedial tool. The obligation to encourage lower income housing, therefore, will hereafter depend on rational long-range land use planning (incorporated into the SDGP) rather than upon the sheer economic forces that have dictated whether a municipality is "developing." Moreover, the fact that a municipality is fully developed does not eliminate this obligation although, obviously, it may affect the extent of the obligation and the timing of its satisfaction. The remedial obligation of municipalities that consist of both "growth areas" and other areas may be reduced, based on many factors, as compared to a municipality completely within a "growth area."

There shall be a heavy burden on any party seeking to vary the foregoing remedial consequences of the SDGP designations.

(3) *Mount Laurel* litigation will ordinarily include proof of the municipality's fair share of low and moderate income housing in terms of the number of units needed immediately, as well as the number needed for a reasonable period of time in the future. "Numberless" resolution of the issue based upon a conclusion that the ordinance provides a realistic opportunity for *some* low and moderate income housing will be insufficient. Plaintiffs, however, will still be able to prove a prima facie case, without proving the precise fair share of the municipality, by proving that the zoning ordinance is substantially affected by restrictive devices, that proof creating a presumption that the ordinance is invalid.

The municipal obligation to provide a realistic opportunity for low and moderate income housing is not satisfied by a good faith attempt. The housing opportunity provided must, in fact, be the substantial equivalent of the fair share.

(4) Any future *Mount Laurel* litigation shall be assigned only to those judges selected by the Chief Justice with the approval of the Supreme Court. The initial group shall consist of three judges, the number to be increased or decreased hereafter by the Chief Justice with the Court's approval. The Chief Justice shall define the area of the State for which each of the three judges is responsible: any *Mount Laurel* case challenging the land use ordinance or a municipality included in that area shall be assigned to that judge. . . .

(5) The municipal obligation to provide a realistic opportunity for the construction of its fair share of low and moderate income housing may require more than the elimination of unnecessary cost-producing requirements and restrictions. Affirmative governmental devices should be used to make that opportunity realistic, including lower-income density bonuses and mandatory set-asides. Furthermore the municipality should cooperate with the developer's attempts to obtain federal subsidies. For instance, where federal subsidies depend on the municipality providing certain municipal tax treatment allowed by state statutes for lower income housing, the municipality should make a good faith effort to provide it. Mobile homes may not be prohibited, unless there is solid proof that sound planning in a particular municipality requires such prohibition.

(6) The lower income regional housing need is comprised of both low and moderate income housing. A municipality's fair share should include both in such proportion as reflects consideration of all relevant factors, including the proportion of low and moderate income housing that make up the regional need.

(7) Providing a realistic opportunity for the construction of least-cost housing will satisfy a municipality's *Mount Laurel* obligation if, and only if, it cannot otherwise be satisfied. In other words, it is only after *all* alternatives have been explored, *all* affirmative devices considered, including, where appropriate, a reasonable period of time to determine whether low and moderate income housing is produced, only when everything has been considered and tried in order to produce a realistic opportunity for low and moderate income housing that least-cost housing will provide an adequate substitute. Least-cost housing means what it says, namely, housing that can be produced at the lowest possible price consistent with minimal standards of health and safety.

(8) Builder's remedies will be afforded to plaintiffs in *Mount Laurel* litigation where appropriate, on a case-by-case basis. Where the plaintiff has acted in good faith, attempted to obtain relief without litigation, and thereafter vindicates the constitutional obligation in *Mount Laurel*-type litigation, ordinarily a builder's remedy will be granted, provided that the proposed project includes an appropriate portion of low and moderate income housing, and provided further that it is located and designed in accordance with sound zoning and planning concepts, including its environmental impact.

(9) The judiciary should manage *Mount Laurel* litigation to dispose of a case in all of its aspects with one trial and one appeal, unless substantial considerations indicate some other course. . . . The trial court will appoint a master to assist in formulating and implementing a proper remedy whenever that course seems desirable.

(10) The *Mount Laurel* obligation to meet the prospective lower income housing need of the region is, by definition, one that is met year after year in the future, throughout the years of the particular projection used in calculating prospective need. In this sense the affirmative obligation to provide a realistic opportunity to construct a fair share of lower income housing is met by a "phase-in" over those years; it need not be provided immediately. Nevertheless, there may be circumstances in which the obligation requires zoning that will provide an immediate opportunity—for instance, zoning to meet the region's present lower income housing need. In some cases, the provision of such a realistic opportunity might result in the immediate construction of lower income housing in such quantity as would radically transform the municipality overnight. Trial courts shall have the discretion, under those circumstances, to moderate the impact of such housing by allowing even the present need to be phased in over a period of years. Such power, however, should be exercised sparingly. The same power may be exercised in the satisfaction of prospective need, equally sparingly, and with special care to assure that such further postponement will not significantly dilute the *Mount Laurel* obligation.

We reassure all concerned that *Mount Laurel* is not designed to sweep away all land use restrictions or leave our open spaces and natural resources prey to speculators. Municipalities consisting largely of conservation, agricultural, or environmentally sensitive areas will not be required to grow because of *Mount Laurel*. No forests or small towns need be paved over and covered with high-rise apartments as a result of today's decision.

As for those municipalities that may have to make adjustments in their lifestyles to provide for their fair share of low and moderate income housing, they should remember that they are not being required to provide more than their *fair* share. No one community need be concerned that it will be radically transformed by a deluge of low and moderate income developments. Nor should any community conclude that its residents will move to other suburbs as a result of this decision, for those "other suburbs" may very well be required to do their part to provide the same housing. Finally, once a community has satisfied its fair share obligation, the *Mount Laurel* doctrine will not restrict other measures, including large-lot and open area zoning, that would maintain its beauty and communal character. [In the *Chester Township* case, one of the five consolidated with the *Mount Laurel II* litigation, the court held that five-acre lot minimums do not invariably violate the *Mount Laurel* doctrine.]

. . .Our scenic and rural areas will remain essentially scenic and rural, and our suburban communities will retain their basic suburban character. But there will be *some* change, as there must be if the constitutional rights of our lower income citizens are ever to be protected. That change will be much less painful for us than the status quo has been for them.

II. Resolution of the Issues . . .

C. CALCULATING FAIR SHARE

The most troublesome issue in *Mount Laurel* litigation is the determination of fair share. It takes the most time, produces the greatest variety of opinions, and engenders doubt as to the meaning and wisdom of *Mount Laurel*. Determination of fair share has required resolution of three separate issues: identifying the relevant region, determining its present and prospective housing needs, and allocating those needs to the municipality or municipalities involved. Each of these issues produces a morass of facts, statistics, projections, theories and opinions sufficient to discourage even the staunchest supporters of *Mount Laurel*. The problem is capable of monopolizing counsel's time for years, overwhelming trial courts and inundating reviewing courts with a record on review of superhuman dimensions. . . .

The restriction of *Mount Laurel* litigation to three judges should simplify and perhaps, in time, substantially eliminate the issues of "region" and "regional need" from litigation. Of the three major issues in this area, their determination is most susceptible to judicial treatment. . . .

The determination of region and regional need by any of these judges shall be presumptively valid as to all municipalities included in the region unless the judge hearing the matter indicates otherwise for reasons stated in his or her decision. Given the importance of these determinations, municipalities not named as parties may attempt to intervene or the court may require their joinder if, all things considered, it is thought advisable that such a municipality be bound by the determination even though such joinder may complicate the litigation. . . .

In short we foresee that within several years . . . the only issue (other than the adequacy of the housing opportunity provided by the ordinance) that may require serious litigation is a particular municipality's fair share of [regional] need. . . .

[On that issue,] we offer some suggestions. Formulas that accord substantial weight to employment opportunities in the municipality, especially new employment accompanied by substantial ratables, shall be favored; formulas that have the effect of tying prospective lower income housing needs to the present proportion of lower income residents to the total population of a municipality shall be disfavored; formulas that have the effect of unreasonably diminishing the share because of a municipality's successful exclusion of lower income housing in the past shall be disfavored.

In determining fair share, the court should decide the proportion between and low and moderate income housing unless there are substantial reasons not to do so. The provisions and devices needed to produce moderate income housing may fall short of those needed for lower. Since there are two fairly distinct income housing needs, an effort must be made to meet both.

The proportion between the two is, inevitably, a matter for expert testimony. It will depend, as does the fair share itself, on a complex mix of factors. . . .

We recognize that the tools for calculating present and prospective need and its allocation are imprecise and further that it is impossible to predict with precision how many units of housing will result from specific ordinances. What is required is the precision of a specific area and specific numbers. They are required not because we think scientific accuracy is possible, but because we believe the requirement is most likely to achieve the goals of *Mount Laurel.* . . .

D. MEETING THE MOUNT LAUREL OBLIGATION

1. Removing Excessive Restrictions and Exactions

In order to meet their *Mount Laurel* obligations, municipalities, at the very least, must remove all municipally created barriers to the construction of their fair share of lower income housing. Thus, to the extent necessary to meet their prospective fair share and provide for their indigenous poor (and, in some cases, a portion of the region's poor), municipalities must remove zoning and subdivision restrictions and exactions that are not necessary to protect health and safety. . . .

It may be difficult for a municipality to determine how to balance the need to reduce the costs of its regulations against the need to adequately protect health and safety, just as it may be difficult for a court to determine when a municipality has reduced these costs enough. There are, however, relatively objective guides that can help both the municipality and the court. Particularly helpful, though in no way conclusive as to what the minimum standards should be in a particular community, are the Department of Housing and Urban Development's Minimum Property Standards and the suggestions as to minimum zoning and subdivision standards made by the Rutgers Center for Urban Policy Research in [S. Seidel, Housing Costs and Government Regulations (1978)]. With these and other such guides, plus specific evidence submitted by the parties, we believe that a court can determine whether municipally-imposed housing costs have been sufficiently reduced.

Once a municipality has revised its land use regulations and taken other steps affirmatively to provide a realistic opportunity for the construction of its fair share of lower income housing, the *Mount Laurel* doctrine requires it to do no more. For instance, a municipality having thus complied, the fact that its land use regulations contain restrictive provisions incompatible with lower income housing, such as bedroom restrictions, large lot zoning, prohibition against mobile homes, and the like, does not render those provisions invalid under *Mount Laurel*. Obviously, if they are otherwise invalid—for instance if they bear no reasonable relationship to any legitimate governmental goal—they may be declared void on those other grounds. But they are not void because of *Mount Laurel* under those circumstances. *Mount Laurel* is not an indiscriminate broom designed to sweep away all distinctions in the use of land. Municipalities may continue to reserve areas for upper income housing, may continue to require certain community amenities in certain areas, may continue to zone with some regard to their fiscal obligations: they may do all of this, provided that they have otherwise complied with their *Mount Laurel* obligations.

2. Using Affirmative Measures

. . . Satisfaction of the *Mount Laurel* doctrine cannot depend on the inclination of developers to help the poor. It has to depend on affirmative inducements to make the opportunity real. . . .

Therefore, unless removal of restrictive barriers will, without more, afford a realistic opportunity for the construction of the municipality's fair share of the region's lower income housing need, affirmative measures will be required.

There are two basic types of affirmative measures that a municipality can use to make the opportunity for lower income housing realistic: (1) encouraging or requiring the use of available state or federal housing subsidies, and (2) providing incentives for or requiring private developers to set aside a portion of their developments for lower income housing. Which, if either, of these devices will be necessary in any particular municipality to assure compliance with the constitutional mandate will be initially up to the municipality itself. Where necessary, the trial court overseeing compliance may require their use. We note again that least-cost housing will not ordinarily satisfy a municipality's fair share obligation to provide low and moderate income housing unless and until it has attempted the inclusionary devices outlined below or otherwise has proven the futility of the attempt.

a. Subsidies

Because the kinds of lower income housing subsidies available are subject to change—and have in fact changed often—it is more important to establish the municipality's general *Mount Laurel* obligation concerning subsidies than its required role as to any particular existing subsidy. The importance of defining that obligation may depend at any particular time on the then extent and impact of available subsidies; if anything, the quantity of housing subsidies varies even more than the kind. For example, the amount of lower income housing subsidies now available is substantially less than several years ago, and there is no indication that subsidies for lower income housing construction are likely to increase in the near future. They are, nevertheless, apparently a permanent part of the housing scene; the long-term importance of defining the municipality's *Mount Laurel* obligation in relation to such subsidies is that the construction of lower income housing is practically impossible without some kind of governmental subsidy. . . .

On occasion, what is needed to obtain a subsidy may be as simple as a "resolution of need" stating that "there is a need for moderate income housing" in the municipality. N.J.S.A. 55:14J 6(b). In addition to the "resolution of need," the most important federal program for providing lower income housing subsidies (the section 8 low and moderate income housing program; 42 U.S.C. §1437f (1982 Supp.)) requires in New Jersey, as a practical matter, that the municipality grant tax abatements to developers. See N.J.S.A. 55:14J-8(f).

. . .The trial court in a *Mount Laurel* case, therefore, shall have the power to require a municipality to cooperate in good faith with a developer's attempt to obtain a subsidy and to require that a tax abatement be granted for that purpose pursuant to applicable New Jersey statutes where that abatement does not conflict with other municipal interests of greater importance.

b. Inclusionary Zoning Devices

There are several inclusionary zoning techniques that municipalities must use if they cannot otherwise assure the construction of their fair share or lower income housing. Although we will discuss some of them here, we in no way intend our list to be exhaustive; municipalities and trial courts are encouraged to create other devices and methods for meeting fair share obligations.[28]

The most commonly used inclusionary zoning techniques are incentive zoning and mandatory set-asides. The former involves offering economic incentives to a developer through the relaxation of various restrictions of an ordinance (typically density limits) in exchange for the construction of certain amounts of low and moderate income units. The latter, a mandatory set-aside, is basically a requirement that developers include a minimum amount of lower income housing in their projects.

28. For useful discussions of how inclusionary techniques have been utilized [see] Fox & Davis, "Density Bonus Zoning to Provide Low and Moderate Cost Housing," 3 Hastings Const. L.Q. 1015 (1977); Kleven, "Inclusionary Ordinances—Policy and Legal Issues in Requiring Private Developers to Build Low Cost Housing," 21 U.C.L.A.L. Rev. 1432 (1974); H. Franklin, D. Falk, A. Levin, In-Zoning: A Guide for Policy Makers on Inclusionary Land Use Programs (1974).

(i) Incentive Zoning

Incentive zoning is usually accomplished either through a sliding scale density bonus that increases the permitted density as the amount of lower income housing provided is increased, or through a set bonus for participation in a lower income housing program. See Fox & Davis, 3 Hastings Const. L.Q. 1015, 1060-62 (1977).

Incentive zoning leaves a developer free to build only upper income housing if it so chooses. Fox and Davis, in their survey of municipalities using inclusionary devices, found that while developers sometimes profited through density bonuses, they were usually reluctant to cooperate with incentive zoning programs; and that therefore those municipalities that relied exclusively on such programs were not very successful in actually providing lower income housing. Id. at 1067.

Sole reliance on "incentive" techniques (or, indeed, reliance exclusively on any one affirmative device) may prove in a particular case to be insufficient to achieve compliance with the constitutional mandate.

(ii) Mandatory Set-Asides

A more effective inclusionary device that municipalities must use if they cannot otherwise meet their fair share obligations is the mandatory set-aside.[30] According to the Department of Community Affairs, as of 1976 there were six municipalities in New Jersey with mandatory set-aside programs, which varied from a requirement that 5 percent of developments in a certain zone be composed of low and moderate income units (Cherry Hill, Camden County) to a requirement that between 15 and 25 percent of all PUDs be reserved for low and moderate income housing (East Windsor, Mercer County). Apparently, judging from the Handbook itself and from responses to our inquiries at oral argument, lower income housing is in fact being built pursuant to these mandatory requirements.

The use of mandatory set-asides is not without its problems: dealing with the scarcity of federal subsidies, maintaining the rent or sale price of lower income units at lower income levels over time, and assuring developers an adequate return on their investments. Fox and Davis found that the scarcity of federal subsidies has greatly undermined the effec-

---

30. Mandatory set-asides do not give rise to the legal issues treated in Property Owners Ass'n of N. Bergen v. Twp. of N. Bergen, 74 N.J. 327, 378 A.2d 25 (1977). We held in that case that rent control ordinances that exempted units occupied by senior citizens from future rent increases were confiscatory as to the landlord. . . . [T]he builder who undertakes a project that includes a mandatory set-aside voluntarily assumes the financial burden, if there is any, of that condition. There may very well be no "subsidy" in the sense of either the landlord or other tenants bearing some burden for the benefit of the lower income units: those units may be priced low not because someone else is subsidizing the price, but because of realistic considerations of cost, amenities, and therefore underlying values.

tiveness of mandatory set-asides where they are triggered only when a developer is able to obtain such subsidies. Fox & Davis, supra, 3 Hastings Const. L.Q. at 1065-66. Where practical, a municipality should use mandatory set-asides even where subsidies are not available.[32]

As several commentators have noted, the problem of keeping lower income units available for lower income people over time can be a difficult one. Because a mandatory set-aside program usually requires a developer to sell or rent units at below their full value so that the units can be affordable to lower income people, the owner of the development of the initial tenant or purchaser of the unit bay be induced to re-rent or re-sell the unit at its full value.

This problem, which municipalities *must* address in order to assure that they continue to meet their fair share obligations, can be dealt with in two ways. First, the developer can meet its mandatory quota of lower income units with lower cost housing, such as mobile homes or "no-frills" apartments, which may be affordable by lower income families at close to the units' market value. The other, apparently more common, approach for dealing with the re-sale or re-rent problem is for the municipality to require that re-sale or re-rent prices be kept at lower income levels. For example, the Cherry Hill ordinance requires that there be "regulations which reasonably assure that the dwelling units be occupied by [lower income persons]." . . .

In addition to the mechanisms we have just described, municipalities and trial courts must consider such other affirmative devices as zoning substantial areas for mobile homes and for other types of low cost housing and establishing maximum square footage zones, i.e., zones where developers cannot build units with *more* than a certain footage or build anything other than lower income housing or housing that includes a specified portion of lower income housing. In some cases, a realistic opportunity to provide the municipality's fair share may require over-zoning, i.e., zoning to allow for *more* than the fair share if it is likely, as it usually will actually result in such housing.

Although several of the defendants concede that simply removing restrictions and exactions is unlikely to result in the construction of lower income housing, they maintain that requiring the municipality to use affirmative measures is beyond the scope of the courts' authority. We disagree. . . .

The specific contentions are that inclusionary measures amount to a

32. Where set-asides are used, courts, municipalities, and developers should attempt to assure that lower income units are integrated into larger developments in a manner that both provides adequate access and services for the lower income residents and at the same time protects as much as possible the value and integrity of the project as a whole. For a helpful discussion of how this can be done see O. Newman, Community of Interest (1980).

taking without just compensation and an impermissible socio-economic use of the zoning power, one not substantially related to the use of land. Reliance is placed to some extent on Board of Supervisors v. DeGroff Enterprises, Inc., 214 Va. 235, 198 S.E.2d 600 (1973), to that effect. We disagree with that decision. . . . We hold that where the *Mount Laurel* obligation cannot be satisfied by removal of restrictive barriers, inclusionary devices such as density bonuses and mandatory set asides keyed to the construction of lower income housing, are constitutional and within the zoning power of a municipality. . . .

We find the distinction between the exercise of the zoning power that is "directly tied to the physical use of the property," *Madison*, 72 N.J. at 517, 371 A.2d 1192, and its exercise tied to the income level of those who use the property artificial in connection with the *Mount Laurel* obligation, although it obviously troubled us in *Madison*. The prohibition of this kind of affirmative device seems unfair when we have for so long allowed large lot single family residence districts, a form of zoning keyed, in effect, to income levels. The constitutional obligation itself is not to build three bedroom units, or single family residences on very small lots, or high-rise multifamily apartments, but rather to provide through the zoning ordinance a realistic opportunity to construct *lower income housing*. All of the physical uses are simply a means to this end. We see no reason why the municipality cannot exercise its zoning power to achieve that end directly rather than through a mass of detailed regulations governing the "physical use" of land, the sole purpose of which is to provide housing within the reach of lower income families. We know of no governmental purpose relating to zoning that is served by requiring a municipality to ingeniously design detailed land use regulations, purporting to be "directly tied to the physical use of the property," but actually aimed at accommodating lower income families, while not allowing it directly to require developers to construct lower income units. Indirection of this kind has no more virtue where its goal is to achieve that which is permitted—indeed, constitutionally mandated—than it has in achieving that which is prohibited.

3. Zoning for Mobile Homes

As the cost of ordinary housing skyrockets for purchasers and renters, mobile homes become increasingly important as a source of low cost housing. . . . Therefore, subject to the qualifications noted hereafter, we rule that municipalities that cannot otherwise meet their fair share obligations must provide zoning for low-cost mobile homes as an affirmative device in their zoning ordinances.

Townships such as Mount Laurel that now ban mobile homes do so in reliance upon Vickers v. Gloucester, 37 N.J. 232, 181 A.2d (1962), in which this Court upheld such bans. *Vickers*, however, explicitly recognized that changed circumstances could require a different result. *Id.* at 250, 181 A.2d 129. We find that such changed circumstances now exist. As Judge Wood found in *Mount Laurel II*, mobile homes have since 1962 become "structurally sound [and] attractive in appearance." 161 N.J. Super. at 357, 391 A.2d 935. Further, since 1974, the safety and soundness of mobile homes have been regulated by the National Mobile Home Construction and Safety Standards Act, 42 U.S.C. 5401 (1974). *Vickers*, therefore, is overruled; absolute bans of mobile homes are no longer permissible on the grounds stated in that case. . . .

Lest we be misunderstood, we do *not* hold that every municipality must allow the use of mobile homes as an affirmative device to meet its *Mount Laurel* obligation, or that any ordinance that totally excludes mobile homes is per se invalid. Insofar as the *Mount Laurel* doctrine is concerned, whether mobile homes must be permitted as an affirmative device will depend upon the overall effectiveness of the municipality's attempts to comply: if compliance can be just as effectively assured without allowing mobile homes, *Mount Laurel* does not command them; if not, then assuming a suitable site is available, they must be allowed. . . .

4. Providing "Least Cost" Housing

. . . [In most cases,] middle income housing will not satisfy the *Mount Laurel* obligation. This is so despite claims by some defendant-municipalities that the provision of such middle income housing will allow less expensive housing to "filter down" to lower income families. The problem with this theory is that the housing that has been built and is now being built in suburbs such as Mount Laurel is rapidly *appreciating* in value so that none of *it* will "filter down" to poor people. Instead, if the only housing constructed in municipalities like Mount Laurel continues to be middle and upper income, the only "filter down" effect that will occur will be that housing on the fringes of our inner cities will "filter down" to the poor as more of the middle class leave for the suburbs, thereby exacerbating the economic segregation of our cities and suburbs. See A. Downs, [Opening up the Suburbs 9-12 (1973)]. Only if municipalities like Mount Laurel begin now to build lower income or least cost housing will some part of *their* housing stock ever "filter down" to New Jersey's poorer families.

E. JUDICIAL REMEDIES . . .

1. Builder's Remedy

Builder's remedies have been one of many controversial aspects of the *Mount Laurel* doctrine. Plaintiffs, particularly plaintiff-developers, maintain that these remedies are (i) essential to maintain a significant level of *Mount Laurel* litigation, and the only effective method to date of enforcing compliance; (ii) required by principles of fairness to compensate developers who have invested substantial time and resources in pursuing such litigation; and (iii) the most likely means of ensuring that lower income housing is actually built. . . .

. . . We hold that where a developer succeeds in *Mount Laurel* litigation and proposes a project providing a substantial amount of lower income housing,[37] a builder's remedy should be granted unless the municipality establishes that because of environmental or other substantial planning concerns, the plaintiff's proposed project is clearly contrary to sound land use planning. We emphasize that the builder's remedy should not be denied solely because the municipality prefers some other location for lower income housing, even if it is in fact a better site. Nor is it essential that considerable funds be invested or that the litigation be intensive. . . .

. . .Trial courts should guard the public interest carefully to be sure that plaintiff-developers do not abuse the *Mount Laurel* doctrine. Where builder's remedies are awarded, the remedy should be carefully conditioned to assure that in fact the plaintiff-developer *constructs* a substantial amount of lower income housing. Various devices can be used for that purpose, including prohibiting construction of more than a certain percentage of the non-lower income housing until a certain amount of the lower income housing is completed.

2. *Revision of the Zoning Ordinance: the Master*

If the trial court determines that a municipality's zoning ordinance does not satisfy its *Mount Laurel* obligation, it shall order the defendant to revise it. Unless it is clear that the requisite realistic opportunity can be otherwise provided, the trial court should direct the municipality to incorporate in that new ordinance the affirmative devices discussed above most likely to lead to the construction of lower income housing. The trial court shall order the revision to be completed within 90 days of its original judgment against the municipality. For good cause shown, a municipality may be granted an extension of that time period.

To facilitate this revision, the trial court may appoint a special master to assist municipal officials in developing constitutional zoning and land use regulations. . . .

---

37. What is "substantial" in a particular case will be for the trial court to decide. The court should consider such factors as the size of the plaintiff's proposed project, the percentage of the project to be devoted to lower income housing (20 percent appears to us to be a reasonable minimum), what proportion of the defendant municipality's fair share allocation would be provided by the project, and the extent to which the remaining housing in the project can be categorized as "least cost." . . .

III. Resolution of the Cases

A. MOUNT LAUREL II

1. The 1976 Revised Zoning Ordinance . . .

. . . Instead of attempting to amend [its] specific deficiencies, Mount Laurel simply added three new zones to meet its fair share obligation, presumably assuming that such action would conform to the underlying intent of our ruling.

We find that the amended ordinance falls far short of what was required, that it neither corrects the particular deficiencies of the prior ordinance nor otherwise affirmatively provides a realistic opportunity for Mount Laurel's fair share of lower income housing. It is little more than a smoke screen that attempts to hide the Township's persistent intention to exclude housing for the poor. . . .

Nothing has really changed since the date of our first opinion, either in Mount Laurel or in its land use regulations. The record indicates that the Township continues to thrive with added industry, some new businesses, and continued growth of middle, upper middle, and upper income housing.[48] As far as lower income housing is concerned, from the date of that opinion to today (as far as the record before us shows) no one has yet constructed one unit of lower income housing—nor has anyone even tried to.[49] Mount Laurel's lower income housing effort has been either a total failure or a total success—depending on its intention.

We realize that given today's economy, especially as it affects housing, the failure of developers to build lower income housing does not necessarily prove that a town's zoning ordinances are unduly restrictive. One might have expected, however, that in the eight years that have elapsed since our decision, Mount Laurel would have something to show other than this utter cipher—that is, unless one looked at the amended ordinance.

48. Between 1970 and 1977, Mount Laurel added 1,300,000 square feet to its industrial floor space and 700,000 square feet to its office space. Between 1970 and 1980, 2,784 new housing units were built in Mount Laurel, *all* of them under the restrictive conditions that this Court held in *Mount Laurel I* could not produce lower income housing. The total population of Mount Laurel has increased tremendously, from 11,221 in 1970 to 17,614 in 1980, a 57 percent increase during a decade when the total population of the state increased by less than 5 percent and the total population of Burlington Country increased by only 12 percent.

49. There has been a continuing application for construction of mobile homes, but no applications of any kind other than this and certainly none pursuant to the new ordinance. If this continues, and no new lower income housing is built in Mount Laurel to the year 2000, then by that year the percentage of lower income families in the Township will have dropped to 7.7 percent, from 25.5 percent in 1970 and 41.4 percent in 1960. The percentage of lower income families in the Burlington, Gloucester, Camden regions has been, and will, it is assumed, continue to be through 2000, roughly 40 percent.

Mount Laurel's notion of providing a realistic opportunity to build lower income housing has led to the rezoning of less than one-fourth of one percent of its land (about 20 out of 14,700 acres). This minuscule acreage consists of three zones, R-5, -6, and -7, each one owned by a different individual (apparently not residential developers in the cases of R-5 and R-6) who may very well elect never to take "advantage" of the alleged opportunity to build lower income housing.

The zone designated R-5, consisting of 13 acres, allows the construction of townhouses and garden apartments with a maximum of 10 units per acre. It is owned by an industrial developer, is totally surrounded by industrially zoned land, virtually isolated from residential uses, has no present access to other parts of the community, no water or sewer connections nearby, is in the path of a proposed high speed railroad line, and is subject to possible flooding. It would be hard to find (other than R-6) a less suitable parcel for lower income or indeed any kind of housing. Furthermore, as one of plaintiff's experts pointed out, no experienced industrial developer would allow this parcel to become a pocket of protesting residents objecting to his planned industrial uses surrounding them.

The R-6 zone is for detached single family residences on 6,000 square foot lots, which is an effort to comply with the *Mount Laurel I* requirement that there be some residential development permitted on "very small lots." *Mount Laurel I*, 67 N.J. at 187, 336 A.2d 713. It includes, however, only 7.45 acres. It has an extremely serious drainage problem, lying so low compared to the surrounding area that it would cost $10,000 per acre, according to plaintiffs' experts, to raise it so as to minimize that problem. In addition, there are no water or sewer connections nearby. There are cost generating requirements concerning parking, street widths, and others, that will subsequently affect the price of homes, if they are ever to be built. The size of the zone itself is so small that it is highly unlikely that any developer would consider building low and even moderate income housing there, for the necessary economies of scale could never be achieved. Defendant's planner estimated that only 30 units could be built in this zone, and conceded that under no circumstances would *anything* be built for five to six years since there would be no sewer or water access available until then. Lower income housing on this tract is a phantom.

The R-7 zone is somewhat more complex. It does not consist of any specific land but rather is defined as being a maximum of 10 percent of the units to be built in Section VII of an existing approved PUD known as Larchmont. . . .

R-7 is really not a zone at all, but rather a waiver by Mount Laurel of certain restrictions and requirements that would otherwise have been imposed on the Larchmont Section VII units. . . .

Unless something changes radically, it is certain that no builder will construct lower income housing in R-7. There is no evidence that the present developer has any intention to do so, especially in light of the benefits available to him when he builds upper and middle income housing in the R-7 zone. . . .

[Although Mount Laurel asserted that these zones satisfied its fair share obligation, Wilentz, C.J., found the township's analysis of its obligation to be "blatantly self-serving." The Delaware Valley Regional Planning Commission estimated Burlington County's need for lower income housing through the year 2000 at 22,900 dwelling units.] The sole factor used by Mount Laurel's planners in allocating this regional need . . . was "developable land." Its studies indicated that Mount Laurel had 5,963 acres of such land, and Burlington County 263,282 acres, and concluded that this 2.25 percent ratio, when applied to the county need of 22,900 units through the year 2000, meant that Mount Laurel's fair share was 515 units. Vacant developable land, at this point, may be regarded as land not legally committed to other uses. The formula, therefore, assigns the same share to 100 acres located 100 miles from Camden, totally unsuitable for lower income housing and totally devoid of any demand for such use, as it does to 100 acres 10 miles from the center of Camden, near shopping centers, transportation facilities, and highly suited for lower income housing and subject to intensive demand for such use. In fact Mount Laurel's formula equates the highly desirable vacant acreage of Mount Laurel with that of the Pine Barrens. . . .

In sum, we find that Mount Laurel's revised zoning ordinance fails completely to comply with the mandate of *Mount Laurel I*. . . .

We therefore remand this matter to the trial court for further proceedings to determine Mount Laurel's fair share, and upon such determination to require further actions by the municipality to assure the expeditious revision of Mount Laurel's land use regulations (and other actions) all in accordance with this opinion. While we have held that the bona fides of Mount Laurel is irrelevant in determining its compliance with the underlying constitutional obligation, it is not irrelevant in determining the remedy adopted herein. Where, as here, there is evidence of lack of municipal good faith and/or interminable delay, trial courts must closely supervise orders designed to compel compliance. Here that supervision must include the appointment of a master.

2. The Builder's Remedy

Davis Enterprises was permitted to intervene as plaintiff in this case after *Mount Laurel I* was decided. Davis proposed a 535 unit, 107 acre mobile home park for the Township. Davis committed itself to securing federal Section 8 subsidies for 20 percent of the units. Mount Laurel originally rejected the Davis project because its zoning ordinance barred all mobile homes. Although this rationale for excluding Davis is no longer tenable after our overturning of *Vickers*, we must still decide whether Davis is entitled to the builder's remedy it seeks.

The trial court granted the builder's remedy, ordering the Mount Laurel Planning Board to consider the Davis application and review it in a "manner consistent with the least-cost housing principles enunciated in Oakwood v. Madison," 161 N.J. Super. at 359, 391 A.2d 935. We affirm the grant of a builder's remedy. It is clearly appropriate in this case under the new standard enunciated in this opinion. First, the Davis project *will* provide lower income housing for Mount Laurel. Beside the fact that mobile homes are generally much less costly than site-built housing, the trial court's decision requires that Davis construct *at least* 20 percent of its units for lower income persons. In addition, the site chosen by Davis is plainly suited for mobile home development and Mount Laurel has presented no real evidence to the contrary. Finally, we feel that after ten years of litigation it is time that *something* be built for the resident and non-resident lower income plaintiffs in this case who have borne the brunt of Mount Laurel's unconstitutional policy of exclusion.

. . . On December 2, 1980, the trial court . . . ordered Mount Laurel to grant Davis a building permit on condition that Davis apply to HUD for Section 8 subsidies for 20 percent of its units. . . . We now affirm the December 2, 1980, order with the added condition that if Davis is not able to obtain the Section 8 subsidies being sought, the developer must use whatever other means are available to make certain that *at least* 20 percent of the units built are affordable by lower income households, with *at least* half of these being affordable by low income households. . . .

[Unanimous.]

NOTE ON MOUNT LAUREL II

1. *The emphasis on* new *housing for low- and moderate-income families*. In its *Madison* decision in 1977 (supra Casebook p.813), the New Jersey Supreme Court emphasized the importance of removing barriers to the construction of least-cost, unsubsidized housing units. It reasoned then that the production of these new least-cost units, even if they were too expensive for low- and moderate-income families to afford, would help those families by freeing up units in the *used* stock of housing. *Mount Laurel II*, by contrast, emphasized affirmative municipal duties to ensure the production of *new* housing units affordable by low- and moderate-income families.

If homebuilders would lose money on inclusionary units, would *Mount Laurel II* dull their incentives to build housing? In what situations might the entire cost of an inclusionary program be passed backward to owners of undeveloped land? Cf. supra Casebook pp. 735-737.

Was Wilentz, C.J., right to focus on the composition of the flow of new housing units, as opposed to the composition of the used stock of housing? Some simple calculations can sharpen the question. In recent years the annual production of new housing units in New Jersey has equaled about 2 percent of the units in the state's total housing stock. Assume that this level of production would not be affected by *Mount Laurel II* and that half of this production would be subjected to a 20 percent inclusionary requirement. Under these conditions low- and moderate-income families would receive each year housing units equal in number to 0.2 percent of the current New Jersey housing stock. Low- and moderate-income households — that is, households with up to 120 percent of the state's median household income — constitute roughly 60 percent of New Jersey's population. If these numbers are accurate, could the inclusionary component of *Mount Laurel II* be expected to make much of a contribution to the satisfaction of the housing demands of low- and moderate-income households?

What assumptions about the operation of housing markets might lead one to conclude that *Mount Laurel II* would on balance diminish the housing opportunities of the targeted families? What assumptions about the operation of housing markets led Wilentz, C.J., to anticipate that *Mount Laurel II* would help those families? Two articles that attempt to analyze the net effects of inclusionary housing programs are cited infra Supplement p. 177 See also Weicher, Private Production: Has the Rising Tide Lifted All Boats?, in Housing America's Poor 45 (P. Salins ed. 1987). According to Weicher, most evidence suggests that the production of new housing for the well-to-do does more to improve the housing opportunities of the poor than does the production of subsidized housing. A more technical version is Weicher & Thibodeau, Filtering and Housing Markets: An Empirical Analysis, 23 J. Urb. Econ. 21 (1988).

2. Mount Laurel III? Assume that the Township of Mount Laurel, acting under the scrutiny of a master and a trial court, were to adopt an ordinance requiring all housing developers to provide 50 percent of their units below cost to low- and moderate-income families. Assume further that this ordinance would effectively terminate *all* residential development within the Township, in part because developers anticipated that either the Township or the state would soon abandon its inclusionary policies. Would the Township's de facto no-growth policy violate *Mount Laurel II*?

3. *The legislative response.* In 1985 the New Jersey law of exclusionary

zoning became even more idiosyncratic. After lengthy debate the state legislature responded to *Mount Laurel II* by enacting a Fair Housing Act, N.J. Stat. Ann. §§52:27D-301 to :27D-329 (West 1986). The Act transfers to a new administrative agency, the Council on Affordable Housing, many functions formerly performed by the courts. The Council is given responsibility both for determining each municipality's "fair share," and also for hearing cases challenging compliance with municipal obligations. The Act authorizes a court to set aside a Council decision only if "clear and convincing evidence" so requires. The Act also entitles a municipality to transfer up to 50 percent of its fair-share obligations to a receiving municipality, along with a negotiated amount of compensation.

In Hills Dev. Co. v. Township of Bernards, 103 N.J. 1, 510 A.2d 621 (1986), the Supreme Court of New Jersey unanimously held that the provisions of the Fair Housing Act were consistent with the constitutional obligations it had announced in the two *Mount Laurel* decisions. The rules of the Council on Affordable Housing, which now govern the details of a New Jersey municipality's housing obligations, strongly encourage communities to grant density bonuses to builders willing to set aside 20 percent of their units for low- and moderate-income families. See Update on Mount Laurel, Zoning News, Nov. 1986, p.2.

By enabling a suburb to transfer up to half of its obligations to a receiving municipality, most likely a poor city, the Act has turned the *Mount Laurel* doctrine into a vehicle for inner-city revival. Newark, for example, has used funds obtained from suburbs to help low- and moderate-income families buy 15 percent of the units in a new 1,100-unit housing development in the city's Central Ward, the area most devastated in the city's 1967 riots. See N.Y. Times, Dec. 7, 1987, p.16, col. 1. On the issue of whether it is desirable to allow suburbs to transfer fair-share obligations, compare Note, Zoning for the Regional Welfare, 89 Yale L.J. 748 (1980), with McDougall, Regional Contribution Agreements: Compensation for Exclusionary Zoning, 60 Temple L.Q. 665 (1987).

Page 835.   Before "C. Municipal Obligations . . . ," add:

INTRODUCTORY NOTE ON DEVELOPMENTS IN EXCLUSIONARY ZONING LAW

The zigzagging of New Jersey exclusionary zoning law, although perhaps more pronounced than that of other states, is hardly unique. Most state supreme courts that have tackled the issue seem to have found it difficult to develop a stable set of satisfactory rules.

The materials that follow cover major developments in the law of exclusionary zoning in states other than New Jersey during the 1980-1987 period. The first principal case involves the validity of an Illinois county's use of the goal of preserving prime agricultural land as a justification for giant-lot zoning. The remaining materials provide a more general update of legal developments, particularly in Pennsylvania, New York, Michigan, and California—states whose exclusionary zoning law as of mid-1980 was surveyed supra at Casebook pp. 823-826.

WILSON v. COUNTY OF McHENRY

92 Ill. App. 3d 997, 416 N.E.2d 426 (1981)

SEIDENFELD, Presiding Justice: . . .

. . . The county zoning ordinance was amended on November 1, 1979, to provide a 160 acre lot minimum in agricultural zones which were set forth pursuant to the land use plan for McHenry County characterized as the year 2000 plan. The plan was adopted by the McHenry County Board on October 4, 1979, and recited in substance that it was an attempt to channel development toward existing urban centers; particularly recognizing prime agricultural land as a primary, finite material resource to be preserved. The plan also recognized, however, that certain prime agricultural land closer to existing municipalities should be designated for residential use in order to preserve larger, rural tracts of prime agricultural soils. . . .

The Wilson property is a 76 acre parcel located about one-half mile north of the intersection of Greenwood Road and State Route 120 in Greenwood Township, which is currently zoned A-1 Agricultural. The Wilsons sought to rezone to an E-1 Estate classification so that their proposed one acre residential development would be permissible. The county denied the petition and plaintiffs sought relief in the Circuit Court. There was evidence at trial that when the Wilsons purchased the property it was zoned F-Farming under the McHenry County Zoning Ordinance then in effect which provided for a one and one-eighth acre minimum residential lot size. In 1974 the ordinance was amended, raising the minimum lot size to five acres. The present ordinance, adopted on November 1, 1979, requires residential lot sizes of not less than one hundred sixty acres in the zone designated as agricultural. . . .

. . . The trial judge in his final order found that the plaintiffs had failed to establish by a preponderance of the evidence that the proposed use of the subject property is reasonable. . . .

From the testimony it is clear that the predominant zoning in the area is A-1 Agriculture and that the predominant land use is also agricultural. There were other land uses within the two square mile area of the subject property; but the mere fact that exceptions exist to the predominant character of an area does not require a finding that zoning which would preserve the predominant classification is in error. (See, Jackson v. County of DuPage, 10 Ill. App. 3d at 500, 294 N.E.2d 773.) The nonagricultural uses either existed prior to the recent zoning amendments, were more proximate to urban centers and required services, or were distinguishable because of physical characteristics making them unsuitable for farming.

There is testimony in the record as to the loss in value to the owners if the agricultural zoning is applied. There was testimony on behalf of the plaintiffs that the subject property as presently zoned is of a value of less than $4,000 per acre; but that if zoned E-1, allowing for one acre residential development, the value would be $18,000 to $20,000 per lot. There is no testimony in the record as to the cost of development, however. The county does not essentially dispute the valuation testimony offered by the plaintiffs and concedes that the property is worth considerably more for subdivision purposes. A concededly lower value of the property for agricultural use alone is insufficient, however, to overcome the presumption of the validity of the ordinance. (Reeve v. Village of Glenview, 29 Ill. 2d 611, 616, 195 N.E.2d 188 (1963).) . . .

The consideration of the public welfare does not support plaintiffs' argument on the record before us. The plaintiffs do not challenge the constitutionality of the zoning ordinance except as applied. They agree that the preservation of prime farm land is a valid zoning objective but argue, generally, that the county has placed too much of its territory in that category; particularly, that the subject property is not prime farm land which should be preserved. While the plaintiffs produced testimony in support of their argument there was also testimony on behalf of the county which was conflicting.

There was testimony by the coordinator of agricultural programs at McHenry County College that 87% of the property was prime agricultural land under United States Department of Agriculture Standards. . . . There was also testimony that the highest and best use of the land was for agriculture.

While there was testimony that the farm had not been an economic success there was also testimony that under "high level" management the farm would produce between 115-125 bushels per acre rather than the approximate 100 bushels per acre the owners claimed they were producing; that the average yield for farm land in McHenry County was 104 bushels per acre; and that although the small size of the farm would have a bearing on its being a good economic unit, it could be combined with other property and more effectively managed.

Another significant aspect in the case is the county's adoption of a comprehensive plan for the area. One commentator has stated with respect to agricultural zoning: "In determining the validity of a particular zoning ordinance, the court will examine whether there exists a reasonable comprehensive plan for the area." (Rohan, "Zoning and Land Use Controls," Vol. 3, Sec. 19.02(2), pp. 19-13.) The adoption of a comprehensive plan which incorporates valid zoning goals increases the likelihood that the zoning of a particular parcel in conformity therewith is not arbitrary or unrelated to the public interest. . . .

Plaintiffs rely on Smeja v. County of Boone, 34 Ill. App. 3d 628, 339 N.E.2d 452 (1975) and Pettee v. County of DeKalb, 60 Ill. App. 3d 304, 376 N.E.2d 720 (1978), where agricultural zoning was held arbitrary in relation to the properties in question. However, those cases present a very different circumstance. In *Smeja*, the property was a 50 acre tract, 35 acres wooded and 15 acres "sub-marginal" land. Thus preserving the tract as farm land was found to bear no relation to the health, safety, morals, comfort or general welfare. In *Pettee*, the 80 acre tract had severe drainage problems on 25 acres and the court found that it was at best marginal farm land. Although concluding that farm land could be characterized as an essential natural resource, the benefit to the public of the marginal farm land was minimal whereas the hardship imposed upon the plaintiff was substantial.

On the record before use we conclude that the plaintiffs have neither overcome the presumption of the validity of the legislative judgment nor satisfied their burden of proving by clear and convincing evidence that the ordinance, as applied, is arbitrary, unreasonable, and without substantial relation to the public health, welfare and safety. . . .

Affirmed.

APPEAL OF M.A. KRAVITZ

501 Pa. 200, 460 A.2d 1075 (1983)

ZAPPALA, Justice.

This is an appeal from a decision of the Commonwealth Court, reversing the decision of the Court of Common Pleas of Bucks County, which had affirmed the Board of Supervisors of Wrightstown Township in its finding that the Township Zoning Ordinance of 1971 was not exclusionary. The appellee, M. A. Kravitz Co., Inc., petitioned the Board on May 7, 1976 for a curative amendment to the Zoning Ordinance and approval of a proposed townhouse development on a 96 acre parcel of land which it owned. The land is located in an area zoned R-2 Residential, permitting only single-family dwellings. The basis for Kravitz's substantive challenge was the Ordinance's alleged unconstitutional exclusion of townhouses. . . .

. . . In finding the Wrightstown Township Zoning Ordinance to be unconstitutionally exclusionary, the Commonwealth Court followed a line of its own decisions, beginning with Camp Hill Development Co. v. Zoning Board of Adjustment, Borough of Dauphin, 13 Pa. Cmwlth. 519, 319 A.2d 197 (1974). . . . Treating townhouses as "an accepted form of development entitled . . . to the same recognition accorded by *Girsh* to apartments," *Camp Hill*, 13 Pa. Cmwlth. at 525, 319 A.2d at 200, the Commonwealth Court developed the rule that an ordinance which prohibits or unreasonably fails to provide for townhouses is unconstitutional. In the present case, the court reviewed the Ordinance and determined that the only district which conceivably allows for more than single-family detached residential uses, "cannot be reasonably construed to incorporate the separate and distinctly provided for single-family attached townhouse use." 53 Pa. Cmwlth. at 627, 419 A.2d at 230. Concluding that the Ordinance "fails to provide a home for [the] legitimate and necessary development [of townhouses]", 53 Pa. Cmwlth. at 628, 419 A.2d at 230, the court declared the Ordinance unconstitutional and directed approval of the proposed development. We reverse.

Central to the Commonwealth Court's decision in *Camp Hill* and, consequently, in this case, is the assumption that townhouses, being a legitimate and accepted form of residential use, are entitled to the same protection afforded to apartments in *Girsh*. This assumption ignores significant facts which bore on our decision in *Girsh* and thus, while tracing the rule of that case, it outruns the reasoning which supports that rule. . . .

. . . [T]he ordinance challenged in *Girsh* made no provision for any form of residence other than single-family units. The developer sought to build multi-unit high rise apartments, but the zoning ordinance did not permit any form of multiple dwelling. Indeed, Girsh argued that he used the term "apartments" to include all forms of multiple dwellings. (Brief of Appellant Joseph Girsh, p.11). The importance of these observations becomes apparent in light of the rationale which supported our holding. . . .

. . . A fair reading of *Girsh* makes it clear that there, as in *National Land*, we were concerned with the exclusion of population growth. . . .

. . . In *Girsh* we were not faced with, and therefore did not address, the issue whether the failure to provide for apartments in an area where other types of multiple dwellings were available, which presumably would not have the effect of excluding population growth, would also be [constitutionally impermissible.]

. . . The question which this case presents is whether a community must affirmatively provide for a particular architectural design in its plan for development. In no case has this Court held that a municipality's zoning ordinance must affirmatively provide for *any* specific use—residential, commercial, industrial, or otherwise. Our holdings have been limited to statements that an ordinance may not prohibit certain uses, because total prohibitions "cannot be premised on the fundamental reasonableness of allocating to each type of activity a particular location in the community." *Exton Quarries*, 425 Pa. at 59, 228 A.2d at 179. As applied to residences, we have found ordinances which fail to provide for a particular use unreasonable where they exclude population growth generally. *Girsh Appeal*. We have never found an ordinance unreasonable solely because it fails to provide for a particular use. We will not do so here. . . .

Kravitz argues that the 40 acres zoned for multi-family housing out of a total Township area of 6,491 acres, approximately 0.6%, is patently only a token provision for multi-family housing. The percentage of land available for multi-family needs is not to be considered in isolation, however. Given the projected population figures for the township and the region, and more importantly the projected housing needs, it is apparent that Wrightstown in its 1971 Zoning Ordinance more than provided for anticipated population growth. We note that according to the Bucks County Housing Plan, the total number of new dwelling units *of all types* projected to be needed in the Township by 1985 was projected in 1974 at 259 units. (Bucks County Housing Plan, p.57). The R-4 multi-family district alone would permit construction of 320 dwelling units, more than the total number projected for the Township. (Findings of Fact, ¶19, p.5).

In addition to the foregoing, we note that the Board also made findings regarding the inadequacy of local roads and the absence of mass transportation in the Township. [Wrightstown Township is approximately 37 miles from Philadelphia and 18 miles from Trenton, but no major highways link the Township with those cities.] It is clear that the Township may not avoid its responsibilities to provide for its fair share of population growth by failing to provide necessary increases in municipal services which accompany such growth. *National Land; Girsh*. It is also clear, however, that not all such services are entirely within the Township's ability to provide. Major highways, for example, are typically county or state projects, and mass transportation is now primarily a regional undertaking. Wrightstown has indicated no reluctance to provide those community services, such as local road improvements, schools, etc., which are its responsibility. . . .

This Court has repeatedly eschewed the role of "superboard of adjustment" or "planning commission of last resort." We have anticipated "that zoning boards and governing bodies in the exercise of their special expertise in zoning matters, will develop and consider any number of factors relevant to the need for and distribution of local and regional housing." *Surrick*, 476 Pa. at 194, 382 A.2d at 111, n.12. We acknowledge that the appellee here presented to the Board testimony of experts and other evidence that population would be expanding rapidly into the Wrightstown area creating a great demand for townhouses and other varieties of multi-family housing; and that the proposed development could be achieved without any adverse effect on traffic, sewage, or other municipal concerns. On the whole we must conclude, however, that in relying on the authorities which it accepted, rather than on those offered by Kravitz, the Board gave "a balanced and weighted consideration to the many factors which bear upon local and regional housing needs and development." *Surrick*, 476 Pa. at 191, 382 A.2d at 110.

For the forgoing reasons, the Order of the Commonwealth Court is reversed, and the Order of the Common Pleas Court is reinstated.

NIX, Justice, dissenting.

I dissent. I would affirm the order of the Commonwealth Court for the reasons set forth in its well analyzed opinion. See In Re: Appeal of M. A. Kravitz Co., Inc., 53 Pa. Commonwealth Ct. 622, 419 A.2d 227 (1980). The relaxed judicial review of suburban zoning decisions reflected in the plurality's view permits virtually unlimited freedom to developing municipalities to erect exclusionary walls on their boundaries, according to local whim, and to use the zoning power for aims far beyond its legitimate purposes.

LARSEN, J., joins in this dissenting opinion.

HUTCHINSON, Justice, dissenting. . . .

Where a municipality totally excludes a recognized residential use two distinct interests are foreclosed: (1) the rights of property owners to be free from "an unreasonable intermeddling with the private ownership of property." *Exton Quarries*, [425 Pa. 43 (1967)]; and (2) the interest of our growing population looking "to hitherto undeveloped areas in search of a comfortable place to live." *Girsh Appeal*. Such total exclusion of otherwise legitimate uses cannot be justified by concluding the Township is not in the path of development under the "fair share" test announced by a plurality of this Court in *Willistown* and a bare majority in *Surrick*. The simple fact that someone is anxious to build townhouses in this Township is a strong indication that people desire them. We do not believe Wrightstown Township can close its doors to these people. See *Girsh Appeal*, 437 Pa. at 245, 263 A.2d at 399. Indeed, the determination of what is a "fair share" and what communities are "in the path of development" will inevitably entangle this Court in problems of regional or community land use planning, problems unsuitable to judicial determination. . . .

NOTE ON PENNSYLVANIA EXCLUSIONARY ZONING LAW

The Pennsylvania Supreme Court elaborated its views in Appeal of Elocin, Inc., 501 Pa. 348, 461 A.2d 771 (1983), decided contemporaneously with *Kravitz*. In *Elocin* the plaintiff landowner desired to build 872 dwelling units in townhouses and high- and mid-rise apartment buildings on a parcel of 64 acres of land, much of which was tree-covered and heavily sloped. The defendant township's zoning ordinance made provision for neither townhouses nor high- and mid-rise apartment buildings, but did allow construction of "twin homes" and low-rise apartment buildings with no more than four dwelling units per building. Units of the latter two types made up about 12 percent of the township's total housing stock. The Pennsylvania Supreme Court divided 4-3, just as it had in *Kravitz*. The majority rejected the landowner's constitutional challenge to the zoning scheme, saying in part:

> ... in determining whether a municipality meets the fair share test, a court is to look to whether the zoning reflects a balanced consideration of regional needs and development. It is necessary to inquire into whether the municipality is a logical area for population growth and whether it is already highly developed. It is also necessary to inquire into the actual effect of a zoning ordinance on the availability of multi-family dwellings.
>
> In the instant case, Springfield is in an area that has experienced growth in population. Springfield itself has grown and developed significantly in recent decades. Its development has reached a high level and covered most of its land area. Twelve percent of its housing units are in multifamily dwellings. We find that to be a fair share for such use under the criteria established in our prior cases. We make that finding not only on the basis of the percentage of multi-family dwelling units, but also on the basis of the degree of development and the small amount of undeveloped land.We further find that given the nature of the Elocin tract, the refusal to allow the proposed development is reasonably related to the public health, safety and welfare of Springfield. Under the circumstances, the ordinance is not unconstitutionally exclusionary.
>
> Elocin claims that the ordinance is improper in failing to provide for townhouses and mid- and high-rise apartments. It argues that these are legitimate uses for which reasonable provision must be made. We do not agree that a municipality must necessarily provide for every conceivable use. Where a municipality provides for a reasonable share of multi-family dwellings, as Springfield has done, it need not provide for every conceivable subcategory of such dwellings. ...

461 A.2d at 773.

Responding to its Supreme Court's pair of decisions, a lower court in Pennsylvania held that a municipality that is *not* in a logical area for growth and development could totally prohibit multifamily uses. In a renewed burst of anti-exclusionary sentiment, the Pennsylvania Supreme Court reversed by a 5-2 margin. The majority reasserted that it would be highly suspicious of *any* municipality that totally excluded "a basic form of housing such as apartments." Fernley v. Board of Supervisors, 509 Pa. 413, 502 A.2d 585 (1985).

To what extent has the Pennsylvania Supreme Court retreated from its stance during the *National Land/Girsh* era? To what extent has it made exclusionary-zoning litigation in Pennsylvania more complicated? Are the new complications justified?

SUFFOLK HOUSING SERVICES v. TOWN OF BROOKHAVEN

70 N.Y.2d 122, 511 N.E.2d 67, 517 N.Y.S.2d 924 (1987)

WACHTLER, Chief Judge.

Plaintiffs seek a judgment, among other things, declaring the zoning ordinance of the Town of Brookhaven void in its entirety because of the Town's failure to exercise its zoning power (Town Law §261) to enable development of sufficient low-cost shelter and ordering the Town to take affirmative action to rectify the perceived housing shortage. Both lower courts held that the Town of Brookhaven properly exercised its land use authority. In view of the affirmed findings, and because plaintiffs in this litigation, in essence, ask this court to undertake the legislative function of rezoning the Town of Brookhaven, we must affirm the order of the court below.

I

The facts of this case, as well as a description of the pertinent provisions of the zoning ordinance at issue, are fairly set forth in the opinion of the Appellate Division (109 A.D.2d 323, 491 N.Y.S.2d 396). In essence, plaintiffs allege that there is a critical need for low-cost, multifamily rental housing, the development of which the Town is accused of actively discouraging through its zoning practices. Although plaintiffs originally contended that the Town ordinance itself contained several exclusionary devices (among them, excessive minimum acreage and site area requirements), they concede on this appeal that the ordinance "on its face does not betray the Town's opposition" to low-income, multifamily housing. Their core contention is that the Town has impeded low-income housing through its *implementation* of the ordinance. Plaintiffs point to the requirement that a developer wishing to construct any housing other than a single-family dwelling obtain a special permit. Thus, under the

Brookhaven zoning scheme, a developer may apply for permission to "cluster" developments in single-family residential districts ("the section 281" application) (see, Town Law §281). Only after a public hearing may the Town Board by resolution grant the developer permission to build multifamily housing at densities already allowed in the underlying single-family zone. Alternatively, a developer may apply for rezoning to one of two multifamily (MF-1 or MF-2) districts — a process that allows development at densities higher than those allowed in the single-family zones, but, according to the plaintiffs, like the "section 281" application, exposes approval of the project to vehement community opposition. The plaintiffs allege that the failure of the Town to "pre-map" some 49,100 acres of vacant land for multifamily housing has two principal effects: first, it inflates the cost of housing because a developer must submit to a protracted and expensive approval process; and, second, the process usually ends in failure because the Town Zoning Board inevitably bows to strong public sentiment against low-cost housing projects.

Both lower courts concluded that plaintiffs had failed to overcome the presumption of the constitutionality of the Brookhaven zoning ordinance, a conclusion we now affirm.

II

. . . Implicit in our rulings is a recognition of the principle that a municipality may not legitimately exercise its zoning power to effectuate socioeconomic or racial discrimination (Berenson v. Town of New Castle, supra, 38 N.Y.2d at 108; Matter of Golden v. Planning Bd., 30 N.Y.2d at 378). Thus, we have scrutinized carefully the talismanic invocation of seemingly legitimate police power purposes (see, Town Law §§261, 263) by municipalities to discern whether they seek to conceal exclusionary zoning practices.

In this case, however, our scope of review is limited by affirmed factual findings, for which there is support in the record (Huntley v. State of New York, 62 N.Y.2d 134). Here, both lower courts found that numerous developer applications for multifamily and subsidized housing were approved despite the special permit procedures. Moreover, there are affirmed findings that a significant reason for inadequate development of low-cost, multifamily housing was not, as plaintiffs claim, the chilling effect of the application procedures but the lack of developers willing to undertake such projects due to factors such as rising construction and financing costs and economic stagnation. Plaintiffs, in sum, have failed to demonstrate that efforts by the Town caused the claimed shortage of shelter.

We need not address whether the Town of Brookhaven zoning ordinance also meets the standards set forth in Berenson v. Town of New Castle, 38 N.Y.2d 102. In *Berenson*, plaintiffs challenged only the *facial* validity of a per se exclusion of multifamily dwellings from a zoning ordinance. Plaintiffs here challenge not facial validity, but illegitimate implementation of the ordinance; as we have already held, there has been a failure of proof on this point.

III

Zoning, we have already recognized, is an essentially legislative task, and it is therefore anomalous that courts should be required to perform the tasks of a regional planner (Robert E. Kurzius, Inc. v. Incorporated Vil. of Upper Brookville, 51 N.Y.2d, at 347; Berenson v. Town of New Castle, supra, 38 N.Y.2d at 111). The present plaintiffs, none of whom has proved that he or she has been denied housing by virtue of the Town's zoning practices,* ask the courts to undertake radical rezoning of some 49,100 acres of vacant residential land and an unspecified number of parcels. They seek this relief although they have failed to present a direct challenge to the denial of a specific special permit application pertaining to a particular parcel affected by defendants' land use practices (see, Klostermann v. Cuomo, 61 N.Y.2d 525, 535 ["(t)he paramount concern is that the judiciary not undertake tasks that the other branches are better suited to perform"]).

The desirability of a more particularized claim directed at a specific parcel of land or project or plan for housing is apparent from our cases. Historically, the law of zoning in this State has been concerned with development of *individual* plats. In more recent years, we have required a regional approach—the considered balance of development of the individual parcel with implementation of a comprehensive plan, taking into account community needs (Berenson v. Town of New Castle, supra, 38 N.Y.2d, at 110-111). This approach is necessary to ensure the interests of the public by counterbalancing the parochial tendency of local planning boards to insulate their communities from an influx of "less desirable" residents.

In sum, plaintiffs in this case propose no solution short of drastic, essentially legislative intervention by the judiciary. It should be emphasized that our decision does not mean that any of the present plaintiffs will be denied low-income housing. As noted, the plaintiffs include institutions which obviously have no personal housing needs and certain designated individuals. The institutional plaintiffs concede on this appeal

* Plaintiffs are public interest organizations, low-income individuals already residing within the Town or in Suffolk County, and Brookhaven taxpayers. [Footnote in original.—Ed.]

that the individual plaintiffs cannot be located and thus their present housing needs cannot be determined. This factor underscores the abstract character of the case and of the relief sought. Moreover, although we affirm the disposition of the Appellate Division here, we note that "today's decision [should not] be read as revealing hostility to breaking down even unconstitutional zoning barriers that frustrate the deep human yearning of low-income and minority groups for decent housing they can afford in decent surroundings" (Warth v. Seldin, 422 U.S. 490, 528-529 [Brennan, J., dissenting]). In view of the affirmed factual findings, however, we decline to take the legislative action urged by plaintiffs in the context of this lawsuit.

Accordingly, the order of the Appellate Division should be affirmed, without costs.

SIMONS, KAYE, HANCOCK and BELLACOSA, JJ., concur.

ALEXANDER, J., concurs in result only.

TITONE, J., taking no part.

NOTE ON EXCLUSIONARY-ZONING LAW IN OTHER STATES

1. *New York.* The landowner plaintiff in Robert E. Kurzius, Inc. v. Incorporated Village of Upper Brookville, 51 N.Y.2d 338, 414 N.E.2d 680, 434 N.Y.S.2d 180 (1980), invoked *Berenson* (N.Y. 1975, supra Casebook p.825), to attack the validity of five-acre minimum lot zoning in an exclusive area of the defendant Village. The New York Court of Appeals distinguished *Berenson* and unanimously rejected the landowner's challenge:

> ... [I]n this case, because there was insufficient and, indeed, a complete absence of proof of regional needs or a discriminatory purpose and no proof that the zoning ordinance in question has excluded or will exclude persons having a need for housing within the municipality or within the region, the issues are narrowed to the questions of whether five-acre zoning is exclusionary per se and an impermissible exercise of the police power. ...

The court applied a presumption of validity, and held that the landowner had not sustained the burden of proving the unconstitutionality of the zoning classification. The court also rejected the plaintiff's argument that a five-acre minimum lot requirement is per se unconstitutional.

The plaintiff landowner in Blitz v. Town of New Castle, 94 A.D.2d 92, 463 N.Y.S.2d 832 (1983), fared no better. The defendant was the Town of New Castle, the same defendant as in *Berenson*. In response to the Appellate Division's decision supra at Casebook p.830, in 1979 the Town of New Castle rezoned a small portion of its land to a multifamily classification but kept over 90 percent of its land area in single-family zones requiring minimum lot-sizes of at least one acre. The plaintiff Blitz's land had been placed in a two-acre minimum-lot zone. The Appellate Division rejected Blitz's bid to be entitled to undertake denser development because it concluded that Blitz had failed to prove that the Town had not met its *Berenson/Kurzius* obligations.

2. *Michigan.* Robinson Township v. Knoll, 410 Mich. 293, 302 N.W.2d 146 (1981), is a more recent chapter of the litigation cited supra Casebook p.794. The Township's ordinance prohibited the use of mobile homes except in mobile home parks. In a 4-3 decision the Michigan Supreme Court held this restriction lacked a "reasonable basis" and was therefore an unconstitutional exercise of the police power. "A mobile home may be excluded if it fails to satisfy reasonable standards designed to assure favorable comparison of mobile homes with site-built housing which would be permitted on the site, and not merely because it is a mobile home." But see City of Brookside Village v. Comeau, 633 S.W.2d 790 (Tex. 1982).

3. *California.* Arnel Development Co. v. City of Costa Mesa, 126 Cal. App. 3d 330, 178 Cal. Rptr. 723 (1981), cited supra Supplement p. 60, was the first reported instance in which a landowner successfully invoked the *Livermore* rule that a municipality's land-use policies must be reasonably related to the *regional* welfare. In *Arnel* the court invalidated an initiative measure that would have prevented the construction of multifamily buildings on the plaintiff's land.

The California legislature has enacted a number of statutes that might be of help to a party challenging a municipality's exclusionary policies. Each California city and county must prepare a general plan that contains a housing element. "The housing element shall identify adequate sites for housing, including rental housing, factory-built housing, and mobile homes, and shall make adequate provision for the existing and projected needs of all economic segments of the community." Cal. Govt. Code §65583 (West Supp. 1988). The complex provisions of this long statutory section were construed in Buena Vista Gardens Apartments Assn. v. City of San Diego Planning Dept., 175 Cal. App. 3d 289, 220 Cal. Rptr. 732 (1985). A private developer planned to demolish a large but aging apartment complex whose tenants were mostly low-income retirees, and to build twice as many condominium units in its place. The City of San Diego approved the project. The tenants' association then sought a court order enjoining issuance of the permits on the ground that the City's housing element failed to meet statutory requirements. The appellate court approved most features of the City's housing element, but enjoined issuance of the project's permits until the City had adopted an adequate program to conserve its housing stock.

Cal. Govt. Code §65584 establishes a procedure under which super-local agencies decide each locality's share of the housing needs of persons of all income levels in the region affected by the locality's plan. Section 65913.1 requires both general-law and charter cities to have zoning policies that "meet housing needs as identified in the general plan." Moreover, §65913.2 enjoins California localities from having subdivision standards that render "infeasible the development of housing for any and all economic segments of the community." The evolving California statutory matrix is highly complex and hedged about with qualifications.

Page 859.   Before "2. Demand Restrictions," insert:

3. *Update on growth controls.* The Town of Ramapo's schedule for capital improvements proved to be unrealistic, and many civic leaders came to conclude that the program had discouraged desirable forms of development. In 1983 the Town's governing body voted to drop its point system, the heart of its timed-growth program. See Planning, June 1983, at 8.

In 1979 and 1980 the California legislature enacted several statutes that in effect require a municipality that adopts a Petaluma Plan to justify the impact of its program on regional housing supply. See Cal. Evid. Code §669.5 (West Supp. 1983); Cal. Govt. Code §65863.6 (West 1983), construed in Building Indus. Assn. of Southern Cal., Inc. v. City of Camarillo, 41 Cal. 3d 810, 718 P.2d 68, 226 Cal. Rptr. 81 (1986).

There is a burgeoning literature on the effects of growth controls on housing prices. Most of the studies have been done in California, which during the 1972-1980 period contemporaneously experienced a major increment in legal restrictions on development and a remarkable spurt in housing prices. Although they have used different methods, the various investigators have almost invariably found that growth controls do raise housing prices when consumers cannot readily shift to a nearby area where growth has not been controlled.

For example, Michael Elliott of the MIT Department of Urban Studies and Planning gathered house-price data during the 1968-1976 period for 100 growing California cities and their surrounding counties. He found that a city's growth controls seemed to have little effect on housing prices unless the city was situated in a county that also controlled growth. When a city and its county both made growth-control efforts, Elliott found those combined controls tended to produce sharply higher housing prices. Elliott, The Impact of Growth Regulations on Housing Prices in California, 9 AREUEA J. 115 (1981).

See also Katz & Rosen, The Interjurisdictional Effects of Growth Controls on Housing Prices, 30 J.L. & Econ. 149 (1987) (estimating that growth controls in the San Francisco Bay Area have increased house prices there by 17 to 38 percent); Schwartz, Hansen, & Green, Suburban Growth Controls and the Price of New Housing, 8 J. Envtl. Econ. & Mgmt. 303 (1981) (Petaluma's quota, within a few years of its adoption, pushed Petaluma's new house prices 7.8 percent above the new house prices in nearby Santa Rosa); Mercer & Morgan, An Estimate of Residential Growth Controls' Impact on Housing Prices, in Resolving the Housing Crisis 189 (M. Johnson ed. 1982) (water-hookup moratorium in Santa Barbara area was responsible for one-fourth of the rise in real housing prices there during 1972-1979); Land Use and Housing on the San Francisco Peninsula (Stan. Envtl. L. Socy. 1983) (detailed description of growth controls in suburban region with extraordinarily high housing prices); Schwartz, Zorn & Hansen, Research Design Issues and Pitfalls in Growth Control Studies, 62 Land Econ. 223 (1986).

Page 863. Before the last full paragraph on the page, insert:

In United Building & Constr. Trades Council v. Mayor of Camden, 465 U.S. 208 (1984), the Supreme Court held that the Privileges and Immunities Clause of Article IV constrains not only state, but also municipal, policies that discriminate on the basis of residence to the disadvantage of out-of-state residents. A Camden ordinance required that 40 percent of the employees of contractors and subcontractors on city construction projects be Camden residents. Rejecting Camden's argument that municipal ordinances are beyond the reach of the Privileges and Immunities Clause, the Court remanded the case for a determination of whether Camden could show a "substantial reason" for having a policy that adversely affected out-of-state residents. But cf. White v. Massachusetts Council of Constr. Employers, Inc., 460 U.S. 204 (1983) (local-hire ordinance like Camden's held not to violate Commerce Clause).

Page 873. Before *Arlington Heights II*, add:

In HOPE, Inc. v. County of DuPage, 738 F.2d 797 (7th Cir. 1984), a fair housing organization and ten individuals of modest income brought suit against the County of DuPage, a suburban county just west of Cook County. The plaintiffs asserted that DuPage County's land-use policies intentionally excluded low- and moderate-income households and members of racial minorities. The district court held that the plaintiffs had proved a pattern of racially motivated discrimination that violated the Equal Protection Clause. It enjoined the County from applying lot-size and other development standards to proposed low- and moderate-income housing projects and ordered the County to prepare a ten-year plan to increase significantly the number of housing units available to households in those income ranges. On appeal, a divided panel of the Seventh Circuit reversed on the ground that the plaintiffs lacked standing under Warth v. Seldin, 422 U.S. 490 (1975).

Page 877.   Before "2. Lower-Income Families," insert:

5. *The Fair Housing Act (continued).* The United States Department of Justice invoked the provisions of the Fair Housing Act in a 1973 suit against the City of Parma, a large suburb of Cleveland. In 1970 blacks constituted 16 percent of the population of the greater Cleveland area but only 0.05 percent of Parma's population. The United States asserted that Parma had intentionally endeavored to exclude black households from the city. The district court found that Parma had violated the Act and ordered the city to follow a broad remedial plan, including "all efforts necessary to ensure that at least 133 units of low- and moderate-income housing are provided annually in Parma." The City appealed. In 1981, eight years after the United States had filed the action, the Sixth Circuit affirmed in all respects except two: it held that flexible targets were preferable to the rigid target of 133 units, and that the district court should not have appointed a special master to oversee the implementation of the remedial plan. United States v. City of Parma, 661 F.2d 562 (6th Cir. 1981).

In 1980 the United States initiated a lawsuit against the City of Yonkers, New York, to cure what it asserted was a city-maintained pattern of racial segregation in schools and housing. In an opinion that runs 268 pages in the Federal Supplement reporter, Judge Leonard Sand held, among other things, that Yonkers had violated civil rights by intentionally concentrating its subsidized housing in the southwest part of the city. United States v. Yonkers Bd. of Educ., 624 F. Supp. 1276 (S.D.N.Y. 1985). In his subsequent opinion on remedies, Judge Sand ordered the city to cease its discrimination and to provide 200 units of family public housing outside its predominantly minority areas. 635 F. Supp. 1577 (S.D.N.Y. 1986). On appeal Judge Sand's rulings were affirmed in all respects. 837 F.2d 1181 (2d Cir., 1987).

Page 884.   Before Note 5, insert:

4a. *Update on inclusionary zoning.* California's inclusionary housing movement suffered several setbacks during the early 1980s. In 1981 the state legislature greatly limited the Coastal Commission's authority to impose inclusionary requirements on coastal developers. See 1981 Cal. Stat. ch. 1007. And in 1983 Orange County, which had previously administered the largest inclusionary program in the state, voted to phase out its program over a three-year period. The City of San Francisco bucked this tide. In late 1980 it began to require office developers to finance inclusionary housing efforts. To receive approval for a downtown skyscraper, for example, one developer paid $2.4 million to the city's housing fund. See S.F. Chronicle, June 12, 1982, p.2, col. 1. See generally Diamond, The San Francisco Office/Housing Program, 7 Harv. Envtl. L. Rev. 449 (1983).

The New Jersey Supreme Court has rendered two decisions that warmly embrace inclusionary techniques. In *Mount Laurel II*, supra Supplement p. 139, it held that an inclusionary program does not (in the usual case at least) constitute an unconstitutional taking of a developer's property and does not involve impermissible socio-economic classifications. Perhaps more significantly, *Mount Laurel II* strongly encouraged a municipality to impose on its developers a mandatory inclusionary set-aside of at least 20 percent. In a subsequent decision, In re Egg Harbor Associates, 94 N.J. 358, 464 A.2d 1115 (1983), the New Jersey Supreme Court held that the state coastal agency had statutory authority to require a coastal developer to set aside 20 percent of its proposed housing units for low- and moderate-income families and that this exaction did not constitute a taking of property.

New additions to the inclusionary-zoning literature include A. Mallach, Inclusionary Housing Programs (1984); Inclusionary Zoning Moves Downtown (D. Merriam, D. Brower & P. Tegeler eds. 1985); Schwartz & Johnson, Inclusionary Housing Programs, J. Am. Planning Assn. 3 (Winter 1983) (generally favorable review of California programs); Ellickson, The Irony of "Inclusionary Zoning," 54 S. Cal. L. Rev. 1167 (1981) (asserts that an inclusionary program imposes a potentially counterproductive tax on housing construction and is a wasteful and unfair way to provide housing assistance).

Page 896.   Before "5. Absentee Owners," add:

CITY OF CLEBURNE v. CLEBURNE LIVING CENTER

473 U.S. 432, 105 S. Ct. 3249, 87 L. Ed. 2d 313 (1985)

Justice WHITE delivered the opinion of the Court.

A Texas city denied a special use permit for the operation of a group home for the mentally retarded, acting pursuant to a municipal zoning ordinance requiring permits for such homes. The Court of Appeals for the Fifth Circuit held that mental retardation is a "quasi-suspect" classification and that the ordinance violated the Equal Protection Clause because it did not substantially further an important governmental purpose. We hold that a lesser standard of scrutiny is appropriate, but conclude that under that standard the ordinance is invalid as applied in this case.

I

In July, 1980, respondent Jan Hannah purchased a building at 201 Featherston Street in the city of Cleburne, Texas, with the intention of leasing it to Cleburne Living Centers, Inc. (CLC), for the operation of a group home for the mentally retarded. It was anticipated that the home would house 13 retarded men and women, who would be under the constant supervision of CLC staff members. The house had four bedrooms and two baths, with a half bath to be added. CLC planned to comply with all applicable state and federal regulations.

The city informed CLC that a special use permit would be required for the operation of a group home at the site, and CLC accordingly submitted a permit application. In response to a subsequent inquiry from CLC, the city explained that under the zoning regulations applicable to the site, a special use permit, renewable annually, was required for the construction of "[h]ospitals for the insane or feeble-minded, or alcoholic [sic] or drug addicts, or penal or correctional institutions."[3] The city had determined that the proposed group home should be classified as a

---

3. The site of the home is in an area zoned "R-3," an "Apartment House District." App. 51. Section 8 of the Cleburne zoning ordinance, in pertinent part, allows the following uses in an R-3 district:

1. Any use permitted in District R-2.
2. Apartment houses, or multiple dwellings.
3. Boarding and lodging houses.
4. Fraternity or sorority houses and dormitories.
5. Apartment hotels.
6. Hospitals, sanitariums, nursing homes or homes for convalescents or aged, *other than for the* insane or *feeble-minded* or alcoholics or drug addicts.
7. Private clubs or fraternal orders, except those whose chief activity is carried on as a business.
8. Philanthropic or eleemosynary institutions, other than penal institutions.
9. Accessory uses customarily incident to any of the above uses. . . . Id., at 60-61 (emphasis added).

Section 16 of the ordinance specifies the uses for which a special use permit is required. These include "[h]ospitals for the insane or feebleminded, or alcoholic or drug addicts, or penal or correctional institutions." Id., at 63. Section 16 provides that a permit for such a use may be issued by "the Governing Body, after public hearing, and after recommendation of the Planning Commission." All special use permits are limited to one year, and each applicant is required "to obtain the signatures of the property owners within two hundred (200) feet of the property to be used." Ibid.

"hospital for the feebleminded." After holding a public hearing on CLC's application, the city council voted three to one to deny a special use permit.

CLC then filed suit in Federal District Court against the city and a number of its officials, alleging, inter alia, that the zoning ordinance was invalid on its face and as applied because it discriminated against the mentally retarded in violation of the equal protection rights of CLC and its potential residents. . . .

III . . .

Doubtless, there have been and there will continue to be instances of discrimination against the retarded that are in fact invidious, and that are properly subject to judicial correction under constitutional norms. But the appropriate method of reaching such instances is not to create a new quasi-suspect classification and subject all governmental action based on that classification to more searching evaluation. Rather, we should look to the likelihood that governmental action premised on a particular classification is valid as a general matter, not merely to the specifics of the case before us. Because mental retardation is a characteristic that the government may legitimately take into account in a wide range of decisions, and because both state and federal governments have recently committed themselves to assisting the retarded, we will not presume that any given legislative action, even one that disadvantages retarded individuals, is rooted in considerations that the Constitution will not tolerate.

Our refusal to recognize the retarded as a quasi-suspect class does not leave them entirely unprotected from invidious discrimination. To withstand equal protection review, legislation that distinguishes between the mentally retarded and others must be rationally related to a legitimate governmental purpose. This standard, we believe, affords government the latitude necessary both to pursue policies designed to assist the retarded in realizing their full potential, and to freely and efficiently engage in activities that burden the retarded in what is essentially an incidental manner. . . .

IV

We turn to the issue of the validity of the zoning ordinance insofar as it requires a special use permit for homes for the mentally retarded. We inquire first whether requiring a special use permit for the Featherston home in the circumstances here deprives respondents of the equal protection of the laws. If it does, there will be no occasion to decide whether the special use permit provision is facially invalid where the mentally retarded are involved, or to put it another way, whether the city may never insist on a special use permit for a home for the mentally retarded in an R-3 zone. This is the preferred course of adjudication since it enables courts to avoid making unnecessarily broad constitutional judgments.

The constitutional issue is clearly posed. The City does not require a special use permit in an R-3 zone for apartment houses, multiple dwellings, boarding and lodging houses, fraternity or sorority houses, dormitories, apartment hotels, hospitals, sanitariums, nursing homes for convalescents or the aged (other than for the insane or feeble-minded or alcoholics or drug addicts), private clubs or fraternal orders, and other specified uses. It does, however, insist on a special permit for the Featherston home, and it does so, as the District Court found, because it would be a facility for the mentally retarded. May the city require the permit for this facility when other care and multiple dwelling facilities are freely permitted?

It is true, as already pointed out, that the mentally retarded as a group are indeed different from others not sharing their misfortune, and in this respect they may be different from those who would occupy other facilities that would be permitted in an R-3 zone without a special permit. But this difference is largely irrelevant unless the Featherston home and those who would occupy it would threaten legitimate interests of the city in a way that other permitted uses such as boarding houses and hospitals would not. Because in our view the record does not reveal any rational basis for believing that the Featherston home would pose any special threat to the city's legitimate interests, we affirm the judgment below insofar as it holds the ordinance invalid as applied in this case.

The District Court found that the City Council's insistence on the permit rested on several factors. First, the Council was concerned with the negative attitude of the majority of property owners located within 200 feet of the Featherston facility, as well as with the fears of elderly residents of the neighborhood. But mere negative attitudes, or fear, unsubstantiated by factors which are properly cognizable in a zoning proceeding, are not permissible bases for treating a home for the mentally retarded differently from apartment houses, multiple dwellings, and the like. It is plain that the electorate as a whole, whether by referendum or otherwise, could not order city action violative of the Equal Protection Clause, Lucas v. Forty-Fourth General Assembly of Colorado, 377 U.S. 713, 736-737 (1964), and the City may not avoid the strictures of that Clause by deferring to the wishes or objections of some fraction of the body politic. "Private biases may be outside the reach of the law, but the law cannot, directly or indirectly, give them effect." Palmore v. Sidoti, 104 S. Ct. 1879, 1882 (1984).

Second, the Council had two objections to the location of the facility. It was concerned that the facility was across the street from a junior high school, and it feared that the students might harass the occupants of the Featherston home. But the school itself is attended by about 30 mentally retarded students, and denying a permit based on such vague, undifferentiated fears is again permitting some portion of the community to validate what would otherwise be an equal protection violation. The other objection to the home's location was that it was located on "a five hundred year flood plain." This concern with the possibility of a flood, however, can hardly be based on a distinction between the Featherston home and, for example, nursing homes, homes for convalescents or the aged, or sanitariums or hospitals, any of which could be located on the Featherston site without obtaining a special use permit. The same may be said of another concern of the Council—doubts about the legal responsibility for actions which the mentally retarded might take. If there is no concern about legal responsibility with respect to other uses that would be permitted in the area, such as boarding and fraternity houses, it is difficult to believe that the groups of mildly or moderately mentally retarded individuals who would live at 201 Featherston would present any different or special hazard.

Fourth, the Council was concerned with the size of the home and the number of people that would occupy it. The District Court found, and the Court of Appeals repeated, that "[i]f the potential residents of the Featherston Street home were not mentally retarded, but the home was the same in all other respects, its use would be permitted under the city's zoning ordinance." App. 93; 726 F.2d, at 200. Given this finding, there would be no restrictions on the number of people who could occupy this home as a boarding house, nursing home, family dwelling, fraternity house, or dormitory. The question is whether it is rational to treat the mentally retarded differently. It is true that they suffer disability not shared by others; but why this difference warrants a density regulation that others need not observe is not at all apparent. At least this record does not clarify how, in this connection, the characteristics of the intended occupants of the Featherston home rationally justify denying to those occupants what would be permitted to groups occupying the same site for different purposes. Those who would live in the Featherston home are the type of individuals who, with supporting staff, satisfy federal and state standards for group housing in the community; and there is no dispute that the home would meet the federal square-footage-per-resident requirement for facilities of this type. See 42 CFR §442.447 (1984). In the words of the Court of Appeals, "The City never justifies its apparent view that other people can live under such 'crowded' conditions when mentally retarded persons cannot." 726 F.2d, at 202. . . .

The short of it is that requiring the permit in this case appears to us to rest on an irrational prejudice against the mentally retarded, including those who would occupy the Featherston facility and who would live under the closely supervised and highly regulated conditions expressly provided for by state and federal law.

The judgment of the Court of Appeals is affirmed insofar as it invalidates the zoning ordinance as applied to the Featherston home. The judgment is otherwise vacated.

[Justices STEVENS and MARSHALL wrote opinions that concurred in the majority's conclusion that the city had violated the Equal Protection Clause.]

Chapter Nine
Intergovernmental Relations

Page 916.   Before "3. Regional Planning Agencies," insert:

Nine states have developed programs to compensate a local government that allows a hazardous waste facility to be located within its boundaries. See Bacow & Milkey, Overcoming Local Opposition to Hazardous Waste Facilities: The Massachusetts Approach, 6 Harv. Entl. L. Rev. 265, 278 n.78 (1982). Under prodding from the MIT team, Massachusetts has become the leading laboratory for experimentation with the compensation technique. See generally M. O'Hare, L. Bacow, & D. Sanderson, Facility Siting and Public Opposition (1983) (includes five case studies of siting disputes in which compensation was offered to the targeted locality).

Page 920.   Before "C. State Regulation of Land Use," insert:

In 1982 the Reagan Administration revoked OMB Circular A-95, the document that had guaranteed COGs an opportunity to comment upon local applications for federal funds. Executive Order 12372, 47 Fed. Reg. 30959 (1982), encourages states to develop their own procedures for coordinating the delivery of federal financial assistance to state and substate units of government.

Page 930.   Before "Note on State Preemption . . . ," insert:

A useful book on utility siting is M. O'Hare, L. Bacow & D. Sanderson, Facility Siting and Public Opposition (1983). These authors are of course noted for their emphasis on the role of compensation in overcoming local opposition. See also Tarlock, Anywhere But Here: An Introduction to State Control of Hazardous Waste Facility Location, 2 U.C.L.A.J. Envtl. L. & Policy 1 (1982) (asserting that state preemption and other strong measures will be necessary to overcome local opposition to regionally important waste facilities).

Page 945.   Before "b. Imposition of State Planning Goals . . . ," insert:

NOTE ON STATE LAND-USE REGULATION IN FLORIDA

The Florida appellate court's decision in *Estuary Properties* was reversed *sub nom.* Graham v. Estuary Properties, Inc., 399 So. 2d 1374 (Fla.), *cert. denied,* 454 U.S. 1083 (1981). The Florida Supreme Court held both that the Adjudicatory Commission had acted within its statutory mandate when denying the developer's application and that the Commission's decision in this instance did not effect a taking of property in violation of either the Florida or United States constitution.

In 1984-1985 Florida adopted a much more ambitious scheme of state land-use regulation. Like Oregon, Florida now has articulated state planning goals. These are identified in Fla. Stat. Ann. §187.201 (West 1987), which lists 25 "goals" and more than 300 associated "policies." State agencies must prepare functional plans that are consistent with the state comprehensive plan. Secs. 186.021-186.022. The new legislation also sets standards for local and regional comprehensive plans; they too must be consistent with the state comprehensive plan. Sec. 163.3177(9). See generally Pelham, Hyde & Banks, Managing Florida's Growth: Toward an Integrated State, Regional, and Local Comprehensive Planning Process, 13 Fla. St. U.L. Rev. 515 (1985).

Page 952.   At the end of Note 1, insert:

Oregon's state land-use regulation system has continued to be politically controversial and, perhaps as a result, has been periodically reshaped by both the legislature and the LCDC. H. Leonard, Managing Oregon's Growth (1983), is a thorough and largely approving history of the state's program.

An important structural change occurred in 1979 when the Oregon legislature created the Land Use Board of appeals (LUBA). LUBA is a five-member board, appointed by the governor, with "exclusive jurisdiction to review any land use decision of a local government or special district governing body or a state agency." See Or. Laws 1979 ch. 772, *as amended, reprinted in* note preceding Or. Rev. Stat. §197.005 (1981). By creating LUBA, Oregon became the first state to have a specialized agency with adjudicatory jurisdiction over the entire panoply of land-use disputes in which government is a party. In an ordinary case LUBA renders its own decision, which an aggrieved party can then ask the Oregon Court of Appeal to review. However, in a case where LUBA has dealt with an allegation that a local government has violated LCDC's planning goals for the state, LUBA essentially acts only as a hearing officer. It takes evidence and recommends a decision to the LCDC, which is authorized to review the record de novo and render a final decision. Any LCDC decision on the consistency of local action with LCDC goals is then itself subject to judicial review.

Stewart v. City of Eugene, 57 Or. App. 627, 646 P.2d 74 (1982), illustrates LUBA's role when a local government's adherence to LCDC goals is at issue. The local government had amended its plan to redesignate from agricultural to industrial use an 1800-acre territory at the confluence of an airport, rail facilities, and a major highway. Stewart asked LUBA to find that this redesignation violated LCDC's Goal #3, which governs the conservation of agricultural lands. LUBA agreed with Stewart and recommended that the LCDC hold that the plan amendment violated Goal #3. LCDC followed LUBA's recommendation. When the City of Eugene sought judicial review, the Oregon Court of Appeal sustained the LCDC's decision. Was the three-stage adjudicative sequence involved in *Stewart* overly cumbersome? When, if ever, will LUBA serve to expedite the resolution of land-use disputes in Oregon? See Note, Future of Oregon's Land Use Appeals Process, 19 Willamette L.J. 109 (1983) (generally upbeat review of LUBA's performance).

The recession of 1981-1983 battered the Oregon lumber industry and cooled antigrowth sentiment in the state. Nevertheless, in November 1982 Oregon voters rejected, by a margin of 55 to 45 percent, a ballot measure that would have abolished both the LCDC and LUBA. In 21 of Oregon's 36 counties, however, a majority of voters cast ballots against the agencies, and their statewide support was significantly narrower than the LCDC's 61 to 39 percent victory margin in 1978. See Land Use L. & Zoning Dig., Jan. 1983, at 3.

In 1000 Friends of Oregon v. Land Conservation & Dev. Commn., 292 Or. 735, 642 P.2d 1158 (1982), the Oregon Supreme Court signaled that it would strictly scrutinize any LCDC actions to placate the landowners and local officials who had been so critical of the agency. One of the LCDC's most controversial policies had been Goal #14, which required local governments to demarcate "Urban Growth Boundaries" beyond which urbanization would not be permitted. During the 1970s the LCDC required local governments, when setting their Urban Growth Boundaries, to weigh their future housing and employment needs against fiscal and environmental considerations. In the late 1970s the LCDC amended Goal #14 to authorize any city that had determined that its housing and employment needs so required to set its Urban Growth Boundary at its city limits. This meant that the city's entire territory would be urbanizable, regardless of threats posed to the achievement of other LCDC goals. The issue in *1000 Friends* was whether this amendment was within the LCDC's statutory authority. The Oregon Supreme Court held unanimously that the amendment was invalid because the LCDC had paid too little heed to the variety of the legislature's concerns. Morgan & Shonkwiler, Urban Development and Statewide Planning: Challenge of the 1980s, 61 Or. L. Rev. 351 (1982), criticizes Oregon's Urban Growth Boundaries for overly concentrating development in existing population centers.

Page 968.   At the end of the first full paragraph, insert:

The District Court's decision in *Pacific Legal Foundation* was reversed *sub nom.* Pacific Gas & Elec. Co. v. State Energy Resources Conservation & Dev. Commn., 461 U.S. 190 (1983). The Supreme Court accepted California's argument that the state was concerned not with nuclear safety — the field that Congress had preempted — but rather with "economic" issues.

Page 977.   Before "(2) The Coastal Zone Management Act," insert:

In November 1982 Republican George Deukmejian was elected to succeed Democrat Edmund G. Brown, Jr., as Governor of California. Governor Deukmejian's appointments to TRPA tipped that agency toward a more prodevelopment posture. In 1984 TRPA approved some pro-growth amendments to the Tahoe regional plan. John Van De Kamp, the attorney General of California and a Democrat, immediately filed suit for a preliminary injunction enjoining TRPA from approving any projects under the plan. He argued that the plan amendments violated environmental protection criteria set out in the interstate compact. District Judge Edward Garcia granted the preliminary injunction, and was upheld on appeal. People of State of California ex rel. Van De Kamp v. Tahoe Regional Planning Agency, 766 F.2d 1308 (9th Cir. 1985). The case was settled in 1987, on terms that allowed TRPA to approve construction of no more than 300 single-family homes annually for a five-year period. The settlement agreement also set ceilings on other types of new construction. See Tahoe Planners Smooth Path for Growth Plan's Final OK, S.F. Chronicle, June 26, 1987, p.2, col. 4.

Page 978.   Before "c. Development of Interstate Impact . . . ," insert:

The federal flood insurance program has drawn fire from both taxpayer and environmental groups. With Congress's blessing federal administrators have typically set the premiums that policyholders pay at a level below market rates. The program is thus thought to have increased the pace of construction in flood-prone areas. In 1982 opponents of these federal subsidies succeeded in securing legislation that barred the future provision of federal flood insurance for structures on designated barrier islands along the Atlantic and Gulf of Mexico coasts. See 42 U.S.C. 4028 (Supp. 1983).

Page 983.   Before "b. Federal Grants-in-Aid . . . ," insert:

In 1981 Congress repealed the §701 program. Pub. Law 97-35, §313(b), 95 Stat. 398. Its intent was apparently to compel a local planning agency desirous of the benefits of federal aid to try to obtain a piece of its locality's community development block grant (CDBG) funds. HUD distributes about 70 percent of CDBG funds directly to large cities and urban counties and the balance to the states for redistribution to smaller localities. The federal government has placed relatively few strings on the state and local spending of CDBG funds. When a planning agency asks a local governing body to funnel CDBG funds in its direction, it must now compete against other applicants for aid.

Chapter Ten
Government as Landowner, Developer, and Financier

Page 999. Before "4. Land Banking," insert:

4. *From Andrus to Watt.* During 1981-1983 Secretary of the Interior James Watt pursued prodevelopment policies on federal lands and adopted a conciliatory "Good Neighbor" attitude toward the political leaders of western states. This shift in federal policy took the steam out of the Sagebrush Rebellion.

Libertarian analysts have increasingly suggested that the proper federal policy is not to turn the federal lands over to the states—the object of the Sagebrush Rebellion—but rather to auction off federal lands to private owners. See G. Lidecap, Locking up the Range (1981); Private Rights and Public Lands (P. Truluck ed. 1983).

In 1982 Secretary Watt announced that he was considering selling 5 percent of the Interior Department's acreage. This proposal predictably aroused the opposition of environmentalists, who generally prefer retention of current federal land holdings. See, e.g., Hooper, Privatization: The Reagan Administration's Master Plan for Government Giveaways, Sierra 32 (Nov.-Dec. 1982); Sax, Why We Will Not (Should Not) Sell the Public Lands: Changing Conceptions of Private Property, 1983 Utah L. Rev. 313. The proposed privatization of public lands also proved to be controversial with federal lessees, who feared the termination of federal subsidies, and with localists, who worried that outside investors would be the highest bidders at auction. In 1983 Secretary Watt decimated the privatization program and announced that he had been "stupid" in 1982 when he had advocated major sales of federal land. S.F. Chronicle, June 30, 1983, p.10, col. 3.

Page 1007. Before *Pillar of Fire*, insert:

State courts have continued to differ in their interpretations of the public use clauses in their state constitutions. In Poletown Neighborhood Council v. City of Detroit, 410 Mich. 616, 304 N.W.2d 455 (1981), the

Michigan Supreme Court sustained, over two dissents, Detroit's authority to use the power of eminent domain to assemble a site for a General Motors assembly plant. The majority concluded that the city's announced purpose of strengthening its economic base satisfied the public use requirement.

But compare In re City of Seattle, 96 Wash. 2d 616, 638 P.2d 549 (1981). In that case Seattle intended to assemble about a block of downtown land to enable a private consortium to develop a retail shopping district that city leaders hoped would serve as a downtown focal point. The court held by a margin of 6-3 that Seattle not only lacked the statutory authority to employ eminent domain powers for this purpose but that redevelopment to bolster private retail trade was not a constitutionally adequate public use.

Note, Public Use, Private Use, and Judicial Review in Eminent Domain, 58 N.Y.U.L. Rev. 409 (1983), thoughtfully discusses the judicial role in policing governmental exercise of the power of eminent domain.

HAWAII HOUSING AUTHORITY v. MIDKIFF

467 U.S. 229, 104 S. Ct. 2321, 81 L. Ed. 2d 186 (1984)

Justice O'CONNOR delivered the opinion of the Court.

The Fifth Amendment of the United States Constitution provides, in pertinent part, that "private property [shall not] be taken for public use, without just compensation." These cases present the question whether the Public Use Clause of that Amendment, made applicable to the States through the Fourteenth Amendment, prohibits the State of Hawaii from taking, with just compensation, title in real property from lessors and transferring it to lessees in order to reduce the concentration of ownership of fees simple in the State. We conclude that it does not.

I

A

The Hawaiian Islands were originally settled by Polynesian immigrants from the western Pacific. These settlers developed an economy around a feudal land tenure system in which one island high chief, the ali'i nui, controlled the land and assigned it for development to certain subchiefs. The subchiefs would then reassign the land to other lower ranking chiefs, who would administer the land and govern the farmers and other tenants working it. All land was held at the will of the ali'i nui and eventually had to be returned to his trust. There was no private ownership of land.

Beginning in the early 1800's, Hawaiian leaders and American settlers repeatedly attempted to divide the lands of the kingdom among the crown, the chiefs, and the common people. These efforts proved largely unsuccessful, however, and the land remained in the hands of a few. In the mid-1960's, after extensive hearings, the Hawaii Legislature discovered that, while the State and Federal Governments owned almost 49% of the State's land, another 47% was in the hands of only 72 private landowners. The legislature further found that 18 landholders, with tracts of 21,000 acres or more, owned more than 40% of this land and that on Oahu, the most urbanized of the islands, 22 landowners owned 72.5% of the fee simple titles. The legislature concluded that concentrated land ownership was responsible for skewing the State's residential fee simple market, inflating land prices, and injuring the public tranquility and welfare.

To redress these problems, the legislature decided to compel the large landowners to break up their estates. The legislature considered requiring large landowners to sell lands which they were leasing to homeowners. However, the landowners strongly resisted this scheme, pointing out the significant federal tax liabilities they would incur. Indeed, the landowners claimed that the federal tax laws were the primary reason they previously had chosen to lease, and not sell, their lands. Therefore, to accommodate the needs of both lessors and lessees, the Hawaii Legislature enacted the Land Reform Act of 1967 (Act), Haw. Rev. Stat., ch. 516, which created a mechanism for condemning residential tracts and for transferring ownership of the condemned fees simple to existing lessees. By condemning the land in question, the Hawaii Legislature intended to make the land sales involuntary, thereby making the federal tax consequences less severe while still facilitating the redistribution of fees simple.

Under the Act's condemnation scheme, tenants living on single-family residential lots within developmental tracts at least five acres in size are entitled to ask the Hawaii Housing Authority (HHA) to condemn the property on which they live. Haw. Rev. Stat. §§516-1(2), (11), 516-22 (1977). When 25 eligible tenants, or tenants on half the lots in the tract, whichever is less, file appropriate applications, the Act authorizes HHA to hold a public hearing to determine whether acquisition by the State of all or part of the tract will "effectuate the public purposes" of the Act. §516-22. If HHA finds that these public purposes will be served, it is authorized to designate some or all of the lots in the tract for acquisition. It then acquires, at prices set either by condemnation trial or by negotiation between lessors and lessees, the former fee owners' full "right, title, and interest" in the land. §516-25.

After compensation has been set, HHA may sell the land titles to tenants who have applied for fee simple ownership. . . . In practice, funds to satisfy the condemnation awards have been supplied entirely by lessees. While the Act authorizes HHA to issue bonds and appropriate funds for acquisition, no bonds have issued and HHA has not supplied any funds for condemned lots.

[Midkiff challenged the HHA's right to take his land for the ultimate benefit of his tenants. The District Court rejected his challenge, but was reversed by the Court of Appeals for the Ninth Circuit.]

III

The majority of the Court of Appeals ... determined that the Act violates the "public use" requirement of the Fifth and Fourteenth Amendments. On this argument, however, we find ourselves in agreement with the dissenting judge in the Court of Appeals.

A

The starting point for our analysis of the Act's constitutionality is the Court's decision in Berman v. Parker, 348 U.S. 26 (1954). [*Berman* held that the] "public use" requirement is . . . coterminous with the scope of a sovereign's police powers.

There is, of course, a role for courts to play in reviewing a legislature's judgment of what constitutes a public use, even when the eminent domain power is equated with the police power. But the Court in *Berman* made clear that it is "an extremely narrow" one. Id., at 32. . . .

To be sure, the Court's cases have repeatedly stated that "one person's property may not be taken for the benefit of another private person without a justifying public purpose, even though compensation be paid." Thompson v. Consolidated Gas Corp., 300 U.S. 55, 80 (1937). Thus, in Missouri Pacific R. Co. v. Nebraska, 164 U.S. 403 (1896), where the "order in question was not, *and was not claimed to be*, . . . a taking of private property for a public use under the right of eminent domain," id., at 416, at 135 (emphasis added), the Court invalidated a compensated taking of property for lack of a justifying public purpose. But where the exercise of the eminent domain power is rationally related to a conceivable public purpose, the Court has never held a compensated taking to be proscribed by the Public Use Clause. . . .

On this basis, we have no trouble concluding that the Hawaii Act is constitutional. The people of Hawaii have attempted, much as the settlers of the original 13 Colonies did,[5] to reduce the perceived social and

5. After the American Revolution, the colonists in several States took steps to eradicate the feudal incidents with which large proprietors had encumbered land in the Colonies.

economic evils of a land oligopoly traceable to their monarchs. The land oligopoly has, according to the Hawaii Legislature, created artificial deterrents to the normal functioning of the State's residential land market and forced thousands of individual homeowners to lease, rather than buy, the land underneath their homes. Regulating oligopoly and the evils associated with it is a classic exercise of a State's police powers. See Exxon Corp. v. Governor of Maryland, 437 U.S. 117 (1978). We cannot disapprove of Hawaii's exercise of this power.

Nor can we condemn as irrational the Act's approach to correcting the land oligopoly problem. The Act presumes that when a sufficiently large number of persons declare that they are willing but unable to buy lots at fair prices the land market is malfunctioning. When such a malfunction is signalled, the Act authorizes HHA to condemn lots in the relevant tract. The Act limits the number of lots any one tenant can purchase and authorizes HHA to use public funds to ensure that the market dilution goals will be achieved. This is a comprehensive and rational approach to identifying and correcting market failure.

Of course, this Act, like any other, may not be successful in achieving its intended goals. But "whether *in fact* the provision will accomplish its objectives is not the question: the [constitutional requirement] is satisfied if . . . the . . . [state] Legislature *rationally could have believed* that the [Act] would promote its objective." Western & Southern Life Ins. Co. v. State Bd. of Equalization, 451 U.S. 648, 671-672 (1981). When the legislature's purpose is legitimate and its means are not irrational, our cases make clear that empirical debates over the wisdom of takings — no less than debates over the wisdom of other kinds of socioeconomic legislation — are not to be carried out in the federal courts. Redistribution of fees simple to correct deficiencies in the market determined by the state legislature to be attributable to land oligopoly is a rational exercise of the eminent domain power. Therefore, the Hawaii statute must pass the scrutiny of the Public Use Clause.[6]

See, e.g., Act of May 1779, 10 Henning's Statutes At Large 64, ch. 13, §6 (1822) (Virginia statute); Divesting Act of 1779, 1775-1781 Pa. Acts 258, ch. 139 (1782) (Pennsylvania statute). Courts have never doubted that such statutes served a public purpose. See, e.g., Wilson v. Iseminger, 185 U.S. 55, 60-61 (1902); Stewart v. Gorter, 70 Md. 242, 244-245, 16 A. 644, 645 (1889).

6. We similarly find no merit in appellees' Due Process and Contract Clause arguments. The argument that due process prohibits allowing lessees to initiate the taking process was essentially rejected by this Court in New Motor Vehicle Board v. Fox Co., 439 U.S. 96 (1978). Similarly, the Contract Clause has never been thought to protect against the exercise of the power of eminent domain. See United States Trust Co. v. New Jersey, 431 U.S. 1, 19, and n.16 (1977).

B

The Court of Appeals read our cases to stand for a much narrower proposition. First, it read our "public use" cases, especially *Berman*, as requiring that government possess and use property at some point during a taking. Since Hawaiian lessees retain possession of the property for private use throughout the condemnation process, the court found that the Act exacted takings for private use. 702 F.2d, at 796-797. Second, it determined that these cases involved only "the review of . . . *congressional* determination[s] that there was a public use, *not* the review of . . . state legislative determination[s]." Id., at 798 (emphasis in original). Because state legislative determinations are involved in the instant cases, the Court of Appeals decided that more rigorous judicial scrutiny of the public use determinations was appropriate. The court concluded that the Hawaii Legislature's professed purposes were mere "statutory rationalizations." Ibid. We disagree with the Court of Appeals' analysis.

The mere fact that property taken outright by eminent domain is transferred in the first instance to private beneficiaries does not condemn that taking as having only a private purpose. The Court long ago rejected any literal requirement that condemned property be put into use for the general public. "It is not essential that the entire community, nor even any considerable portion, . . . directly enjoy or participate in any improvement in order [for it] to constitute a public use." Rindge Co. v. Los Angeles, 262 U.S., at 707. . . .

Similarly, the fact that a state legislature, and not the Congress, made the public use determination does not mean that judicial deference is less appropriate. Judicial deference is required because, in our system of government, legislatures are better able to assess what public purposes should be advanced by an exercise of the taking power. State legislatures are as capable as Congress of making such determinations within their respective spheres of authority. . . .

IV

The State of Hawaii has never denied that the Constitution forbids even a compensated taking of property when executed for no reason other than to confer a private benefit on a particular private party. A purely private taking could not withstand the scrutiny of the public use requirement; it would serve no legitimate purpose of government and would thus be void. But no purely private taking is involved in these cases. The Hawaii Legislature enacted its Land Reform Act not to benefit a particular class of identifiable individuals but to attack certain perceived evils of concentrated property ownership in Hawaii—a legitimate public purpose. Use of the condemnation power to achieve this purpose is not irrational. Since we assume for purposes of these appeals that the weighty demand of just compensation has been met, the requirements of the Fifth and Fourteenth Amendments have been satisfied. Accordingly, we reverse the judgment of the Court of Appeals, and remand these cases for further proceedings in conformity with this opinion.

It is so ordered.

Justice Marshall took no part in the consideration or decision of these cases.

Page 1059.   Before "b. State Housing Programs," add:

4. *Reagan Administration policies.* Shortly after taking office, President Reagan appointed a commission to recommend changes in federal housing policies. Among other deregulation proposals, the Commission's final report recommended a scaling back of federal housing assistance. In particular, the Commission reviewed the results of the experimental housing allowance program and recommended that federal housing assistance be redirected from the subsidization of newly constructed housing projects to the provision of cash housing allowances to very low income families. See Report of the President's Commission on Housing 17-27 (1982).

The Commission's report marshalled evidence that the §8 new construction program had been much less efficient than federal programs that subsidized the occupancy of existing housing units. Id. at 12-15. In 1983 Congress repealed HUD's §8 new construction budget authority.

Throughout its tenure the Reagan Administration has given priority to housing-allowance programs, such as the §8 certificate program, that enable tenants to find their own apartments in the used stock of housing. Between 1980 and 1986 the number of households receiving §8 assistance doubled to two million. During the same period, largely because of inflation and the expansion of the §8 certificate program, actual federal outlays for housing assistance also doubled. To the dismay of many housing activists, however, Reagan Administration budgets slashed prospective funding for new construction of subsidized housing projects. As a result, housing starts of subsidized units plummeted from 208,000 in 1980 to 70,000 in 1985. See George Sternlieb & David Liskotin, A Review of National Housing Policy, in Housing America's Poor 14, 29 (P. Salins ed. 1987).

The Tax Reform Act of 1986 created a new and potentially significant system of tax credits for low income housing. See I.R.C. §42. To receive the credit a homebuilder must make available, at a low and regulated rent, at least 20 percent of the units in a development to households whose incomes are less than half of the median income in the relevant geographic area. The credit, which the taxpayer takes evenly over a ten-year period, is calculated to have a present value equal to 70 percent of the basis of the units so provided. (The tax credit is limited to 30 percent of basis when the taxpayer has obtained tax-exempt bond financing or federal subsidies, or is acquiring an existing low income housing project.) The aggregate credits available annually to taxpayers for housing projects in a particular state are limited to $1.25 per state resident. Because of this aggregate ceiling, a firm interested in receiving these tax benefits must obtain an allocation of "credit authority" from a designated state or local agency. Each state decides which agency this will be, except in the case of constitutional home-rule cities, which receive a share of the state credit authority as a matter of right. Perhaps because the program was new, in 1987 many states failed to exhaust their rather modest allocations of credit authority. Because the Act forbids a state from carrying forward unallocated credit authority to a subsequent year, these states forfeited the sums not given out. As with the Historic Rehabilitation tax credits, supra Supplement p. 118, an individual taxpayer's maximum low income housing tax credit is, in effect, $7,000 per year.

Major new sources on housing assistance policy include I. Lowry, Experimenting with Housing Allowances (RAND 1982) (RAND's final report, which confirms its preliminary finding that the provision of housing allowances did not inflate the price of housing in either Green Bay or South Bend); Do Housing Allowances Work? (K. Bradbury & A. Downs ed. 1981); R. Struyk & M. Bendick, Housing Vouchers for the Poor: Lessons from a National Experiment (1981); Housing America's Poor (P. Salins ed. 1987). A particularly useful overview is J. Weicher, Housing: Federal Programs and Policies (1980).